A PRACTICAL HANDBOOK OF LEAN SIX SIGMA

Continuous Improvement and Operational Excellence tools

Bhargavi Rao

Copyright © 2024 Bhargavi Rao

All rights reserved

The characters and events portrayed in this book are fictitious. Any similarity to real persons, living or dead, is coincidental and not intended by the author.

No part of this book may be reproduced, or stored in a retrieval system, or transmitted in any form or by any means, electronic, mechanical, photocopying, recording, or otherwise, without express written permission of the publisher.

*This book is dedicated to all those who contributed
to the success of Lean Six Sigma projects, which
I executed, learned from, and understood the
conceptual knowledge of Excellence.*

CONTENTS

Title Page
Copyright
Dedication
Introduction
Prologue
Chapter - 1 — 1
Chapter – 2 — 20
Chapter – 3 — 37
Chapter - 4 — 43
Chapter – 5 — 55
Chapter – 6 — 89
Chapter – 7 — 121
Chapter – 8 — 134
Chapter – 9 — 141
Chapter – 10 — 157
Chapter – 11 — 168
Chapter – 12 — 180
Chapter – 13 — 187
Chapter - 14 — 193
Chapter – 15 — 204
Chapter – 16 — 211

Chapter – 17	217
Chapter – 18	224
Chapter – 19	236
Chapter – 20	253
Chapter – 21	264
Chapter – 22	270
Chapter – 23	276
Chapter – 24	283
Chapter- 24	289
Chapter – 25	296
Chapter – 26	302
Chapter – 27	308
About The Author	335

INTRODUCTION

It all began with a faint, rhythmic drip, drip, drip. A small leak from the faucet in the break room. Nobody thought much of it—just a couple of drops hitting the sink, hardly worth attention. But within a few days, the puddle grew annoying, and someone placed a bucket under the faucet.

Problem solved? Not really.

By the end of the week, the bucket was filling faster than expected. Soon, a rotation of employees took turns emptying it. Someone even suggested, "Why not use the water for the plants or mop the floors?" At first, it seemed clever, even responsible. But soon, the ritual started feeling cumbersome. People were interrupting their work to check the bucket. Emails started flying: "Who emptied the bucket last? It's full again!"

It was clear—our quick fix had only added complexity.

Lean and Six Sigma: Identifying the Real Problem
The bucket became a hot topic during a team meeting. We joked about it, but someone finally said: "Why are we spending so much time managing a leaking tap? Shouldn't we just fix it?"

That question hit like a lightning bolt. We were treating the symptoms but not the root cause—exactly what Lean Six Sigma is designed to avoid.

In Six Sigma, we aim to eliminate defects and unnecessary variability in processes. The leaking tap was a perfect example of a defect. Instead of fixing it, we were adding wasteful steps —muda—by managing the water.

So we asked the right question: What's the simplest, most efficient solution?

Fix The Faucet.

Waste and Muda: The Hidden Costs of Workarounds
Using Lean principles, we mapped out the waste we had unknowingly created:

Wasted Time: Employees spent minutes, sometimes hours, emptying buckets and figuring out water usage.
Wasted Energy: The constant need to monitor the bucket distracted people from more valuable tasks.
Wasted Resources: Instead of solving the core issue, we created an unnecessary process for managing water that shouldn't have been there in the first place.
This was classic muda—waste that adds no value. Lean principles teach us to remove these inefficiencies, and Six Sigma helps by identifying the root cause through problem-solving frameworks like DMAIC (Define, Measure, Analyze, Improve, Control).

Dmaic In Action: Fix The Faucet

Here's how we applied DMAIC to our leaky faucet problem:

Define: The problem is a leaky faucet that creates unnecessary labor and waste.

Measure: We tracked how much time and effort went into monitoring and emptying the bucket.

Analyze: We identified that the root cause of the problem was the defective faucet. No amount of water reuse could eliminate the waste caused by the leak.

Improve: The improvement was clear—call the plumber and fix the faucet.

Control: We documented the issue in our maintenance logs and established a routine inspection process to prevent future leaks from going unnoticed.

Once the faucet was fixed, the bucket was no longer needed, and the unnecessary tasks vanished.

The Lean Lesson: Focus on Value, Eliminate Waste
What started as a clever workaround had become an energy-draining distraction. The moment we applied Lean and Six Sigma thinking, it became clear: workarounds aren't solutions—they're traps.

In a Lean environment, every task should add value. Managing a bucket of water didn't add any real value—it only created non-value-adding activity (muda). By focusing on the root cause and eliminating unnecessary processes, we restored efficiency and freed up time for more meaningful work.

A Culture of Problem Solving: Fix It, Don't Manage It
When the faucet was finally repaired, we all felt relieved. It

wasn't just about stopping the leak—it was about learning a valuable lesson. Lean Six Sigma isn't about managing problems creatively; it's about solving them at their source.

Next time something goes wrong, we won't ask "How can we manage it?" Instead, we'll ask: "How can we eliminate the problem entirely?"

Because the smartest way to deal with a leaky faucet is to fix it.

PROLOGUE

Scene: The Turning Point in a Lean Six Sigma Project

Location: Conference Room, Head Office of a Leading Company.

You sit at the head of a long table, surrounded by department heads, managers, and executives. A Lean Six Sigma project you've been leading has reached a critical juncture—eliminating an outdated, stagnant process and introducing a radically new approach. But this change isn't small. It touches multiple functions, requires cross-departmental buy-in, and needs several levels of approval. Convincing them won't be easy.

The Challenge

You click to the next slide on the projector, showing a flowchart of the current process. "This," you say, "is what we've been using for years. It served us well once, but now it's slow, repetitive, and full of bottlenecks. It's costing us time and effort."

The room murmurs—some nodding, others shifting uncomfortably in their chairs. Someone from the finance team raises an eyebrow. "We get that it's not efficient, but introducing an entirely new process? That's risky. What's the return on this change?"

Another manager leans forward, skeptical. "Replacing the old process means overhauling our workflows, retraining staff, and integrating new tools. Without solid numbers, we can't approve this. How do we know the benefits will outweigh the costs?"

Abstract Ideas Vs. Hard Data

You've prepared for this moment. Experience has taught you that abstract ideas—no matter how compelling—won't sway a room full of business leaders. What they need is concrete evidence.

You take a breath and switch to the next slide: a spreadsheet filled with data projections. Forecasts, simulations, and performance comparisons between the current and future processes fill the screen.

"I hear you," you say. "That's exactly why we modeled the financial and operational impact."

You gesture to the chart. "We ran simulations using historical data and ran different scenarios to predict the outcomes."

Current Process:

Average processing time: 4 hours per task
Labor cost per month: $50,000
Error rate: 6%
New Process (Projected):

Average processing time: 2 hours per task
Labor cost savings: 30%
Error rate: 1.5%

"With these numbers," you continue, "we expect the new process to save us $18,000 per month in labor alone. Over a year, that's over $200,000 saved—and that's before factoring in lower error rates, fewer delays, and improved customer satisfaction."

The room goes quiet as the projections sink in.

The Power of Forecasting: Showing the Road Ahead
"But what if the new process doesn't perform as expected?" a senior executive asks.

You were ready for this too. You switch to the next slide, showing a sensitivity analysis. "Great question," you respond. "We've accounted for multiple scenarios—best case, worst case, and likely case."

Worst Case: Process takes 2.5 hours instead of 2 hours—still 37% faster than today.

Best Case: Savings hit 35%, accelerating implementation across other departments.

Likely Case: On track with a 30% cost reduction and a 4-month break-even period for transition costs.

The numbers are clear. Even in the worst-case scenario, the

company comes out ahead.

Securing Buy-In Through Data-Driven Confidence
The SVP, seated at the far end of the table, leans back thoughtfully. "This is solid forecasting," she says. "We're talking real savings and reduced errors. And it's measurable. I like that."

The operations manager chimes in. "If we can get the training done within the proposed timeline, the new process could actually set us up for more agile operations down the line."

You nod. "Exactly. And once we stabilize, we can introduce continuous improvements—our typical Lean Six Sigma cycles—to refine the process even further."

The SVP smiles and glances around the room. "Alright. You've convinced me. I'll support this—but only if we track performance closely from day one."

The Decision: Data Wins The Day

You feel the tension in the room release. Heads nod, people exchange glances, and the objections begin to dissolve. The skepticism has been replaced with confidence—not because you had brilliant ideas, but because you backed your ideas with data.

The finance head closes his notebook. "I'll fast-track the budget approvals," he says. "With these projections, it makes sense to move forward."

You smile. The hard work isn't over yet—there will be challenges in implementation. But you know that in Lean Six Sigma, good ideas become great solutions when supported by solid data and continuous measurement.

As the meeting adjourns, you make a mental note: this wasn't just about replacing a process. It was about changing the mindset—convincing people to embrace improvements through evidence, not gut feeling.

And in the world of Lean Six Sigma, data isn't just a tool—it's your most persuasive argument.

CHAPTER - 1
A3 Report

In Lean Six Sigma and continuous improvement practices, one of the most valuable tools for structured problem-solving is the A3 report. Developed by Toyota, this report offers a concise, visual method to document an entire problem-solving process. The A3 format derives its name from the size of the paper it is traditionally written on (11 x 17 inches), but its real power lies in its ability to streamline problem-solving by cutting through unnecessary details and focusing on critical information.

By following the Plan-Do-Check-Act (PDCA) cycle, A3 reports drive clarity, accountability, and measurable results. The steps outlined in an A3 report are designed to take a team from problem identification to a measurable solution using root cause analysis, countermeasures, and follow-up activities. This chapter will walk you through the practical aspects of creating and using A3 reports with real-world examples and illustrations, so you can apply these techniques to your own processes.

The A3 Report Structure: A Logical Approach to Problem-Solving

The problem	Target condition
As perceived through the customer/patient's eyes	Chart of new ideal process to be achieved through countermeasures
Background	
Context and importance	
	Implementation plan
Current condition	What? / Who? / When? / Where?
Chart of current process derived from direct observation	
	Follow-up plan
	• Performance anticipated • When to follow-up and measure
Cause analysis	**Results**
Derived from 5-Whys and/or fishbone diagram	• Measurement and date • Variance from predicted measure

The A3 report is divided into two major sections: the left side where the problem is analyzed, and the right side where solutions are designed and implemented. Each side contains clearly labeled blocks, guiding the team step-by-step through the process. The left-hand section includes blocks for the theme, background, current condition, and cause analysis, while the right-hand section houses the target condition, implementation plan, and follow-up activities.

Practical Illustration: Imagine a retail warehouse struggling with late deliveries to customers. The A3 report could be used to systematically break down the issue and find practical solutions. We will walk through each section using this example.

Left Section: Problem Analysis

1. **Theme (Problem Statement):**
   The theme is a short, focused statement that captures the problem. For the warehouse issue, the problem might be: "Increase in customer complaints regarding late deliveries, with a rise from 2% to 5%

over the last three months."

Example:
"Customer complaints have increased by 3% in Q3 due to late deliveries, exceeding acceptable levels by 2%."

2. **Background:**
   This section provides context. The goal is to understand why the problem matters and how it impacts the business. Key data points should be included, such as customer satisfaction metrics, operational costs, and any relevant historical information.

Practical Illustration:
The warehouse may have expanded its service area, increasing delivery times. Additionally, data might show that new hires are still learning processes, which could be contributing to delays.

3. **Current Condition:**
   Here, a detailed value-stream map of the current delivery process should be created, including time frames for each step and bottlenecks. Quantitative data (such as takt time or average lead time) should be included, along with any issues that are visible in the current workflow.

Practical Illustration:
A value-stream map of the warehouse shows that packaging time increased by 15 minutes per order due to bottlenecks in picking and packing. This is coupled with delays in dispatch coordination.

4. **Cause Analysis:**
   The root cause of the issue is explored here, often using tools like the 5 Why's or Fishbone diagram. The goal is to dig deep enough to discover the true source of the problem.

Practical Illustration:

The team uses the 5 Why's to analyze the warehouse delays.

Why #1: Why are orders delayed?
Answer: Packaging takes too long.

Why #2: Why does packaging take too long?
Answer: Pickers are struggling with item location.

Why #3: Why are pickers struggling with item location?
Answer: Items are not logically organized.

Why #4: Why are items disorganized?
Answer: Recent inventory expansion was not incorporated into the storage system.

Why #5: Why was the inventory expansion not planned for?
Answer: No formal process for reconfiguring the layout when inventory changes.

Right Section: Solution Development and Implementation

1. **Target Condition (Countermeasures):**
   Based on the root cause analysis, countermeasures are identified. These are the actions intended to improve the situation. Each countermeasure should be specific and address the root cause directly.

Practical Illustration:
The team proposes reorganizing the storage system to create better alignment with the new inventory, as well as implementing a training program for staff on the new layout. Another countermeasure includes adding clear signage and improving item location software.

2. **Implementation Plan:**
   In this phase, the team develops a timeline

for executing the countermeasures, assigns responsibilities, and sets target dates for each action. Visual tools like Gantt charts or simple timelines can be helpful here.

Practical Illustration:

- **Week 1:** Reorganize inventory layout
- **Week 2:** Install new location software
- **Week 3:** Train staff on new processes
- **Week 4:** Pilot test with smaller batches of orders

The team establishes that the new layout must reduce the average picking time by 10% by the end of the pilot phase.

3. **Follow-Up:**
   This final block ensures that results are tracked after implementation. If issues arise, they should be documented for future improvement. Additionally, metrics from the first phase (theme/problem statement) should be revisited to assess whether the countermeasures have been effective.

Practical Illustration:

After the first month, customer complaints about late deliveries decrease to 2%, aligning with the target. The picking time has been reduced by 12%, which exceeds the target of 10%. However, some staff report challenges with using the new location software, so further training is scheduled.

Using A3 Reports for Proposals and Storyboards

While the A3 report is primarily a problem-solving tool, it can also be adapted for other purposes, such as proposals or storyboards.

Proposal A3 Report:

A proposal A3 report focuses on suggesting new initiatives or improvements. For instance, a retail company looking to expand its e-commerce platform may use a proposal A3 report to lay out the reasons for the expansion, the benefits, potential risks, and the implementation timeline.

Storyboard A3 Report:
A storyboard A3 report is a way to visually present a narrative of a project, often used in communication and training. It can be especially useful for retail environments where visual representation of workflows, customer journeys, or product displays is essential for strategic planning.

Real-World Application in Retail

In the world of retail and e-commerce, A3 reports are invaluable for identifying bottlenecks in the supply chain, optimizing customer service processes, or improving in-store operations. For example, if a retail store notices an increase in stock-outs for popular products, an A3 report can be used to trace the issue back through the supply chain, identify the root causes (perhaps vendor delays or forecasting errors), and then design countermeasures like better inventory management or supplier collaboration.

Practical Example:
In an e-commerce setting, A3 reports could help identify pain points in the customer's checkout process. If data shows a high rate of cart abandonment, the A3 report could help the team pinpoint the exact stage of abandonment, analyze why customers are leaving (e.g., unclear shipping policies), and propose targeted solutions such as improving the user interface or offering transparent shipping costs.

By standardizing the process through A3 reports, teams are not only able to solve current issues but also build a foundation for ongoing continuous improvement.

This breakdown of the A3 report emphasizes its adaptability and power in real-world problem-solving, particularly within retail and e-commerce settings. The structured format ensures that teams focus on the essential aspects of problem-solving while avoiding unnecessary information overload, allowing for effective, targeted improvements.

How to create A3?

A Step-by-Step Guide

Creating an A3 report involves a structured, systematic approach that guides teams through identifying and solving problems. It emphasizes visual clarity and data-driven analysis. Whether you are addressing inefficiencies, proposing a new project, or illustrating a process, following the A3 format ensures consistency and thoroughness. Below is a detailed guide to help you create an A3 report from start to finish, with practical tips and examples.

1. Understand the Purpose of the A3 Report

Before diving into creating an A3 report, it is essential to define its purpose. The A3 report can be used for:

- **Problem-solving**: Identifying a problem, analyzing root causes, and implementing solutions.
- **Proposals**: Presenting a case for change or improvement.
- **Storyboarding**: Mapping out a project plan or process narrative visually.

Practical Tip: Use the A3 report when you need to summarize complex problems or proposals on a single sheet of paper, using concise text, diagrams, and data.

2. Prepare the A3 Template

The A3 report template consists of clear, labeled sections organized into two main areas: the **problem analysis** (left-hand side) and the **solution design/implementation** (right-hand side). These sections are divided into blocks, which you can label in advance.

A basic A3 template should look like this:

Left Section (Problem Analysis)

- **Theme (Problem Statement)**
- **Background**
- **Current Condition**
- **Cause Analysis**

Right Section (Solution and Implementation)

- **Target Condition (Countermeasures)**
- **Implementation Plan**
- **Follow-Up**

You can create this template using simple software like Microsoft Excel, PowerPoint, or dedicated Lean tools like Minitab, but the focus should always be on clarity and conciseness.

---

3. Define the Problem (Theme)

Start by clearly stating the problem or issue at hand in the **Theme** section. This should be concise, typically 1-2 sentences, and based on real data. This is the most critical part of the report because everything else flows from here.

Example (Warehouse Delays):
"Increased customer complaints about late deliveries, with the rate rising from 2% to 5% over the past three months."

Practical Tip: Make the problem statement specific and data-driven. Avoid vague or broad descriptions, as they can mislead the analysis.

4. Provide Background Information

Next, you'll need to describe the **Background**, giving context for why the problem exists and why it is important to address. Include any relevant historical data or trends that support the problem.

Example:
"The warehouse expanded its service area in June, adding 50 new SKUs to the inventory. As a result, delays began to occur, primarily in order picking and dispatch times."

Practical Tip: Focus only on relevant information that helps others understand the scope of the problem. Use charts or tables to display historical trends if necessary.

5. Describe the Current Condition

In this section, document how the process currently works and what is happening in real-time. You'll typically create a **Value Stream Map (VSM)** or another visual diagram to depict the workflow. Highlight any bottlenecks or inefficiencies.

Example (Warehouse):
A VSM shows that the average order-picking time increased from 10 to 25 minutes, primarily due to inefficient storage arrangements. Packaging delays are also noted due to lack of coordination with dispatch.

Practical Tip: Incorporate diagrams, flowcharts, or process maps to visually communicate the current state. Include quantitative data to make the analysis objective (e.g., lead times, wait times).

6. Conduct Cause Analysis

Here, you identify the root cause of the problem. Use root cause analysis techniques like the **5 Why's** or a **Fishbone Diagram (Ishikawa)** to break down the causes of the current condition.

Example (Warehouse Using the 5 Why's):

1. **Why are orders late?**
   Answer: Picking takes too long.

2. **Why does picking take too long?**
   Answer: Items are hard to locate.

3. **Why are items hard to locate?**
   Answer: Inventory is not well-organized after expansion.

4. **Why wasn't the inventory reorganized?**
   Answer: No plan for reconfiguring storage when inventory grew.

5. **Why was there no plan?**
   Answer: Expansion was rushed without involving the operations team.

Practical Tip: Make sure your root cause analysis goes deep enough to address the core issue, not just the symptoms.

---

7. Set Target Condition (Countermeasures)

Once you've identified the root cause, propose **Countermeasures**—specific actions that will address the problem. These should be realistic, actionable, and measurable.

Example (Warehouse):
Reorganize the storage area to optimize item location based on demand frequency. Implement software updates to track item locations efficiently. Schedule training for the team on the new system.

Practical Tip: Countermeasures should directly address the root causes and be formulated with measurable outcomes. These actions must move the system toward a desired future state.

---

8. Develop an Implementation Plan

Now, detail the steps necessary to implement the countermeasures, including timelines, responsibilities, and resources needed. Use a **Gantt chart** or **timeline** for clarity.

Example (Warehouse Implementation Plan):

- **Week 1:** Reorganize warehouse storage (Team A)
- **Week 2:** Implement new item-location software (IT team)
- **Week 3:** Train staff on the new system (Team Leader B)
- **Week 4:** Pilot test with high-demand items (Operations Manager)

Practical Tip: Be as specific as possible. Assign tasks to individual team members and set clear deadlines. You may also add checkpoints for progress reviews.

9. Create Follow-Up Activities

In this final section, you will track whether the implemented countermeasures are effective. Use **Key Performance Indicators (KPIs)** to compare the outcomes with the problem defined in the Theme section. This is a feedback loop that helps adjust or standardize the process.

Example (Warehouse):
After implementation, the team measures the average picking time. If it decreases from 25 minutes to 15 minutes within a month, the improvement is verified. If issues remain, document them and plan for further adjustments.

Practical Tip: Don't stop once the initial goals are reached. Regular follow-ups can reveal new areas for improvement and standardize successful processes for future use.

10. Enhance with Visuals and Data

A key feature of the A3 report is the integration of visuals such as charts, graphs, diagrams, and tables. These elements enhance the communication of complex data and make the report easier to understand at a glance. Use visuals to represent trends, performance gaps, or workflow processes wherever possible.

Practical Tip: Visuals should not overwhelm the report but should clarify and support your points. Simple bar charts, pie charts, or even hand-drawn diagrams can be used effectively.

Practical Example: A3 Report for Warehouse Delays (Summary)

1. **Theme**: Increased customer complaints due to late deliveries, rising from 2% to 5% in the last quarter.
2. **Background**: Warehouse expansion and the addition of 50 SKUs led to longer order picking times.
3. **Current Condition**: Picking time increased from 10 to 25 minutes due to disorganized inventory. A value-stream map shows bottlenecks at the picking and packing stages.
4. **Cause Analysis**: The root cause was a lack of planning for reorganizing storage after expansion.
5. **Target Condition**: Reorganize storage layout, implement a tracking software, and train staff.
6. **Implementation Plan**: Four-week plan with specific tasks assigned to teams for reorganization, software implementation, and training.
7. **Follow-Up**: Monitor picking times for the next month and compare results with pre-expansion performance.

Conclusion: The Power of the A3 Report

By following these steps, you will be able to create an effective A3 report that not only clarifies the problem but also provides a roadmap for continuous improvement. A3 reports help teams stay focused, drive accountability, and deliver measurable results, making them an essential tool in Lean problem-solving methodologies.

Can I customize A3?

Yes, you can absolutely customize an A3 report to fit the specific needs of your organization, team, or project. The A3 report is inherently flexible, allowing you to modify the format and content to better suit your objectives, industry, or unique problem-solving approach. Customizing the A3 report helps tailor it to the context of your work, making it even more effective.

How to Customize an A3 Report

Below are key ways you can customize an A3 report, along with practical examples and tips for each:

1. Adjust Sections for Your Process

The traditional A3 report has sections like **Theme**, **Background**, **Current Condition**, **Cause Analysis**, **Target Condition**, **Implementation Plan**, and **Follow-Up**. However, you can rename or reframe these sections based on your organization's needs or the specific problem you're addressing.

Examples:

- **Proposal A3**: If you're using the A3 to propose a new initiative (like implementing a new software system), you could modify the sections to include:
    - **Business Case**: Explains why the initiative is needed.
    - **Benefits and Risks**: Outlines the advantages and potential challenges.
    - **Cost Estimate**: Includes financial projections.
    - **Timeline**: Breaks down the implementation phases.
- **Strategic Planning A3**: You could use an A3 report

for strategy development by customizing sections like:

- **Vision and Objectives**: What is the long-term goal?
- **Current State of the Market**: Understanding where the business stands.
- **Opportunities and Threats**: Instead of root cause analysis, use SWOT analysis.
- **Key Initiatives**: What are the key projects or programs to be launched?
- **Resource Allocation**: How will resources be distributed?

Practical Tip: Customize the A3 structure to match the process or methodology you're using (e.g., Agile, Kaizen, Lean Six Sigma, etc.). This will help ensure your A3 report aligns closely with your project goals and the team's way of working.

---

2. Include Custom Metrics

Instead of sticking to generic metrics, include Key Performance Indicators (KPIs) that are specific to your business or project. These could be operational, financial, or customer-related metrics that measure success in your specific domain.

Example:

For a **manufacturing team**, your metrics could include:

- **Cycle time**: How long it takes to produce one unit.
- **First-pass yield**: The percentage of products made correctly without rework.
- **Takt time**: The rate at which products must be produced to meet customer demand.

For a **marketing team**, you might use:

- **Customer acquisition cost (CAC)**: How much you

spend to acquire a new customer.
- **Conversion rate**: Percentage of website visitors who become customers.

Practical Tip: In the **Current Condition** or **Follow-Up** sections, integrate customized KPIs that are meaningful to the stakeholders and the problem you're solving.

---

3. Incorporate Your Company's Branding and Visual Style

You can modify the visual appearance of the A3 report to align with your company's branding or preferred presentation style. This could include:

- **Colors and fonts**: Use the same color schemes and fonts that your company uses in reports or presentations.
- **Logos and headers**: Incorporate your company's logo and customize headers to reflect internal terminology or branding.

Example:

For a **tech startup**, you might opt for a sleek, minimalist design with vibrant colors to reflect a modern brand identity. Meanwhile, a **traditional manufacturing company** might use a more structured format with conservative fonts and colors to align with corporate standards.

Practical Tip: While aesthetics matter, the core focus should remain on clarity and conciseness. Don't overload the A3 with excessive visuals or branding elements that detract from the message.

---

4. Modify the Layout for Different Audiences

The A3 report format is flexible enough to be customized based on who will review it. Different stakeholders may require different levels of detail.

Example:

- **For Executives:** You can simplify the report to focus on high-level metrics, business impact, and key decisions needed. For example, in a proposal A3, you might minimize the technical details and focus on strategic insights like ROI, risks, and timelines.
- **For Frontline Teams:** A report aimed at operators or team members on the ground may include more granular details about process changes, specific timelines, and task assignments. You might add sections for tool changes, safety procedures, or employee feedback.

Practical Tip: Always consider the needs and expectations of your audience. If your audience prefers visuals, use more charts and diagrams. If they want hard data, focus on tables and analytics.

5. Add Additional Tools or Techniques

You can expand the A3 report by incorporating other Lean or Six Sigma tools to better suit the nature of your problem-solving process. Some examples include:

- **Fishbone Diagram (Ishikawa):** Add this for a more detailed cause-and-effect analysis in the Cause Analysis section.
- **SWOT Analysis:** Use this to explore strengths, weaknesses, opportunities, and threats in a strategy-focused A3.
- **Pareto Chart:** Include this to show which factors contribute the most to a problem (the 80/20 rule).

Example:

If you're working on a complex problem in a **healthcare**

environment—say, reducing patient wait times—your cause analysis could include both a Fishbone Diagram (to identify various root causes) and a Pareto Chart (to prioritize the most impactful issues).

Practical Tip: Don't overload the A3 with too many tools, but strategically include the ones that best support your analysis and problem-solving efforts.

6. Create a Digital Version

In today's digital workplace, you can easily create a digital A3 report that allows for real-time collaboration, feedback, and updates. Tools like Microsoft Teams, Miro, or specialized Lean software like **KaiNexus** and **Minitab** allow for live updates and integration with other project management tools.

Example:

For a globally dispersed team working on a **supply chain improvement project**, creating an A3 report in a shared online document (e.g., Google Docs or a project management platform) allows for collaboration across time zones, with everyone contributing in real time.

Practical Tip: Ensure your digital A3 still follows the principle of clarity and simplicity. Hyperlinks to supplementary data, additional analysis, or supporting documentation can be added without cluttering the main report.

7. Use A3 Reports for Different Purposes

While A3 reports are traditionally used for problem-solving, they can be customized for other use cases such as:

- **Project Planning A3**: Detailing the timeline, resources, and stakeholders for a new project.
- **Training A3**: Providing a visual, structured guide for onboarding or staff training.

- **Customer Journey Mapping A3**: Mapping out each step in the customer experience, highlighting pain points and opportunities for improvement.

Example (Training A3 Report for Retail Staff):

- **Theme**: Improve checkout experience by reducing cashier errors.
- **Background**: High percentage of checkout errors due to inadequate training.
- **Current Condition**: 10% error rate during peak hours.
- **Target Condition**: Reduce errors to below 2% by Q4.
- **Implementation Plan**: Provide updated cashier training, roll out new software, and schedule weekly refresher courses.

Practical Tip: Customizing the A3 for non-problem-solving scenarios opens up a range of possibilities for structured communication and planning.

Final Thoughts

Customizing an A3 report is not only possible but often necessary to make it more relevant and effective for your specific context. The key to customization is keeping the core principles of the A3—clarity, conciseness, and a focus on continuous improvement—while adapting it to suit your organization's needs. Whether you're working on manufacturing issues, project proposals, or strategic initiatives, an A3 report can be tailored to align with your goals and audience, making it a truly versatile tool in any improvement process.

CHAPTER – 2
Affinity Diagrams

Organizing Chaos to Drive Quality Improvement

Affinity Diagramming

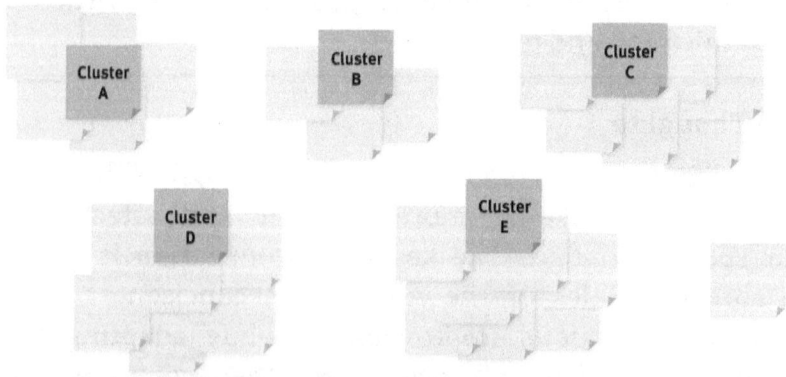

An **Affinity Diagram**, also known as an affinity chart or thematic analysis, is a tool that helps organize a large number of ideas or facts into natural relationships. Whether you are tackling a complex issue, analyzing brainstorming sessions, or sorting through vast data, the affinity diagram method enables the team to identify and group related thoughts, streamlining the chaotic process into structured insights.

Origin and Purpose

The affinity diagram was developed in the 1960s by Japanese anthropologist Jiro Kawakita. Its primary purpose is to foster creativity, intuition, and group collaboration by allowing participants to organize ideas without preconceived categories. It is often used after brainstorming sessions, or when data seems too complex to interpret logically. Affinity diagrams excel in situations where vast amounts of verbal data, such as survey results, need to be structured. It is an excellent tool for identifying patterns, themes, or categories, particularly in collaborative settings.

When to Use an Affinity Diagram

The application of an affinity diagram is particularly useful in these common scenarios:

- After a brainstorming exercise where many ideas have been generated.
- When analyzing qualitative data from interviews, surveys, or feedback forms.
- When there is a need to find connections between seemingly unrelated ideas.
- When a large group consensus is necessary to organize or reduce information into actionable themes.

In practical terms, the affinity diagram is indispensable when a problem appears too overwhelming or complex, and its nature defies easy categorization. By leveraging the creative synergy of a group, an affinity diagram helps translate that chaos into comprehensible and actionable solutions.

The Affinity Diagram Process

The affinity diagram process has four primary steps, and each step guides participants through a methodical organization of ideas.

Step 1: Generating Ideas

First, ideas are generated, typically through brainstorming. Each idea is written on a sticky note or card, and the goal is to create a random, unstructured collection of ideas. No organization is applied at this stage. The sticky notes are placed on a large surface like a wall or table to ensure that all ideas are visible.

Example 1:
A retail operations team is brainstorming potential customer service improvements. They generate ideas such as:

- Faster checkout times.
- Implementing a loyalty program.
- Improving in-store signage.
- Reducing stockouts on key products.
- Providing mobile customer support.

Each idea is written on a sticky note and placed randomly on a board for further analysis.

Step 2: Grouping Ideas by Similarity

In this step, team members silently group related ideas side by side without talking. By allowing ideas to be grouped intuitively rather than through discussion, the group avoids the limitations of habitual thinking and opens space for creativity. Often, these groups emerge naturally as relationships between the ideas become clearer.

Example 2:
The retail team begins grouping their sticky notes based on common themes. Ideas like "faster checkout times" and "mobile customer support" may be grouped under "Technology Solutions," while "improving in-store signage" and "reducing

stockouts" may fall under "Operational Efficiency."

By the end of the silent sorting process, five distinct groups may have emerged:

- Technology Solutions
- Operational Efficiency
- Customer Loyalty
- In-Store Experience
- Marketing Initiatives

Step 3: Creating Group Headers

Once the ideas have been grouped, the team begins discussing the underlying relationships. A critical part of this step is creating header cards for each group, which summarize the essence of the ideas in that group. The headers should capture the core theme of the grouping.

Example 3:

In a hospital setting, a team is working to understand barriers to the on-time delivery of medications. After grouping their ideas, they create the following headers based on the emerging themes:

- **Staffing Issues**
- **Pharmacy Operations**
- **Technology Gaps**
- **Patient Communication**

Each header reflects the commonalities within the ideas and allows the team to focus on specific areas for further investigation.

Step 4: Refining and Supergrouping

In the final stage, teams may choose to create "supergroups," which are broader categories that encompass several of the initial groupings. Supergroups provide a higher-level understanding of the overarching themes.

Example 4:

In the example of a company seeking to streamline employee onboarding (Company SQBOK), four distinct supergroups emerge:

- **Training**: Issues related to orientation, company-specific classes, and office procedures.
- **Paperwork**: Delays in receiving key documents like parking passes and citizenship paperwork.
- **Regulatory**: Problems with drug testing and regulatory compliance.
- **Technology**: Delays in system logons, laptop configuration, and other IT-related hurdles.

These supergroups help the team focus on specific action points and assign responsibilities to relevant departments.

Benefits of Affinity Diagrams

The true value of an affinity diagram lies in its ability to make complex data comprehensible and actionable. It allows teams to break down large volumes of information into manageable categories and stimulates meaningful discussion. By fostering a nonverbal, intuitive process of organizing ideas, affinity diagrams encourage out-of-the-box thinking, enabling the discovery of relationships that might otherwise remain hidden.

Moreover, the collaborative nature of the process ensures that every team member's input is valued, leading to group consensus on the final categories and themes. This can be particularly valuable when tackling cross-functional issues or when the team comprises members from different departments with unique perspectives.

In the world of **continuous improvement and operational**

excellence, affinity diagrams serve as an essential tool for translating data into actionable insights. By engaging team members at every level, from brainstorming to grouping ideas, this technique fosters creativity and enhances problem-solving capabilities.

Illustrative Case Studies

Case Study 1: Lean Six Sigma Project in Retail

A large retail company wanted to improve its customer checkout experience. Using an affinity diagram, the project team categorized 50 potential improvements generated during brainstorming sessions. The ideas ranged from "implementing self-checkout machines" to "enhancing cashier training." After grouping related ideas, the team identified key categories: **Technology Enhancements**, **Staff Training**, and **Store Layout Improvements**. These categories became the focus for the next phase of process improvement, driving changes that led to faster checkouts and higher customer satisfaction.

Case Study 2: Improving E-commerce Delivery Times

An e-commerce company was facing delays in its order fulfillment process. After collecting ideas from different departments during a brainstorming session, they used an affinity diagram to group ideas into themes such as **Warehouse Efficiency**, **Logistics and Shipping**, **Technology Solutions**, and **Customer Communication**. Each theme represented an area for improvement, and the company was able to focus its Lean Six Sigma efforts on the most impactful areas, significantly reducing delivery times.

What are next steps?

Next Steps After Creating an Affinity Diagram

An affinity diagram provides a visual and organized way to understand large amounts of ideas and data, but it is not an endpoint in itself. After creating an affinity diagram, teams should take additional steps to move toward solutions, deeper analysis, and actionable outcomes. The following steps will guide the transition from organizing ideas to implementing change or improvements.

1. Analyze Groupings for Root Causes

Once the affinity diagram has grouped ideas into categories, the next step is to conduct a more detailed analysis. This can be done using tools like a **cause-and-effect diagram** (also known as a fishbone or Ishikawa diagram) or an **interrelationship diagram**.

- **Cause-and-Effect Diagram**: This tool helps drill down into the root causes of a problem by visually mapping out potential reasons that contribute to each category identified in the affinity diagram.
- **Interrelationship Diagram**: This method identifies cause-and-effect relationships between different categories and helps determine the most influential factors that need to be addressed.

Example:
In the hospital example from earlier, where the team grouped ideas related to barriers in on-time medication delivery, the group might use a cause-and-effect diagram to further explore the underlying causes of the "Staffing Issues" and "Pharmacy Operations" categories. This deeper dive helps the team identify specific bottlenecks, like understaffing during peak hours or delays in medication preparation.

2. Prioritize Key Categories or Issues

Not all groupings or categories from an affinity diagram will have equal importance or urgency. After organizing ideas, the team should prioritize which categories to address first, based on impact, feasibility, and urgency. This can be done using prioritization tools like a **Pareto chart**, **weighted scoring**, or simple **voting** among team members.

- **Pareto Principle (80/20 rule)**: By focusing on the categories that represent the biggest proportion of the problem (usually 20% of causes that lead to 80% of the issues), the team can target the most impactful areas for improvement.

Example:
In the onboarding example for Company SQBOK, the team may prioritize fixing issues in the **Technology** and **Paperwork** categories first, as these were found to cause the most delays. Addressing technology access and incomplete paperwork might resolve the majority of onboarding delays.

3. Develop Action Plans

Once the key areas for improvement are identified, the team should create specific action plans for addressing these issues. These plans should define the following:

- **Goals**: Clear objectives for what the team aims to achieve.
- **Actions**: Specific tasks that need to be undertaken to address each category.
- **Responsibilities**: Assign team members or departments to take ownership of specific tasks.
- **Timelines**: Set deadlines for when tasks should be completed.
- **Metrics**: Identify ways to measure success and track improvements.

Example:
After identifying "Technology Gaps" in the hospital's medication delivery process, the team might develop an

action plan that includes upgrading pharmacy management software, streamlining the IT request process for medication order systems, and assigning an IT team member to the project with a two-month timeline for implementation.

4. Use Other Quality Tools to Continue Problem-Solving

An affinity diagram is often just one step in a broader quality improvement or problem-solving process. The next step might be to apply other **Lean Six Sigma** tools or **Total Quality Management** (TQM) techniques to further break down the issue or monitor progress:

- **Process Mapping**: Use a flowchart or process map to visualize the current process and identify inefficiencies or redundancies.
- **Failure Mode and Effects Analysis (FMEA)**: Assess potential risks or failures in the identified categories to prioritize corrective actions.
- **Control Charts**: Monitor key metrics to ensure improvements are maintained over time.

Example:
In a manufacturing setting, after using an affinity diagram to organize performance issues (e.g., quality, equipment maintenance, safety), the team might develop a process map to visualize how different factors are affecting each other. This can help identify specific points of failure in equipment maintenance or unsafe work practices.

5. Implement and Monitor Changes

Once action plans are in place, the team should focus on implementation. During this phase, it's crucial to continuously monitor progress and adjust strategies if necessary. To do this effectively:

- Track key performance indicators (KPIs) associated with each action.

- Hold regular meetings to check in on progress and roadblocks.
- Gather feedback from stakeholders on whether the changes are having the desired impact.

Example:
For Company SQBOK, after implementing changes to improve the onboarding process, HR managers could track KPIs such as the time taken for new employees to gain system access or the percentage of completed paperwork before the first day. Adjustments can be made if the desired improvements are not seen within the established timeline.

6. Reflect and Iterate

The process of creating and using an affinity diagram is iterative. After implementing changes and monitoring their impact, the team should reflect on what worked and what didn't. If issues persist or new challenges arise, the team can revisit the affinity diagram process to generate fresh ideas or refine existing solutions.

- Conduct a **lessons learned** session to discuss what could be improved in future problem-solving efforts.
- Consider using affinity diagrams again when new data or challenges emerge, as they are highly flexible and adaptable to different situations.

Example:
After six months of improving the onboarding process, Company SQBOK may revisit the affinity diagram to address any lingering issues or new challenges that have surfaced. For instance, if technology issues have largely been resolved but training deficiencies remain, the team can regroup to brainstorm new training solutions.

Conclusion (Next Steps)

Affinity diagrams serve as a powerful tool to help teams organize and analyze complex information. However, they are just the beginning. The subsequent steps—analyzing root causes, prioritizing issues, developing action plans, applying other quality tools, implementing changes, and reflecting—are all essential to ensuring that the organized insights from the affinity diagram lead to meaningful improvements and resolutions. By following these next steps, organizations can harness the full potential of their collective ideas and drive real change in their processes and systems.

How do we prioritize?

Prioritization Techniques After an Affinity Diagram

Once you've organized ideas into categories using an affinity diagram, the next step is **prioritizing** those categories or issues. Prioritization helps teams focus on the most impactful or urgent areas, ensuring that resources are used efficiently. Several techniques can be used to prioritize the issues uncovered in an affinity diagram, depending on the team's goals and the complexity of the problem. Below are some of the most commonly used prioritization methods.

1. Pareto Principle (80/20 Rule)

The Pareto Principle, also known as the 80/20 rule, suggests that roughly 80% of the problems are caused by 20% of the issues. This method helps teams focus on the critical few areas that will have the largest impact.

How to Use It:

- **List and categorize** the issues from your affinity diagram.
- **Analyze the frequency or severity** of each category

or problem. For example, if you're addressing customer complaints, determine which categories receive the most complaints.

- **Prioritize** the 20% of categories that represent the most frequent or severe issues, as solving these will likely yield the greatest improvement.

Example:

In a customer service project, a retail team uses the affinity diagram to categorize customer complaints into **"Checkout Delays"**, **"Out-of-Stock Products"**, and **"Unhelpful Staff"**. After analysis, they discover that **Checkout Delays** account for 70% of the complaints, while the other two categories make up the remaining 30%. The team decides to prioritize addressing checkout delays first, as it will have the most significant impact on overall satisfaction.

2. Impact-Effort Matrix (Quick Wins)

The **Impact-Effort Matrix**, also known as a 2x2 grid, helps teams prioritize by balancing the potential impact of each issue with the effort or resources required to address it. This method divides tasks into four quadrants:

- **Quick Wins**: High impact, low effort – prioritize these first.
- **Major Projects**: High impact, high effort – worth tackling but may take more time and resources.
- **Low-Hanging Fruit**: Low impact, low effort – can be handled after quick wins if time allows.
- **Time Wasters**: Low impact, high effort – generally not worth pursuing.

How to Use It:

- **Rank each category** from the affinity diagram based

on the impact (how much improvement it will make) and the effort (resources and time required).
- **Plot** each category on the 2x2 matrix.
- **Prioritize Quick Wins** (high impact, low effort) as they offer the most immediate benefit with the least effort.

Example:

A healthcare team analyzing barriers to on-time delivery of medications identifies categories like **"Staffing Issues"**, **"Pharmacy Delays"**, and **"Technology Gaps"**. After using an impact-effort matrix, they discover that fixing **Pharmacy Delays** is a **Quick Win**: it requires minimal changes (low effort) but could drastically reduce medication delivery times (high impact). Meanwhile, solving **Staffing Issues** is a **Major Project** that will take more time and resources, so it is scheduled for a later phase.

3. Multi-Voting (Nominal Group Technique)

Multi-voting, also known as the **Nominal Group Technique**, is a democratic way for teams to prioritize items by voting. Each team member has a limited number of votes to distribute among the categories or issues, allowing the group to reach consensus on what to prioritize.

How to Use It:

- **List all categories or issues** identified in the affinity diagram.
- Each team member gets a fixed number of votes (e.g., 3 to 5 votes).
- **Vote on the categories** they believe are most important.
- **Tally the votes**, and the categories with the highest

votes become the priorities.

Example:

A software company is looking to prioritize features for an upcoming product update. After an affinity diagram session, they identify 10 potential features. Each team member is given 3 votes to allocate across the features. After voting, the features **"User Interface Enhancements"** and **"Improved Performance"** receive the highest votes, so the team focuses on these in the next development cycle.

4. Weighted Scoring Model

The **Weighted Scoring Model** is a more structured approach where each issue is evaluated based on multiple criteria, such as impact, cost, feasibility, and alignment with strategic goals. Each criterion is assigned a weight, and the team scores each category based on those criteria. This method is useful for making more complex, data-driven decisions.

How to Use It:

- **Define criteria** for prioritization (e.g., impact, cost, feasibility, time required).
- **Assign a weight** to each criterion based on its importance (e.g., Impact = 40%, Cost = 30%, Time Required = 20%, Feasibility = 10%).
- **Score each category** on a scale (e.g., 1 to 5) for each criterion.
- **Calculate a weighted score** for each category by multiplying the scores by their respective weights.
- **Prioritize the categories** with the highest total scores.

Example:

In a manufacturing company, the team uses a weighted

scoring model to prioritize improvements in equipment maintenance. They define criteria such as **Cost to Implement**, **Impact on Production**, **Time Required**, and **Feasibility**. After scoring and weighting the categories, **"Preventive Maintenance Schedules"** receives the highest score due to its high impact on reducing downtime and low cost, so it becomes the top priority.

5. Risk Matrix (Severity vs. Probability)

The **Risk Matrix** method prioritizes issues based on their potential severity (how serious the problem is) and probability (how likely the issue is to occur). This method is often used in risk management to identify and address high-risk items first.

How to Use It:

- **Assess the severity** of each issue (e.g., 1 = minor, 5 = severe).
- **Assess the probability** of each issue occurring (e.g., 1 = rare, 5 = frequent).
- **Multiply the severity and probability scores** to calculate a risk score for each issue.
- **Prioritize issues** with the highest risk scores.

Example:

A hospital safety team uses a risk matrix to prioritize improvements in medication administration. After evaluating the categories from their affinity diagram, they find that **"Pharmacy Staffing Delays"** has a high probability (it happens frequently) and high severity (it can delay critical medications), so it becomes the top priority for immediate action.

6. Critical Path Method (CPM)

For projects that involve multiple interconnected tasks or

categories, the **Critical Path Method (CPM)** helps prioritize by focusing on the sequence of tasks that must be completed on time to avoid delaying the entire project. The method identifies tasks that are critical to overall project success, making it clear where the team should focus its resources first.

How to Use It:

- **Identify the dependencies** between tasks or categories (which tasks must be completed before others can start).
- **Determine the critical path**: the longest sequence of tasks that dictates the project's overall timeline.
- **Prioritize tasks** on the critical path, as any delay in these tasks will delay the entire project.

Example:

In an IT infrastructure project, after creating an affinity diagram of tasks, the project manager uses the critical path method to identify that **"Server Setup"** and **"Network Configuration"** are critical tasks that must be completed before other tasks can begin. These tasks become the top priority to ensure the project stays on schedule.

7. MoSCoW Method (Must Have, Should Have, Could Have, Won't Have)

The **MoSCoW method** is a simple framework for prioritizing tasks or categories based on their importance to the project or outcome:

- **Must Have**: Critical and non-negotiable items that need to be completed.
- **Should Have**: Important but not critical; can be deferred if necessary.
- **Could Have**: Nice-to-have features or solutions, but

not essential.

- **Won't Have**: Items that are not currently a priority or won't be pursued at all.

How to Use It:

- **Categorize each item** from the affinity diagram into Must Have, Should Have, Could Have, or Won't Have categories based on its criticality to the project or outcome.
- **Prioritize** Must Haves first, then Should Haves, and so on.

Example:

A product development team uses the MoSCoW method to prioritize features for a new app. The team categorizes **"Security Features"** as a Must Have, **"User Interface Enhancements"** as a Should Have, and **"Social Media Integration"** as a Could Have. They focus their initial efforts on the security features to ensure the app is compliant before release.

Conclusion

The prioritization process is crucial in translating the insights from an affinity diagram into actionable steps. Whether you use a simple voting system or a more complex weighted scoring model, choosing the right prioritization technique depends on the complexity of the problem, the available data, and the goals of the team. By effectively prioritizing categories or issues, teams can focus on what will drive the most value, making sure that the highest-impact problems are addressed first.

CHAPTER – 3
Andon

Andon is a critical tool in **Lean manufacturing** that empowers employees to signal issues in real time, allowing for immediate resolution to prevent defects and disruptions. The term originates from Japanese, meaning a **paper lantern or signal light**, and in the Lean context, it refers to **visual signals that alert teams to problems on the production line** or in service processes.

Color-Code	Condition	Action
	Production is normal	Proceed to the next step
	Problem appeared	The problem cannot be identified and will need further investigation
	Production has stopped	An operator needs to have a supervisor check the facility

In modern applications, Andon systems go beyond simple visual cues to encompass audio alerts, dashboards, or software notifications. Andon aligns with Lean principles by ensuring **quality control and continuous improvement**, fostering a culture where problems are **identified and fixed immediately**.

What is Andon in Lean?

Andon is a **visual management system** that provides a signal

—often a **light, buzzer, or software notification**—to indicate an issue that requires attention. It allows operators to **stop the production process or request help** when an abnormality occurs, such as a defect, equipment malfunction, or supply shortage. The Andon system ensures that **problems are tackled at their source (in real-time)**, preventing defective products from moving further in the process.

The primary goal of Andon is to **empower frontline employees** to stop and signal issues without fear of repercussions. This practice reduces errors, improves quality, and ensures that operations **run smoothly**.

How Does Andon Work?

An **Andon system** typically consists of:

1. **Signal Mechanism:** A button, cord, or sensor that workers use to activate the Andon signal.
2. **Visual or Audio Indicator:** This can be **lights (e.g., green, yellow, red)**, buzzers, or notifications on a digital screen.
3. **Response Protocol:** When the signal is triggered, supervisors or support teams are **alerted to address the issue** immediately.
4. **Problem Resolution:** The issue is either **resolved on the spot**, or production is halted until the cause is identified and corrected.

Types of Andon Signals

- **Manual Andon:** The operator activates the Andon signal by **pulling a cord or pressing a button** when a problem is detected.
- **Automatic Andon:** Sensors on equipment trigger the signal when **a predefined condition** is violated (e.g.,

machine stops due to overheating).

- **Digital Andon:** In modern facilities, **dashboard displays and software alerts** notify teams of issues in real-time. Remote operations can also track performance using cloud-based Andon systems.

Benefits of Andon in Lean Manufacturing and Service Operations

1. **Improved Quality Control:**
   - Issues are identified early, preventing defective products from continuing through the process.
   - **Example:** An operator notices a misaligned part and activates Andon to halt the assembly line before defects multiply.

2. **Faster Response Times:**
   - Teams respond to alerts immediately, minimizing downtime.
   - **Example:** If a machine stops unexpectedly, maintenance teams are notified instantly to resolve the issue.

3. **Employee Empowerment:**
   - Workers are encouraged to **proactively report problems**, creating a culture of accountability.
   - **Example:** In a contact center, an agent reports a recurring software glitch using a digital Andon system, ensuring IT can address it before it affects service levels.

4. **Reduced Waste (Muda):**
   - Stopping production when problems occur prevents unnecessary rework, scrap, or overproduction.

5. **Continuous Improvement:**
    - Andon alerts provide **real-time data** that can be analyzed for patterns, helping teams identify **root causes** and drive improvement efforts.

Andon in Action: Practical Illustrations

Example 1: Automotive Manufacturing

An automotive factory uses a **manual Andon cord** on the assembly line. If an employee detects a defect, they pull the cord to **stop production immediately**. A flashing yellow light and audio alarm notify supervisors, who arrive promptly to assist. If the problem can't be resolved within a specific time, the light turns **red**, halting the line until the issue is addressed.

Example 2: E-commerce Warehouse

In a **distribution center**, sensors detect if a conveyor belt is running too slowly or if boxes are incorrectly labeled. When the issue is identified, the **Andon system triggers a red light**, and the **warehouse manager receives a digital alert**. This proactive system **prevents shipping delays** by resolving the issue before incorrect orders reach customers.

Example 3: Healthcare Operations

In a hospital, nurses use a **digital Andon system** to signal when patient beds require urgent cleaning or when equipment needs maintenance. Alerts are displayed on a central dashboard, allowing housekeeping staff to respond quickly, ensuring that **patients do not experience delays in care**.

How Andon Supports Lean and Six Sigma Applications

1. **Lean Manufacturing:**
    - Andon **reduces waste** by preventing defective products from being processed further.

- It enhances the **flow of operations**, ensuring that problems are solved immediately without disrupting the entire process.

2. **Six Sigma:**
    - By **capturing real-time data on production issues**, Andon provides insights that can be analyzed for process improvement.
    - It contributes to **variation reduction** by identifying patterns of recurring defects or bottlenecks, aligning with Six Sigma's focus on eliminating defects and variability.

3. **Jidoka (Autonomation):**
    - Andon aligns with the **Jidoka principle** of building intelligence into processes—allowing machines or employees to stop work when a defect is detected.
    - This combination ensures **quality control at every step**, making it possible to correct errors before they escalate.

Challenges in Implementing Andon

While Andon offers significant benefits, some challenges include:

1. **Employee Reluctance:** Some workers may feel hesitant to stop the process for fear of disrupting operations or receiving negative feedback.
2. **Overuse or False Alarms:** Frequent or unnecessary Andon signals can reduce their effectiveness and distract teams.
3. **Integration with Existing Systems:** In digital environments, **integrating Andon systems with other IT systems** can be complex and require investment.

Best Practices for Andon Implementation

1. **Train Employees:** Educate workers on the importance of Andon and empower them to **use the system confidently**.
2. **Establish Clear Response Protocols:** Define who should respond to Andon alerts and within what time frame.
3. **Analyze Data:** Use Andon alerts as a source of **continuous improvement data**, identifying root causes and preventing future issues.
4. **Pilot the System:** Start with a **small-scale implementation** and scale up as the team becomes comfortable using the system.
5. **Use Andon with Other Lean Tools:** Combine Andon with tools like **Kanban and Heijunka** for a fully optimized production system.

Conclusion

Andon is a vital component of **Lean operations**, ensuring that issues are identified and resolved in real-time to prevent disruptions and defects. By **empowering workers and creating visual management systems**, Andon fosters a culture of accountability and continuous improvement. Its applications extend beyond manufacturing into services, healthcare, logistics, and other industries where **real-time problem-solving is critical**.

Through proper training, clear protocols, and integration with other Lean tools like **Kanban and Jidoka**, Andon becomes a powerful ally in achieving **operational excellence and sustainable growth**.

CHAPTER - 4
Arrow Diagram

Understanding the Arrow Diagram for Project Management and Scheduling

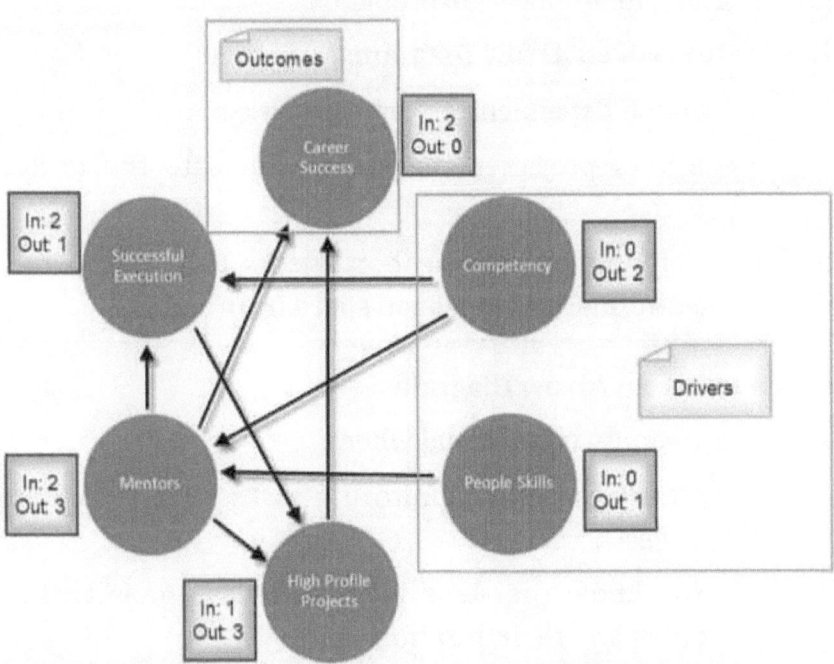

In complex projects with numerous interrelated tasks, it is crucial to plan and sequence activities effectively to ensure smooth execution and timely completion. The **Arrow Diagram** (also known as an activity network diagram or critical path method chart) is a vital tool that helps in this process. It graphically represents the sequence of tasks in a project, identifies dependencies, and pinpoints the critical path, which highlights the essential activities that must be completed on time to avoid project delays. This chapter provides a step-by-step guide to creating and using an arrow diagram, along with examples to solidify your understanding.

What is an Arrow Diagram?

The arrow diagram is a visual representation used to sequence project tasks, assess the interdependencies between tasks, and determine the **critical path**—the series of tasks that directly impact the project's completion date. It illustrates the required order of tasks, allows for better scheduling, and helps foresee potential resource allocation problems.

Key Features of an Arrow Diagram:

- Shows dependencies between tasks.
- Allows project managers to calculate the critical path.
- Helps in identifying bottlenecks and areas where additional resources can speed up progress.

When to Use an Arrow Diagram

An arrow diagram is beneficial when:

- Scheduling and monitoring tasks within complex projects.
- You know the steps involved in the project, their order, and their duration.
- Project deadlines are critical, and delays or early completion can significantly impact the project.

Step-by-Step Guide to Creating an Arrow Diagram

Materials Needed

- Sticky notes or cards
- Markers
- A large writing surface (newsprint, whiteboard, or flipchart)

Step 1: Listing the Tasks

Write down all the necessary tasks that need to be completed for the project. Each task should be concise and descriptive. To organize them visually, write each task on the top half of a sticky note or card. In the center of the card, draw a horizontal arrow pointing to the right, representing the flow of time.

Example: Let's say we're managing a project for launching a new product. Tasks might include:

- Conduct market research
- Develop product prototype
- Test product prototype
- Design packaging
- Launch marketing campaign

Step 2: Determine the Sequence of Tasks

Determine the correct sequence of these tasks by asking:

1. Which tasks must happen before this one can begin?
2. Which tasks can be done simultaneously?
3. Which tasks should happen immediately after this one?

Tip: Use a table to organize these relationships. For example:

Prior Task	This Task	Simultaneous Tasks	Following Task
-	Conduct market	-	Develop product

	research		prototype	
Conduct market research	Develop product prototype	Test product prototype	Design packaging
Develop product prototype	Test product prototype	-	Launch marketing campaign

Step 3: Draw the Network

Arrange the tasks in sequence on a large surface, ensuring that time flows from left to right. Align concurrent tasks vertically to represent simultaneous activities.

- **Events:** Circles are used to mark the start and end of each task. These are called events. Label them with numbers (e.g., 1, 2, 3) to make it easier to reference specific tasks.
- **Dummy Arrows:** Sometimes, two tasks start and end at the same event but are not truly independent. Use **dummy arrows** (dotted lines) to separate these tasks logically.

Example Diagram:

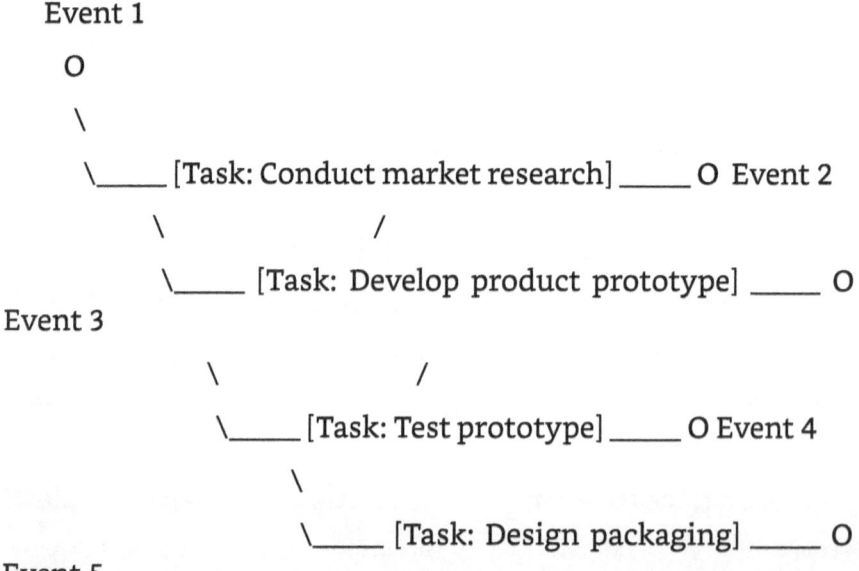

```
   Event 1
     O
      \
       \____ [Task: Conduct market research] ____ O Event 2
         \                /
          \____ [Task: Develop product prototype] ____ O
Event 3
              \                /
               \____ [Task: Test prototype] ____ O Event 4
                  \
                   \____ [Task: Design packaging] ____ O
Event 5
```

\
_____ [Task: Launch marketing]
_____ O Event 6

Figure 1: Dummy separating simultaneous tasks

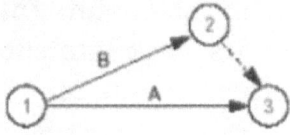

Figure 2: Dummy keeping sequence correct

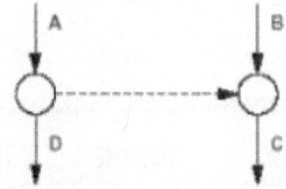

Figure 3: Using an extra event

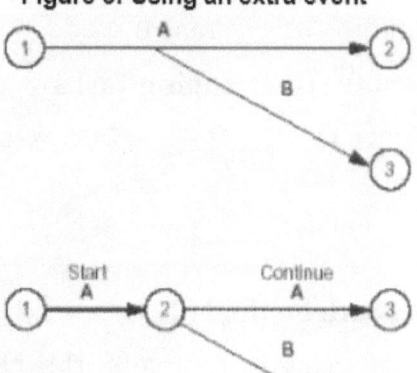

Step 4: Detect Common Problem Situations and Fix Them

You might encounter certain common issues in your task flow. Use dummies or extra events to resolve them. Here are three common scenarios:

1. **Simultaneous tasks that start and end at the same**

events: Add a dummy and extra event to separate the tasks (Figure 1).

2. **A task depends on two prior tasks, but a fourth task only depends on one:** Use a dummy arrow to correctly sequence the tasks (Figure 2).
3. **A second task can start before the first task is fully done:** Split the first task into subtasks and add an event between them (Figure 3).

Figure 1: Dummy Separating Simultaneous Tasks

O ____ Task A ____ O ____ Task C

|____ Task B ____|

Figure 2: Dummy Keeping Sequence Correct

O ____ Task A ____ O ____ Task C

\

__ Dummy __ O ____ Task B

Figure 3: Extra Event for Overlapping Tasks

O ____ Task A (part 1) ____ O ____ Task A (part 2) ____ O Task C

|___ Task B ____|

Scheduling: Critical Path Method (CPM)

Once the network of tasks is complete, the next step is to schedule the tasks using the **Critical Path Method (CPM)**. This will help determine which tasks are critical and must be completed on time to avoid delaying the project.

Step 5: Calculate Task Durations

Estimate the time each task will take and write this duration on the corresponding arrows. Use consistent units like days, weeks, or hours throughout the diagram.

Step 6: Identify the Critical Path

The critical path is the longest sequence of tasks from start to finish. It determines the shortest time in which the project can be completed. To find the critical path, calculate the earliest start (ES) and earliest finish (EF) times for each task, followed by the latest start (LS) and latest finish (LF) times.

- **Earliest Start (ES):** The largest EF of the preceding tasks.
- **Earliest Finish (EF):** ES + task duration.

Then, work backward from the final task to calculate LS and LF:

- **Latest Finish (LF):** The smallest LS of the succeeding tasks.
- **Latest Start (LS):** LF - task duration.

The tasks on the critical path will have no slack (LS = ES and LF = EF).

Step 7: Calculate Slack Times

For tasks not on the critical path, calculate the slack time—the amount of time a task can be delayed without affecting the project timeline. The formula for total slack is:

Total Slack: LS - ES or LF - EF

Tasks with slack time can be postponed without delaying the overall project. Those on the critical path have zero slack.

Arrow Diagram Example

Let's consider an example project with the following tasks and durations (in days):

Task	Duration	Predecessor
A	3	-

B	2	A
C	4	A
D	1	B, C

The arrow diagram with the critical path highlighted might look like this:

plaintext

Copy code

```
O ____(3)____ O ____(2)____ O
    Task A     Task B   Task D (Critical Path)
          |___(4)___|
             Task C
```

In this case, the critical path is A → B → D, and the total project duration is 6 days.

Conclusion

An arrow diagram is a powerful tool for visualizing task dependencies, sequencing activities, and identifying the critical path in complex projects. It provides clarity on what must be prioritized and helps avoid delays, ensuring timely project completion. By learning how to create and use arrow diagrams effectively, project managers can navigate intricate tasks and resources with precision and confidence.

How do I calculate ES?

How to Calculate Earliest Start (ES) in an Arrow Diagram

The **Earliest Start (ES)** of a task is the earliest time at which a task can begin, given the completion of all preceding tasks. To calculate the ES, you need to work from the start of the project to the end. This process is known as the **forward pass** in Critical Path Method (CPM).

Here's a detailed step-by-step guide to calculating the **Earliest Start (ES):**

Step 1: Set the Earliest Start of the First Task to Zero

The project starts with the first task, and since it is the first activity, its **Earliest Start (ES)** is always **0**.

Example:

- Task A is the first task.
    - **ES of Task A = 0**

Step 2: Determine the Earliest Start for Other Tasks

For every other task, the **Earliest Start (ES)** is determined by the **Earliest Finish (EF)** of its immediate predecessor(s). The ES of a task is equal to the **Earliest Finish** of the task that comes right before it. If a task has multiple preceding tasks, the ES is the latest of those preceding tasks' **Earliest Finish** times.

Formula:

ES of a task=max (EF of all predecessor tasks)\text{ES of a task} = \max(\text{EF of all predecessor tasks})ES of a task=max(EF of all predecessor tasks)

- If a task has a single predecessor, the **Earliest Start** is simply the **Earliest Finish** of that predecessor.
- If a task has multiple predecessors, the **Earliest Start** is the largest **Earliest Finish** value among those predecessors.

Example:

Let's say Task B follows Task A, and Task C follows both Task A and Task B.

1. **Task A** has no predecessors, so **ES = 0**.
2. Assume **Task A** takes 3 days, so its **Earliest Finish**

(EF) is 3.
- EF of Task A = ES + Duration = 0 + 3 = 3
3. **Task B** can begin after Task A finishes, so **ES of Task B = EF of Task A = 3**.
4. Assume **Task B** takes 2 days, so **EF of Task B = ES + Duration = 3 + 2 = 5**.
5. **Task C** can only start after both Task A and Task B finish. If Task C depends on both, its **Earliest Start** will be the later of the **Earliest Finish** of Task A or Task B. In this case:
   - **ES of Task C = max(EF of Task A, EF of Task B) = max(3, 5) = 5**

Step 3: Calculate the Earliest Finish (EF)

To calculate the **Earliest Start** (ES) for the next task, you will need to compute the **Earliest Finish** (EF) for the current task. The formula for **Earliest Finish** is:

$$EF = ES + Duration$$

This helps in determining when the next task can start. The **Earliest Finish** (EF) of a task becomes the **Earliest Start (ES)** for the next task in line.

Example:

Let's assume we have the following task details:

- **Task A**: Duration = 3 days, no predecessor → ES = 0
- **Task B**: Duration = 2 days, follows Task A → EF = 3
- **Task C**: Duration = 4 days, follows Task B → EF = 5

Thus:

- **ES of Task A = 0, EF of Task A = 3**
- **ES of Task B = 3, EF of Task B = 5**

- ES of Task C = 5, EF of Task C = 9

Example Walkthrough

Let's go through a full example where we calculate the **Earliest Start (ES)** and **Earliest Finish (EF)** for several tasks in a project.

Project Details:

Task	Duration (days)	Predecessor
A	3	-
B	2	A
C	4	A
D	1	B, C

1. **Task A:**
    - No predecessor.
    - **ES of Task A = 0** (because it's the first task).
    - **EF of Task A = ES + Duration = 0 + 3 = 3.**
2. **Task B:**
    - Predecessor: Task A.
    - **ES of Task B = EF of Task A = 3.**
    - **EF of Task B = ES + Duration = 3 + 2 = 5.**
3. **Task C:**
    - Predecessor: Task A.
    - **ES of Task C = EF of Task A = 3** (since it can begin right after Task A finishes).
    - **EF of Task C = ES + Duration = 3 + 4 = 7.**
4. **Task D:**
    - Predecessors: Task B and Task C.
    - Since Task D cannot begin until both Task B and Task C are completed, we take the later **EF** from Tasks B and C.

- ES of Task D = max(EF of Task B, EF of Task C) = max(5, 7) = 7.
- EF of Task D = ES + Duration = 7 + 1 = 8.

Resulting Early Start and Finish Schedule:

Task	Duration (days)	ES (Earliest Start)	EF (Earliest Finish)
A	3	0	3
B	2	3	5
C	4	3	7
D	1	7	8

Conclusion

In an arrow diagram, the **Earliest Start (ES)** for each task is calculated by working forward from the start of the project, using the **Earliest Finish (EF)** of preceding tasks. By calculating the ES for each task, you can develop a clear timeline and identify critical tasks that affect the overall project completion.

CHAPTER – 5
Balanced Scorecard (BSC)

Implementing the Balanced Scorecard (BSC) for Continuous Improvement

Importance Rating (1 to 10)	6	6	10	8	7	Weighted Score	
Strategy / Initiative	Reduce COPQ	Reduce Inventory	Improve Market Share	Retain Talent	Improve Productivity		
Reduce attrition rate	3	3	3	9	3	159	TOP PRIORITY
Reduce casting rejection	9	3	1	0	9	145	NEXT PRIORITY
Reduce product development time	1	3	9	3	1	145	
Improve training effectiveness	3	3	1	9	3	139	
Eliminate rework at pump assembly	9	1	0	0	9	123	
Reduce pump failures	9	1	3	0	1	97	
Improve accuracy of bill of materials	0	9	1	0	3	85	
Reduce set up time on bottleneck machine	0	3	0	0	9	81	
Reduce time to make engineering changes	1	1	3	0	1	49	
Improve store accuracy	1	3	0	0	3	45	QUEUE
Reduce time to fix field problems	3	0	0	0	0	18	
Reduce energy consumption	1	0	0	0	1	13	

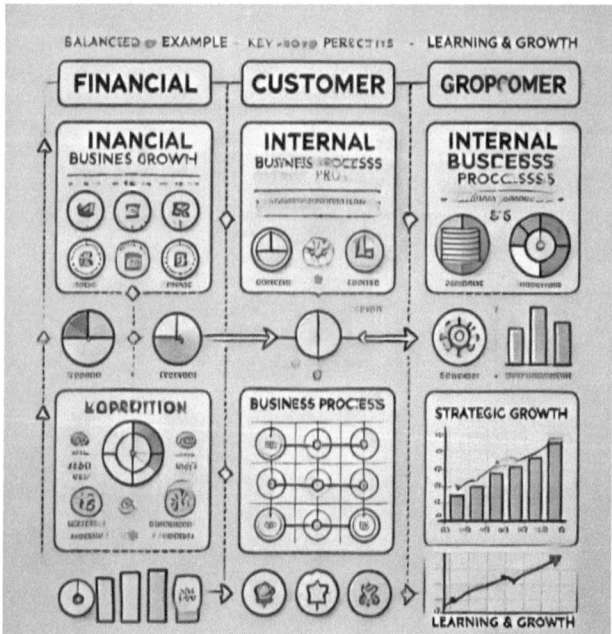

The Balanced Scorecard (BSC) is a vital strategic management tool that helps organizations track, measure, and improve both internal processes and external outcomes, leading to enhanced strategic performance. By integrating perspectives on financial performance, customer experience, internal business processes, and learning and growth, a BSC offers a comprehensive view of organizational health and alignment with long-term goals.

1. Introduction to the Balanced Scorecard

The BSC was introduced in the early 1990s by Robert Kaplan and David Norton to provide a holistic view of organizational performance, beyond just financial metrics. They argued that while financial measures provide insight into past performance, they are insufficient to predict future success. In today's knowledge-driven world, a focus on customers, processes, innovation, and learning is crucial for sustained growth.

2. The Four Perspectives of the Balanced Scorecard

A balanced scorecard typically assesses an organization's performance from four key perspectives:

1. **Financial Perspective**
   This perspective answers the question: "How do we look to our shareholders?"
   Financial measures such as revenue growth, profit margins, and return on investment (ROI) remain essential. However, they are now seen as part of a broader picture. The focus is on ensuring profitability and value creation through the strategic implementation of initiatives that enhance customer satisfaction and internal efficiencies.

Example:
A retail company might track its gross profit margins, aiming for a 5% improvement year-on-year, while also measuring cash flow from operational activities.

Illustration: A line graph showing the company's gross profit margin over time, with a target line highlighting the desired 5% growth.

2. **Customer Perspective**
   This perspective considers: "How do customers see us?"
   It focuses on customer satisfaction, retention, and market share. The idea is to assess how well the organization meets customer needs and expectations. A strong customer perspective is directly linked to future revenue growth.

Example:
An ecommerce platform might measure customer satisfaction through Net Promoter Score (NPS), aiming to increase it by 10 points over the next quarter.

Illustration: A customer satisfaction survey displaying an increase in NPS score from 50 to 60 over three months, with key improvement initiatives listed (e.g., enhanced customer service, faster delivery).

3. Business Process Perspective

This focuses on internal processes and asks: "What must we excel at to meet both customer and shareholder expectations?"

The goal is to identify the critical processes that lead to financial success and satisfied customers. This might include operational efficiencies, quality assurance, or supply chain management.

Example:

In a retail business, streamlining the supply chain could reduce delivery times from 7 days to 3 days, leading to higher customer satisfaction and reduced operational costs.

Illustration: A process flow diagram showing the original supply chain steps and the new optimized process, highlighting time savings and cost reductions.

4. Learning and Growth Perspective

This perspective answers: "How can we continue to improve and create value?"

It focuses on developing the skills, capabilities, and culture needed for long-term success. This includes employee training, leadership development, and fostering innovation.

Example:

A company might implement continuous learning programs, aiming for a 15% increase in employee skill certifications related to Lean Six Sigma principles over the next year.

Illustration: A bar chart showing the growth in employee certifications over time, with specific Lean Six Sigma belts (e.g., Green Belt, Black Belt) highlighted.

3. Developing Metrics and Targets

For each perspective, the Balanced Scorecard requires the development of specific metrics and targets. These metrics should be actionable, measurable, and aligned with the organization's overall strategy.

- **Financial Example:** Increase return on investment (ROI) from 12% to 15% within 12 months.
- **Customer Example:** Achieve a customer retention rate of 90% by the end of the next fiscal year.
- **Business Process Example:** Reduce average product defect rates from 3% to 1% within six months.
- **Learning and Growth Example:** Increase internal promotion rates by 20% over the next two years by implementing robust leadership development programs.

4. The Benefits of a Balanced Scorecard

Implementing a Balanced Scorecard offers several benefits:

- **Strategic Alignment:** It ensures that every department and employee understands and works towards the organization's overarching goals. This alignment drives consistency and focus across the board.
- **Enhanced Communication:** The BSC establishes a shared language around metrics and performance. It creates clear communication lines between departments, allowing for the efficient exchange of information and ideas.
- **Performance Tracking:** Regular reviews of the scorecard enable leadership to track progress and take corrective action when necessary. Metrics

provide insight into areas that need improvement and those that are performing well.

- **Fostering a Culture of Continuous Improvement:** With the Learning and Growth perspective, employees are empowered to innovate and improve, driving long-term success.

5. Example of a Balanced Scorecard Implementation in Retail

Scenario:
Let's consider a retail business that has been facing declining market share and increasing customer complaints about slow deliveries. By implementing a BSC, the company can focus on the following:

1. **Financial Perspective:**
   Target: Achieve a 10% increase in market share within 12 months.
   Metric: Monthly market share percentage.

2. **Customer Perspective:**
   Target: Reduce delivery times by 50% within 6 months.
   Metric: Average delivery time (in days) and customer satisfaction scores.

3. **Business Process Perspective:**
   Target: Streamline internal processes to reduce operational costs by 15%.
   Metric: Operational cost per delivery.

4. **Learning and Growth Perspective:**
   Target: Train 80% of staff in Lean Six Sigma methodologies to improve process efficiency.
   Metric: Percentage of staff certified in Lean Six Sigma.

Illustration: A retail dashboard showing each of these metrics with a traffic light system (green for on track, yellow for at risk, red for behind), highlighting progress and areas for attention.

6. Conclusion: Achieving Continuous Improvement with the BSC

The Balanced Scorecard offers a structured and dynamic approach to performance management. By balancing short-term financial goals with long-term strategic initiatives, organizations can ensure sustainable success. It provides the feedback loops necessary for continuous improvement, allowing businesses to refine strategies, improve processes, and invest in innovation.

As you continue to implement the Balanced Scorecard, remember to review your metrics regularly, adjust targets based on performance, and ensure that your teams remain aligned with the organization's vision.

How to set BSC goals?

Setting effective Balanced Scorecard (BSC) goals is crucial for ensuring that your organization's strategy translates into actionable, measurable outcomes. To do this successfully, follow a structured process that aligns BSC goals with your company's vision, mission, and strategy across the four perspectives: Financial, Customer, Internal Business Processes, and Learning & Growth. Below is a step-by-step guide to setting BSC goals, accompanied by examples and best practices.

1. Understand the Organization's Strategic Vision and Mission

Before setting specific BSC goals, it is essential to understand the organization's long-term vision and mission. Your BSC goals should directly contribute to achieving these high-level strategic objectives.

- **Vision**: Where the organization aspires to be in the long term.
- **Mission**: What the organization does to achieve its vision.

For example, if your organization's vision is to become the leading e-commerce platform in customer satisfaction, your BSC goals should support initiatives that enhance the customer experience.

2. Break Down the Strategy into Specific Objectives

Translate the strategic vision into actionable objectives across the four perspectives of the BSC. These objectives should be clear, measurable, and directly related to improving performance.

Examples:

- **Financial Objective**: Increase revenue by expanding into new markets.
- **Customer Objective**: Improve customer retention by enhancing the shopping experience.
- **Internal Business Process Objective**: Streamline operations to reduce order processing time.
- **Learning & Growth Objective**: Enhance employee skills through targeted training programs.

3. Develop SMART Goals for Each Perspective

When setting BSC goals, ensure they follow the **SMART** criteria:

- **Specific**: Clear and well-defined.
- **Measurable**: Quantifiable, with metrics to track progress.
- **Achievable**: Realistic given the available resources and time.

- **Relevant**: Aligned with strategic priorities.
- **Time-bound**: Linked to a specific timeline.

Let's look at how to apply SMART goals for each perspective of the BSC:

- **Financial Perspective**
  Goal: "Increase gross profit margins by 5% in the next 12 months by reducing product costs through better supplier negotiations."
- **Customer Perspective**
  Goal: "Improve Net Promoter Score (NPS) by 10 points within 6 months by implementing a 24/7 customer service chatbot."
- **Internal Business Process Perspective**
  Goal: "Reduce product return rates from 5% to 2% within 9 months by improving quality control processes."
- **Learning & Growth Perspective**
  Goal: "Increase the percentage of employees trained in project management from 30% to 60% in the next 12 months."

4. Identify Key Performance Indicators (KPIs)

For each SMART goal, you need to define **Key Performance Indicators (KPIs)** to measure progress and success. KPIs are quantifiable metrics that track performance over time. Each BSC perspective should have relevant KPIs that help monitor whether you're on track to achieving your goals.

Examples of KPIs for Each Perspective:

- **Financial Perspective**:
  - Revenue growth rate
  - Return on investment (ROI)
  - Cost of goods sold (COGS) as a percentage of

revenue
- **Customer Perspective**:
  - Customer satisfaction score (CSAT)
  - Net Promoter Score (NPS)
  - Customer retention rate
- **Internal Business Process Perspective**:
  - Average order fulfillment time
  - Process error rate
  - Production efficiency
- **Learning & Growth Perspective**:
  - Employee engagement score
  - Training completion rate
  - Internal promotion rate

5. Set Performance Targets

Each KPI should have a **performance target**—the desired level of performance within a specific time frame. Targets provide benchmarks to assess whether you're achieving your goals.

Examples:

- **Financial KPI**: Target ROI of 12% within 12 months.
- **Customer KPI**: Achieve an NPS of 75 by the end of the fiscal year.
- **Process KPI**: Reduce order fulfillment time to under 48 hours within six months.
- **Learning & Growth KPI**: Ensure 80% of employees complete leadership training within the next year.

6. Align Goals Across the Organization

To ensure that all departments and teams contribute to the overarching goals, BSC goals should be cascaded down through the organization. Each department may have specific goals that align with the company's broader strategic objectives.

Example of Cascading Goals:

- **Company-Level Financial Goal**: Increase profit margins by 5% in the next 12 months.
  - **Sales Department Goal**: Increase average deal size by 10%.
  - **Procurement Goal**: Negotiate 7% lower costs with key suppliers.
  - **Operations Goal**: Reduce manufacturing costs by 8% through process optimization.

7. Regularly Monitor and Adjust Goals

Once BSC goals and KPIs are set, it's important to establish a system for regular monitoring and review. Progress should be evaluated at predetermined intervals (e.g., monthly or quarterly) to assess whether you are on track.

- **Create Dashboards**: Use dashboards to visualize real-time progress on each KPI and performance target.
- **Conduct Regular Reviews**: Hold review meetings with key stakeholders to discuss performance, identify areas needing improvement, and adjust goals if necessary.

Example:

A quarterly review might reveal that customer satisfaction scores are not improving as expected. In response, you may decide to increase investment in customer service training or adjust the chatbot to handle more complex queries.

8. Communicate Goals and Progress Across the Organization

For BSC goals to be effective, they must be clearly communicated throughout the organization. Every employee should understand how their role contributes to the broader organizational strategy.

Best Practices for Communication:

- **Town Hall Meetings**: Present company goals and explain how each department can contribute.
- **Team Huddles**: Department heads should regularly meet with their teams to communicate progress and adjust tactics.
- **Internal Newsletters**: Share updates on BSC performance and recognize teams or individuals who are contributing to success.

9. Examples of Balanced Scorecard Goals for Different Industries

- **Manufacturing Company**:
    - **Financial**: Increase operating margin from 15% to 20% over the next 2 years.
    - **Customer**: Improve on-time delivery rates from 85% to 95% within 6 months.
    - **Process**: Decrease production cycle time by 10% in the next year.
    - **Learning & Growth**: Increase workforce productivity by 15% through skill development programs.
- **Healthcare Organization**:
    - **Financial**: Reduce operational costs by 8% through better resource allocation.
    - **Customer**: Increase patient satisfaction scores from 80 to 90 within the next year.
    - **Process**: Decrease patient wait times from an average of 30 minutes to 15 minutes within six months.
    - **Learning & Growth**: Train 100% of staff on new healthcare regulations within 3 months.

10. Conclusion

Setting Balanced Scorecard goals requires a thoughtful and strategic approach that aligns with the overall organizational vision. By developing SMART goals, identifying relevant KPIs, setting performance targets, and ensuring continuous monitoring and communication, your BSC will become a powerful tool for driving strategic success and continuous improvement.

As you work to implement the BSC framework, remember that flexibility is key—be willing to adjust goals as conditions change and new opportunities or challenges emerge.

Tips for Effective Balanced Scorecard (BSC) Implementation

Implementing the Balanced Scorecard (BSC) effectively is crucial for achieving strategic alignment and driving organizational performance. While the BSC offers a structured framework for tracking goals across multiple perspectives, its success depends on careful planning, clear communication, and continuous monitoring. Below are key tips for implementing the BSC in your organization.

1. Start with Clear Strategic Goals

The foundation of a successful BSC implementation lies in having clear, well-defined strategic goals. These goals should be derived from your organization's vision and mission.

- **Tip**: Break down high-level strategic goals into actionable, specific objectives for each of the four BSC perspectives (Financial, Customer, Internal Processes, Learning & Growth). Ensure these objectives are directly aligned with your long-term strategy.

Example:
If the strategic goal is to become the market leader in customer satisfaction, the Customer Perspective might include goals like improving customer service response times or increasing the Net Promoter Score (NPS).

2. Gain Leadership Buy-In and Commitment

Top management support is critical for the successful implementation of a BSC. Without leadership commitment, it will be difficult to secure the resources and attention required for success.

- **Tip**: Involve key executives early in the process. Ensure that they understand the importance of the BSC, how it aligns with the company's vision, and what role they play in driving its success.

Example:
Hold executive meetings to explain how the BSC will improve decision-making by providing a clear view of strategic progress, helping leaders to prioritize initiatives.

3. Start Small and Scale Gradually

It can be tempting to implement the BSC across the entire organization immediately. However, starting with a small pilot program allows you to refine the process and iron out any issues before a full-scale implementation.

- **Tip**: Begin by introducing the BSC to one department or business unit, preferably one that is critical to your organization's strategic goals. Once the framework is working effectively in this area, scale it to other departments.

Example:
A manufacturing company may start by implementing the BSC in its operations department to focus on improving production efficiency, then roll it out to the sales and marketing teams after reviewing initial success.

---

4. Involve Employees at All Levels

Successful BSC implementation requires the involvement of employees at all levels of the organization. Their understanding of the goals and their role in achieving them is essential for success.

- **Tip**: Ensure that employees are informed about the BSC framework and how their daily activities contribute to the company's strategic objectives. Use regular training and communication channels like team meetings, newsletters, or internal portals.

Example:
When implementing the BSC in a customer service department, conduct workshops to help employees understand how improving response times or resolving more issues on the first call ties into the broader Customer and Process objectives.

---

5. Develop Meaningful KPIs and Metrics

Key Performance Indicators (KPIs) are the backbone of the BSC. However, KPIs must be meaningful and relevant to your organization's goals. Metrics should be actionable, providing insights into what needs improvement rather than just data collection.

- **Tip**: Avoid overcomplicating your KPIs. Focus on a few critical indicators for each perspective that will provide the most value in tracking progress toward strategic goals. Ensure these KPIs are easy to understand and measure.

Example:
For the Financial Perspective, use metrics like profit margin, return on investment (ROI), and cash flow, instead of focusing on dozens of financial ratios. For the Customer Perspective, focus on NPS and customer retention rates.

---

6. Set Realistic Performance Targets

The BSC is designed to push organizations toward strategic goals, but unrealistic performance targets can demotivate employees and cause frustration.

- **Tip**: Ensure that the performance targets set for each KPI are challenging but achievable. Involve employees and managers in the target-setting process to get their input and ensure buy-in.

Example:
Instead of setting a target of improving customer satisfaction by 20 points in 3 months, consider a more realistic target of a 5-point improvement over the next quarter, followed by incremental improvements.

---

7. Establish a System for Continuous Monitoring and Feedback

The BSC is not a one-time tool; it requires continuous monitoring to ensure that performance stays on track. Establish regular reviews to evaluate performance and adjust strategies as needed.

- **Tip**: Create a dashboard or automated reporting system to track KPIs in real-time. Hold monthly or quarterly review meetings with leadership to discuss progress, adjust goals, and address areas where performance is lagging.

Example:
An e-commerce company might have a dashboard showing real-time customer metrics like satisfaction scores and average response times, which managers can review weekly to ensure targets are being met.

8. Link the BSC to Incentives

Incentives and rewards can significantly boost motivation for achieving BSC goals. Aligning employee incentives with BSC performance ensures that everyone is working toward the same objectives.

- **Tip**: Use the BSC to inform bonuses, promotions, or other rewards. Ensure that rewards are tied not only to financial metrics but also to customer satisfaction, internal processes, and learning and growth achievements.

Example:
Tie bonuses in the customer service department to metrics such as first-call resolution rates and average customer satisfaction scores, not just to financial performance.

9. Ensure Flexibility and Adaptability

While the BSC provides a structured approach, it's important to remain flexible. Business environments are constantly changing, and your BSC should be adaptable to shifts in strategy or market conditions.

- **Tip**: Regularly review and update your goals, KPIs, and performance targets. Be willing to revise objectives if market conditions change or if certain initiatives aren't delivering the expected results.

Example:
If a new competitor enters the market, you may need to adjust your customer satisfaction goals or introduce new initiatives

focused on customer retention.

10. Foster a Culture of Continuous Improvement

The BSC is a dynamic tool that promotes continuous improvement. Encourage a culture where employees regularly seek ways to enhance processes, learn new skills, and contribute to the organization's success.

- **Tip**: Integrate continuous improvement initiatives into the Learning and Growth Perspective. Encourage employees to share feedback on how processes can be optimized, and reward innovation.

Example:
A tech company may implement a suggestion system where employees can propose process improvements, linking those ideas to internal process KPIs on the BSC.

11. Use Technology to Support Implementation

Leveraging technology can simplify the tracking and reporting of BSC metrics. There are numerous software solutions designed to automate data collection, reporting, and analysis.

- **Tip**: Invest in BSC software tools that allow you to easily track KPIs, generate reports, and visualize data. These tools can help automate the process of collecting and reviewing performance data, freeing up time for analysis and decision-making.

Example:
A cloud-based BSC tool can automatically pull data from various systems (like sales, customer support, and HR systems) and update dashboards in real-time for managers to review.

12. Communicate the Value of the BSC

To ensure widespread adoption, employees at all levels need to understand the value of the BSC. Effective communication helps to align the entire organization around the shared goals represented in the scorecard.

- **Tip**: Share the successes achieved through the BSC. Highlight case studies or examples within the organization where BSC-driven improvements have led to measurable results. This reinforces the importance of the tool and encourages further engagement.

Example:
If a department hits its BSC targets and significantly improves customer satisfaction, share this success across the organization via newsletters, town halls, or internal social networks.

Conclusion

Implementing the Balanced Scorecard is a powerful way to align an organization's strategy with measurable actions and goals. By following these tips—starting with a clear strategy, gaining leadership buy-in, involving employees, setting meaningful KPIs, and regularly reviewing progress—you can ensure that the BSC becomes a driver of strategic success and continuous improvement.

Flexibility, communication, and technology are key to sustaining the BSC over time, making it a living tool that helps the organization adapt and thrive in a constantly changing environment.

Common Balanced

Scorecard (BSC) Challenges and How to Overcome Them

While the Balanced Scorecard (BSC) is an effective tool for aligning strategy with measurable performance, its implementation is not without challenges. Many organizations face hurdles when integrating the BSC into their management systems, ranging from misaligned goals to data tracking issues. Here are some of the most common challenges faced during BSC implementation, along with tips on how to overcome them.

1. Lack of Clear Strategic Objectives

One of the most common challenges in BSC implementation is the absence of clearly defined strategic objectives. Without clear, specific goals, it becomes difficult to create meaningful metrics and align performance across the organization.

- **Symptoms**: Vague goals, difficulty in setting measurable KPIs, misalignment across departments.
- **Solution**: Start by clarifying the organization's vision and mission. Break down the high-level strategy into specific, actionable objectives for each of the four BSC perspectives (Financial, Customer, Internal Processes, Learning & Growth). Ensure these objectives are specific, measurable, and directly linked to the organization's overall goals.

Example:

Instead of setting a general goal like "improve customer satisfaction," define a specific target such as "increase Net Promoter Score (NPS) by 10 points in the next 12 months."

2. Overcomplicating the Scorecard

Another common challenge is the tendency to overcomplicate the BSC by including too many metrics or KPIs. This can overwhelm teams, dilute focus, and make it difficult to track progress effectively.

- **Symptoms**: Too many KPIs to manage, data overload, lack of focus on critical objectives.
- **Solution**: Prioritize a few key metrics for each BSC perspective. Focus on the most important KPIs that align with your strategic goals. A balanced scorecard should ideally have no more than 20–25 metrics in total, ensuring that each one is critical for decision-making.

Example:
Instead of tracking every possible metric for customer satisfaction, focus on high-impact ones like customer retention rate, first-call resolution, and NPS.

3. Misaligned Organizational Goals

If departments or teams are not aligned with the overall organizational strategy, the BSC will not be effective. Misalignment often occurs when individual departments pursue their own priorities, which may not fully support the company's overall objectives.

- **Symptoms**: Conflicting departmental goals, siloed decision-making, teams working on initiatives that don't contribute to strategic objectives.
- **Solution**: Use the cascading approach to BSC

implementation. Ensure that departmental and individual goals align with the company's broader strategic goals. Encourage cross-functional collaboration and align incentives across departments.

Example:
If the company's strategic goal is to improve operational efficiency, the sales team should focus on high-margin products, while the operations team focuses on reducing production cycle time.

4. Poor KPI Selection

Choosing the wrong Key Performance Indicators (KPIs) can lead to ineffective performance tracking. Some organizations may focus on easily measurable KPIs that don't necessarily drive strategic progress or pick too many indicators that don't tell the full story.

- **Symptoms**: KPIs that don't provide actionable insights, difficulty measuring intangible goals, metrics that focus on outputs rather than outcomes.
- **Solution**: Choose KPIs that are directly linked to strategic objectives and that measure performance in a meaningful way. For more qualitative objectives (e.g., customer satisfaction, employee engagement), use indirect measures like surveys or interviews to capture relevant data.

Example:
Instead of measuring the number of customer service calls handled, measure the percentage of issues resolved on the first contact (First Call Resolution), which ties directly to customer satisfaction.

5. Lack of Employee Buy-In

A major challenge in BSC implementation is getting employees to understand and commit to the system. Without proper buy-in, employees may view the BSC as just another management tool with little relevance to their daily work.

- **Symptoms**: Resistance to new processes, lack of engagement in performance reviews, employees not linking their roles to the broader strategy.
- **Solution**: Communicate the purpose and benefits of the BSC clearly to all employees. Show them how their roles contribute to the company's strategic objectives and explain how performance on the BSC impacts organizational success. Involve employees in the goal-setting process to give them ownership over their KPIs.

Example:
Hold workshops or team meetings to explain how a customer service representative's daily performance affects company-wide goals like improving the Net Promoter Score (NPS).

6. Inconsistent Data Collection and Tracking

For the BSC to work, you need reliable and consistent data collection. Many organizations struggle with incomplete data or inconsistent measurement, making it difficult to accurately assess performance.

- **Symptoms**: Gaps in performance data, outdated reports, lack of standardized measurement methods across departments.
- **Solution**: Standardize the data collection process across the organization. Invest in tools or software that automate data gathering and reporting. Ensure that all teams are trained in how to measure and report their KPIs consistently.

Example:
If you're tracking customer satisfaction, ensure that every department uses the same method (e.g., customer surveys, NPS) and collects data at the same frequency (e.g., weekly or monthly).

---

7. Failure to Review and Adjust the BSC

Some organizations treat the BSC as a one-time project, failing to regularly review and adjust it. As business environments and strategies evolve, the BSC must be continuously monitored and updated.

- **Symptoms**: Stagnant KPIs, outdated goals, lack of flexibility in adjusting to changes in the market or strategy.
- **Solution**: Set a schedule for regular reviews (e.g., quarterly or semi-annually) to assess the effectiveness of the BSC. Adjust KPIs, goals, and targets as necessary based on changing market conditions or internal priorities. Ensure that the BSC remains a dynamic tool, not a static report.

Example:
If a new competitor enters the market and disrupts customer preferences, adjust your customer-related goals and KPIs to focus more on retention or product differentiation.

---

8. Lack of Leadership Involvement

BSC implementation often fails when senior leaders are not actively involved. Without leadership driving the initiative, the BSC can lose momentum and become less of a priority.

- **Symptoms**: Low accountability for BSC performance, lack of strategic direction, BSC not integrated into decision-making processes.

- **Solution**: Ensure that senior leaders champion the BSC and are actively involved in its implementation and review. Leadership should regularly discuss BSC progress in management meetings and hold departments accountable for their performance.

Example:
The CEO and senior leadership team should regularly review BSC metrics as part of their strategic discussions, making decisions based on the insights provided by the scorecard.

9. Inflexibility in Goal Setting

Rigidly sticking to original goals, even when market conditions or internal priorities change, can hinder the effectiveness of the BSC. Organizations need to adapt goals as needed.

- **Symptoms**: Irrelevant or outdated goals, difficulty responding to new opportunities or challenges.
- **Solution**: Maintain flexibility in setting and adjusting BSC goals. Regularly revisit goals to ensure they remain relevant. Be open to revising targets and metrics as market conditions shift or new information emerges.

Example:
If a global economic downturn affects your sales targets, consider adjusting financial goals and shifting focus to customer retention or operational efficiency.

10. Disconnect Between Strategy and Execution

In some cases, there's a disconnect between the high-level strategy reflected in the BSC and the day-to-day execution. When the scorecard remains at the strategic level and doesn't trickle down to daily operations, its impact diminishes.

- **Symptoms**: KPIs that are not actionable, strategy not reflected in day-to-day activities, employees unaware of how their work ties into BSC goals.
- **Solution**: Ensure that BSC goals are cascaded down to every level of the organization. This means translating high-level strategic goals into specific, actionable tasks for each department and employee. Align individual performance reviews with BSC metrics to keep execution aligned with strategy.

Example:
If the strategic goal is to improve operational efficiency, the operations team should have daily targets around reducing production time or cutting costs, directly contributing to the overall BSC goals.

Conclusion

Implementing the Balanced Scorecard is a valuable way to drive strategic alignment and improve organizational performance. However, like any management tool, it comes with challenges that need to be carefully managed. By addressing issues such as lack of clarity, overcomplicated metrics, misaligned goals, and inconsistent data tracking, organizations can overcome these obstacles and fully realize the benefits of the BSC.

Flexibility, leadership commitment, and continuous communication are essential for ensuring that the BSC remains a dynamic tool for driving organizational success.

Tools that Support Balanced Scorecard

(BSC) Implementation

The Balanced Scorecard (BSC) requires effective data tracking, reporting, and alignment across various departments to function properly. A variety of software tools are designed to support these needs, helping organizations streamline their BSC process, automate data collection, and monitor performance in real-time. These tools facilitate the implementation, management, and reporting of BSC, making it easier for businesses to align strategic objectives with day-to-day operations.

Below are some of the most popular and widely used tools that support BSC implementation.

---

1. BSC Designer

Overview:
BSC Designer is a specialized tool designed specifically for creating, managing, and tracking balanced scorecards. It allows users to define strategic goals, build strategy maps, set Key Performance Indicators (KPIs), and track performance. The tool offers real-time dashboards and scorecards, making it easy to visualize performance data.

Key Features:

- Strategy mapping and cascading goals
- Real-time dashboards for tracking KPIs
- Automated data collection from various systems
- Collaboration tools for sharing and aligning scorecards across departments
- Integration with financial and business tools

Best For:
Organizations looking for a comprehensive, BSC-specific tool

with advanced features like strategy mapping and real-time KPI tracking.

2. ClearPoint Strategy

Overview:
ClearPoint Strategy is another tool tailored for managing the Balanced Scorecard. It offers a comprehensive suite of features for strategy management, including performance tracking, automated reporting, and strategy maps. ClearPoint also allows for easy collaboration and alignment across teams and departments, helping ensure that all parts of the organization are aligned with the strategic goals.

Key Features:

- Drag-and-drop strategy maps
- Performance tracking and dashboards
- Automated reporting
- Customizable templates for different industries
- Role-based access control for different teams

Best For:
Organizations that need a customizable BSC solution with strong reporting and collaboration features.

3. SAP BusinessObjects

Overview:
SAP BusinessObjects is a robust business intelligence platform that supports BSC implementation by allowing organizations to analyze and report on key data points. While not a dedicated BSC tool, it provides extensive capabilities for tracking and visualizing KPIs. With its strong integration capabilities, SAP BusinessObjects can collect data from various departments and systems to provide a holistic view of business performance.

Key Features:

- Business intelligence and analytics reporting
- KPI tracking and performance management
- Custom dashboards and reports
- Data integration from multiple sources
- Real-time data visualization

Best For:
Large enterprises looking for an all-in-one business intelligence solution with the ability to track BSC metrics along with other business analytics.

---

4. QuickScore

Overview:
QuickScore is a performance management software that is specifically designed for implementing the Balanced Scorecard. It helps users manage strategic goals, track KPIs, and visualize performance through scorecards and strategy maps. QuickScore is cloud-based, allowing users to access their scorecards from anywhere, and offers various tools for automated reporting and collaboration.

Key Features:

- Customizable strategy maps and scorecards
- Real-time KPI tracking
- Automated performance reports
- Integration with other business tools like Excel
- Collaboration tools for teams

Best For:
Organizations seeking a cloud-based, user-friendly BSC tool with strong collaboration and real-time performance tracking features.

5. Tableau

Overview:
Tableau is a powerful data visualization and business intelligence tool that can support BSC by helping users create interactive dashboards for KPI tracking. While it's not a dedicated BSC tool, Tableau's strength lies in its ability to integrate with a wide variety of data sources and present performance metrics in a highly visual format.

Key Features:
- Real-time data integration from various sources
- Interactive dashboards and visual reports
- KPI tracking and trend analysis
- Customizable performance scorecards
- Advanced analytics and drill-down capabilities

Best For:
Organizations that need powerful data visualization and dashboard creation to track BSC metrics alongside other business performance data.

6. IBM Cognos Analytics

Overview:
IBM Cognos Analytics is a comprehensive business intelligence platform that supports performance management and KPI tracking, making it suitable for BSC implementations. It offers powerful analytics, dashboard creation, and reporting features, allowing organizations to visualize and manage their BSC metrics. The tool integrates well with other data sources, making it easy to automate the collection of KPI data.

Key Features:
- Advanced analytics and reporting
- Real-time data tracking

- Custom dashboards and scorecards
- Integration with various data sources
- Automated KPI tracking and performance analysis

Best For:
Large enterprises that need an enterprise-grade solution with extensive analytics and reporting capabilities to manage their BSC.

7. Spider Strategies

Overview:
Spider Strategies offers a cloud-based performance management platform that is ideal for implementing the Balanced Scorecard. The tool allows organizations to create and track scorecards, monitor KPIs, and generate real-time reports. It also offers a range of visualization tools like strategy maps, heat maps, and dashboards, making it easy to communicate performance across the organization.

Key Features:

- Customizable strategy maps and scorecards
- Real-time performance dashboards
- Heat maps for visualizing KPI performance
- Automated reporting and alerts
- Data integration with external sources

Best For:
Organizations looking for a cloud-based BSC tool with strong data visualization and reporting capabilities.

8. Smartsheet

Overview:
Smartsheet is a flexible, cloud-based collaboration tool that, while not specifically designed for BSC, can be adapted

for BSC tracking and management. It allows teams to create scorecards, track KPIs, and monitor progress through customizable dashboards. Smartsheet's strength lies in its simplicity and collaborative features, making it ideal for smaller teams or organizations.

Key Features:

- Customizable scorecards and dashboards
- Task management and collaboration features
- Integration with third-party apps and data sources
- Real-time performance tracking
- Automation and reporting features

Best For:
Small to medium-sized organizations looking for a simple, flexible, and collaborative tool to track BSC metrics.

9. Domo

Overview:
Domo is a cloud-based business intelligence tool that helps organizations visualize and manage KPIs, including those associated with the Balanced Scorecard. It offers real-time data tracking and dashboards, making it easy to monitor progress across all BSC perspectives. Domo integrates with various data sources, allowing seamless KPI tracking from multiple departments.

Key Features:

- Real-time KPI tracking and performance dashboards
- Data integration from multiple sources
- Custom reports and visualizations
- Collaborative tools for team alignment
- Automated alerts for performance tracking

Best For:
Organizations that want to track BSC metrics along with broader business intelligence in a cloud-based platform.

10. Microsoft Power BI

Overview:
Microsoft Power BI is a widely used business intelligence tool that can support BSC by providing powerful KPI tracking, data visualization, and reporting features. It integrates easily with other Microsoft tools like Excel and SharePoint, making it a versatile solution for organizations that need to track performance and visualize BSC metrics in real-time.

Key Features:

- Interactive dashboards and reports
- Real-time KPI tracking and trend analysis
- Data integration from a wide variety of sources
- Customizable performance scorecards
- Integration with Microsoft Office tools

Best For:
Organizations that are heavily invested in the Microsoft ecosystem and need a versatile tool for BSC tracking and broader business analytics.

Conclusion

Choosing the right tool for Balanced Scorecard implementation depends on the size of your organization, your existing technology stack, and your specific needs. Whether you need a specialized tool like **BSC Designer** or **QuickScore**, or a more versatile business intelligence platform like **Tableau** or **Power BI**, the key is to select a tool that aligns with your strategic objectives, supports KPI tracking, and offers real-time reporting to ensure continuous monitoring and adjustment of your BSC metrics.

CHAPTER – 6
Box and Whisker Plots

Understanding Box and Whisker Plots: A Tool for Visualizing Data Distribution

Introduction to Box and Whisker Plots

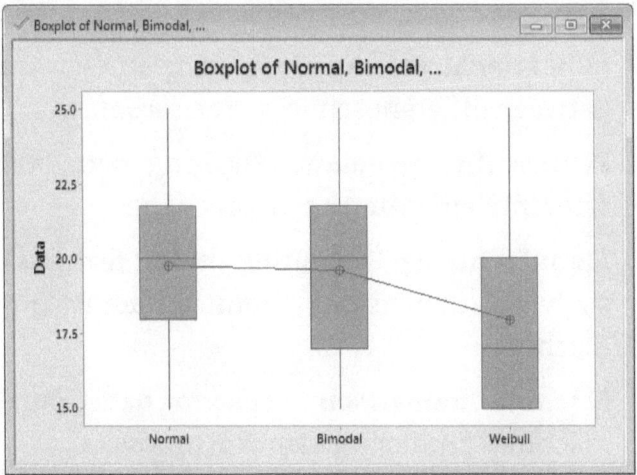

Box and whisker plots, also known as box plots, are a powerful graphical tool for visualizing the distribution and variation in a dataset. While a histogram is often sufficient for showing the frequency of values in a dataset, a box and whisker plot provides additional detail, such as the median, quartiles, and potential outliers, in a compact and easy-to-read format. This makes it especially useful when comparing multiple datasets side by side.

Why Use a Box and Whisker Plot?

Box and whisker plots are excellent for summarizing large datasets from multiple sources, enabling quick comparisons of variations across categories or conditions. They can be used to assess the spread of data, identify outliers, and make comparisons between different groups. These attributes make box and whisker plots effective for:

- Simplifying large data into a single view.
- Offering an intuitive visual representation of data distribution.
- Allowing side-by-side comparison of multiple data sets.

Example Use Cases:

- **Educational Testing**: Comparing student test scores between different schools or classrooms.
- **Process Improvement**: Showing data before and after implementing a process change.
- **Manufacturing**: Evaluating similar features in parts, such as dimensions from different production machines.
- **Machine Comparison**: Displaying data from different machines producing identical products.

Key Components of a Box and Whisker Plot

Before diving into how to create a box and whisker plot, let's first explore its key components:

1. **Minimum Value**: The smallest value in the dataset, represented by the start of the "whisker."

2. **First Quartile (Q1)**: The value below which the lower 25% of the data fall, representing the start of the box.

3. **Median**: The middle value of the dataset, represented by a line inside the box. This divides the data into two halves.

4. **Third Quartile (Q3)**: The value above which the upper 25% of the data fall, representing the end of the box.

5. **Maximum Value**: The largest value in the dataset, represented by the end of the "whisker."

In addition, **outliers**—data points that fall significantly outside the expected range—can also be represented as dots or asterisks outside the whiskers.

How to Create a Box and Whisker Plot

Let's walk through the steps for creating a box and whisker plot, using an example dataset.

Example Data Set:

Here are 20 sample measurements from a manufacturing process:

No.	Data
1	113
2	116
3	119
4	121
5	124
6	124
7	125
8	126
9	126

10	126
11	127
12	127
13	128
14	129
15	130
16	130
17	131
18	132
19	133
20	136

From this dataset, we can compute the following values:

- **Minimum**: 113
- **First Quartile (Q1)**: 124
- **Median**: 126.5 (the average of 126 and 127)
- **Third Quartile (Q3)**: 130
- **Maximum**: 136

This data can be used to construct a box and whisker plot, as illustrated below.

Illustration: Box and Whisker Plot Example

Imagine a plot with a rectangular box starting at 124 (Q1) and ending at 130 (Q3). A line inside the box at 126.5 represents the median. Two whiskers extend from the box, one down to 113 (minimum) and the other up to 136 (maximum). This shows the full range of data distribution. Outliers, if present, would appear as dots outside the whiskers.

Comparison Example: Evaluating Manufacturing Lathes

Now, let's consider a practical scenario where we compare the performance of three lathes responsible for turning motor shafts to a specified diameter. Each lathe produces shafts with slight variations, and we want to compare the diameter measurements visually using a box and whisker plot.

Design Specification: 18.85 mm ± 0.1 mm.

Measurements:

We gather diameter measurements from each lathe, which we plot in Figure 2. Each lathe's data distribution can be represented as follows:

- **Lathe 1**: The distribution is centered within the specification, with low variation, indicating good performance.
- **Lathe 2**: The distribution shows excessive variation, with some shafts falling below the minimum allowable diameter.
- **Lathe 3**: The variation is less than Lathe 2, but the measurements are consistently close to the lower specification limit, with some shafts falling out of tolerance.

Illustration: Box and Whisker Plot of Lathe Comparison

Imagine three box and whisker plots side by side, one for each lathe. The box for Lathe 1 is neatly centered within the specification limits. Lathe 2's box is wider, with whiskers extending below the lower tolerance limit. Lathe 3's box is narrower than Lathe 2 but shifted toward the lower end, showing that it produces shafts close to the minimum limit.

This type of visualization quickly communicates not only the variation between lathes but also highlights potential issues, such as Lathe 2's excessive variability and Lathe 3's tendency to produce undersized parts.

Advantages of Using Box and Whisker Plots

Box and whisker plots offer several advantages, particularly when comparing multiple data sets:

- **Easy Comparison**: The ability to display multiple datasets side by side makes it easy to compare different categories or conditions.
- **Clear Summary**: Box plots provide a clear summary of the key statistics in the data, including median, quartiles, and outliers.
- **Outlier Detection**: They are excellent for identifying outliers that may require further investigation.
- **Effective for Non-Normal Data**: Unlike histograms, box and whisker plots are effective even for datasets that do not follow a normal distribution.

Conclusion

Box and whisker plots are a versatile and effective tool for summarizing and comparing data distributions. Whether you are evaluating process improvement, comparing machinery, or analyzing performance across different teams or products, this type of plot offers valuable insights that can lead to more informed decision-making.

Incorporating box and whisker plots into your data analysis toolkit will allow you to visualize variation, spot trends, and identify areas that require attention. Whether you are working in education, manufacturing, or service industries, box and whisker plots are a simple yet powerful tool for enhancing data-driven decisions.

Outliers: Definition,

Importance, and Examples

What are Outliers?

Outliers are data points that are significantly different from the rest of the dataset. They appear as extreme values that lie far away from the central range of the data. In most cases, outliers are either much higher or much lower than the other data points, making them stand out visually, especially in graphical methods like box and whisker plots.

Key Characteristics of Outliers:

1. **Extreme Values**: Outliers are unusually large or small compared to other values in the dataset.
2. **Influence on Averages**: Outliers can distort summary statistics like the mean, giving a misleading impression of the dataset's overall characteristics.
3. **Unexpected Occurrences**: Outliers may indicate anomalies, errors, or unique conditions.

Why Are Outliers Important?

Outliers are crucial to understand and interpret because they can provide valuable insights or indicate potential problems in your data collection or process. There are several reasons why detecting outliers is important:

1. **Identifying Errors**: Outliers may indicate measurement errors, data entry mistakes, or anomalies that should be corrected or removed.
2. **Spotting Unusual Conditions**: Sometimes, outliers

represent rare or exceptional cases that warrant further investigation. For example, in a manufacturing process, an outlier might indicate a defective part.

3. **Influencing Statistical Analysis**: Outliers can have a substantial impact on statistical calculations, especially the mean and variance, which might skew the interpretation of the data.
4. **Improving Decision Making**: Understanding outliers allows analysts to make informed decisions about whether they should be excluded or whether they represent important trends that should be explored.

How to Identify Outliers

One common way to identify outliers is through the use of a **box and whisker plot**, which highlights outliers visually. In such plots, outliers appear as points that lie outside the "whiskers" of the box plot. These whiskers extend from the first quartile (Q1) and third quartile (Q3) to the smallest and largest values, respectively, within 1.5 times the interquartile range (IQR). Points outside this range are considered outliers.

Formula for detecting outliers:

Formula for detecting outliers:

- Lower bound: $Q1 - 1.5 \times IQR$
- Upper bound: $Q3 + 1.5 \times IQR$

Any data point outside this range is considered an outlier.

Example of Outliers

Consider the following data set of student test scores:

Test Scores

78

82

85

88

89

90

92

94

95

97

45

In this data set, most test scores range between 78 and 97, but one score (45) is unusually low. When plotted in a box and whisker plot, this value would appear as an outlier, far outside the interquartile range. It might suggest that the student encountered a problem during the test or that there was a recording error.

Illustration: Box and Whisker Plot with Outliers

Imagine a box and whisker plot displaying test scores. The majority of the data is clustered between the lower and upper quartiles, but the outlier score (45) is depicted as a small dot or asterisk outside the lower whisker, indicating that it's an unusual data point.

Dealing with Outliers

Once outliers have been identified, it's important to decide how to handle them. Here are common approaches:

1. **Investigate**: Determine whether the outlier is a result of an error or if it represents a legitimate

observation.

2. **Exclude**: If the outlier is due to a mistake or irrelevant condition, it can be removed from the analysis.

3. **Include and Explain**: If the outlier represents an important event or condition (e.g., a rare but valid occurrence), include it in the analysis and discuss its impact on the overall data interpretation.

Types of Outliers

1. **Global Outliers**: These are data points that deviate significantly from the entire dataset. For example, if most sales figures are in the $10,000 to $15,000 range but one sale is $100,000, this would be a global outlier.

2. **Contextual Outliers**: These outliers are abnormal in a specific context but not in others. For example, ice cream sales might be unusually high in winter compared to typical winter sales but would be considered normal during summer.

3. **Collective Outliers**: These occur when a group of data points behave unusually as a whole but may not appear anomalous individually. For example, a cluster of low test scores within a high-performing class could be a collective outlier.

Real-World Examples of Outliers

1. **Stock Market Data**: In financial markets, large deviations in stock prices during events like recessions or company-specific news (e.g., major announcements or scandals) can cause outliers in stock performance.

2. **Manufacturing**: Outliers in a manufacturing process

might indicate defective products or machine malfunctions. For instance, if most parts measure between 9.85 and 10.15 mm but one part measures 7.5 mm, that is an outlier that suggests a defect.
3. **Medical Research**: In a clinical trial, an outlier might represent an individual who reacts unusually well or poorly to a treatment, signaling a potential subgroup that responds differently from the rest of the population.

Conclusion

Outliers are an essential aspect of data analysis, providing valuable insights into unusual or extreme data points. Understanding how to detect, interpret, and handle outliers helps improve data quality, supports informed decision-making, and reveals hidden patterns or anomalies. Whether outliers are errors or critical findings, they deserve careful consideration in any analysis.

What Causes Outliers?

Outliers are data points that significantly deviate from the rest of a dataset. They may arise due to various reasons, ranging from natural variability in the data to errors in data collection or processing. Understanding the causes of outliers is critical in determining whether they should be addressed, corrected, or incorporated into further analysis.

1. Measurement or Recording Errors

One of the most common causes of outliers is human or instrument error during data collection. These errors can distort the data and produce outlier values.

- **Human error**: Mistakes made while entering data, such as typos (e.g., entering 1000 instead of 100) or misreading instruments.

- **Instrument malfunction**: Faulty sensors or malfunctioning equipment may report incorrect values that fall outside the expected range.

Example: A broken thermometer might report an extremely low or high temperature, creating an outlier in a dataset of daily temperatures.

2. Sampling Issues

Outliers can occur when the data sample does not adequately represent the population, often due to poor sampling methods or sampling bias.

- **Small sample size**: A small sample might inadvertently include an extreme value, which would not appear unusual in a larger dataset.
- **Sampling bias**: If the sample over-represents a specific group, the data may include values that do not align with the overall population.

Example: If a survey about income only samples high-income neighborhoods, the results may contain extreme values compared to a more representative sample.

3. Data Entry or Processing Errors

Outliers can also result from errors introduced during the processing of the data after collection. This can include mistakes made while converting units, aggregating data, or performing transformations.

- **Incorrect unit conversions**: Errors in converting units (e.g., converting inches to centimeters) can result in outliers.
- **Faulty data cleaning**: Data cleaning processes that improperly remove or modify data points may lead to outliers.

Example: A dataset with heights measured in both centimeters and meters might contain outliers if the units are mixed up (e.g., entering 1.75 meters as 175 centimeters).

4. Natural Variability in Data

Sometimes, outliers occur naturally due to the inherent variability of a process or population. These outliers are not mistakes; they reflect rare but possible occurrences.

- **Random variability**: Even in well-functioning systems, extreme data points can occur due to random chance.
- **Rare events**: Some outliers are rare but valid events that happen infrequently. For example, in biological studies, a person with an extremely high or low heart rate may represent the natural limits of human variability.

Example: In meteorology, an unusually hot or cold day might be a natural outlier in a dataset of temperatures.

5. Skewed Distributions

In some cases, outliers occur in datasets that do not follow a normal (bell-curve) distribution. Skewed distributions often result in extreme values being present at one end of the data range.

- **Right-skewed distributions**: When the distribution is skewed to the right, the data contains extreme high values. Examples include income distributions, where a few individuals may earn much more than the rest.
- **Left-skewed distributions**: In left-skewed distributions, extreme low values appear, such as in life expectancy data for certain populations.

Example: A dataset on housing prices may have many homes clustered around a median price but with a few extremely expensive homes creating right-skewed outliers.

6. Changes in Process or Environment

Sudden shifts in a process, system, or environment can lead to outliers if the system has not yet stabilized or if it has been disrupted.

- **Process changes**: Modifications to a manufacturing process or system may temporarily produce outliers until the process stabilizes.
- **Environmental changes**: Sudden changes in external factors, such as market conditions or weather events, can create temporary outliers in the data.

Example: A factory that updates its machinery might produce unusually good or bad products while workers and equipment adjust to the new process.

7. Outliers as True Exceptional Cases

In some cases, outliers may represent real and important phenomena rather than errors or anomalies. These outliers may reveal exceptional or unique circumstances that merit further investigation.

- **Breakthrough performance**: In business or sports, an individual or entity might achieve exceptionally high performance that stands apart from the norm.
- **Rare events**: Outliers may reflect once-in-a-lifetime events, such as a financial market crash or a scientific discovery.

Example: In a dataset of athletic performance, an outlier might represent an athlete who set a new world record.

8. External Influences

Sometimes, external factors, such as weather, regulatory changes, or market forces, may cause outliers in data. These external influences can lead to unexpected deviations from normal trends.

- **Natural disasters**: Sudden natural events, like hurricanes or earthquakes, can create outliers in data on weather, infrastructure, or market performance.
- **Economic shifts**: Major policy changes, such as new trade laws or financial regulations, may temporarily cause outliers in economic or business data.

Example: A sudden economic downturn might cause an outlier in a company's sales figures for that period.

Example of Causes of Outliers in Different Scenarios

1. **Manufacturing Process:**
   - **Measurement error**: A machine producing parts might have a faulty sensor, leading to an outlier in part dimensions.
   - **Process change**: A temporary adjustment to the machine settings might cause extreme values until it is calibrated properly.

2. **Financial Data:**
   - **Market crash**: A stock market crash can create outliers in stock price data that deviate dramatically from normal trends.
   - **Data entry error**: A mistyped value for a stock price might result in an unusually high or low value.

3. **Healthcare:**
   - **Outlier patient response**: A patient might react exceptionally well or poorly to a new treatment, creating an outlier in clinical trial results.
   - **Measurement variability**: Medical devices

might temporarily malfunction, leading to inaccurate and extreme measurements of vital signs.

Dealing with Outliers

Once the causes of outliers are identified, the next step is deciding how to handle them:

1. **Correct errors**: If the outlier is due to an identifiable error (such as a recording or measurement mistake), correcting or removing the outlier may be necessary.

2. **Analyze the cause**: If the outlier represents a rare but valid event, further investigation can help understand its cause and implications.

3. **Exclude from analysis**: In cases where the outlier skews the results but doesn't represent meaningful data, it can be excluded from specific analyses to avoid distortion.

4. **Incorporate into findings**: If the outlier reveals important information (e.g., exceptional performance or rare events), include it in the analysis and discuss its significance.

Conclusion

Outliers can arise from various causes, such as errors in data collection, natural variability, process changes, or skewed distributions. Whether they are errors or represent rare and important phenomena, outliers provide valuable insights into the nature of the data and must be handled carefully to ensure accurate and meaningful analysis. Recognizing the cause of outliers is essential for making informed decisions on whether to retain, investigate, or correct them.

How to Handle Outliers: A Step-by-Step Guide

Outliers are extreme values in a dataset that differ significantly from other observations. They can provide valuable insights or distort analysis, so it's crucial to handle them appropriately. Here is a structured approach to dealing with outliers:

Step 1: Identify the Outliers

The first step in handling outliers is identifying them in your data. Several methods can be used:

1. **Visual methods**:
    - **Box and whisker plots**: Outliers appear as points outside the "whiskers," or extreme ends of the data range. This is one of the most common methods to detect outliers visually.
    - **Scatter plots**: Outliers are easy to spot in scatter plots as points that deviate noticeably from the overall trend.
    - **Histograms**: In a histogram, outliers appear as isolated bars far from the rest of the data.
2. **Statistical methods**:

- **Z-scores**: Calculate the Z-score for each data point, which measures how far a value is from the mean in terms of standard deviations. Data points with Z-scores beyond ±3 are typically considered outliers.
  - Formula:
    $$Z = \frac{(X - \mu)}{\sigma}$$
    Where:
    - X = data point
    - μ = mean of the dataset
    - σ = standard deviation
- **Interquartile range (IQR)**: Using IQR, any data point that falls 1.5 times above the third quartile (Q3) or below the first quartile (Q1) is considered an outlier.
  - Formula:
    $$\text{Outliers} = [Q1 - 1.5 \times IQR, Q3 + 1.5 \times IQR]$$

Step 2: Investigate the Cause of Outliers

Once outliers are identified, it is important to understand why they exist. This will help determine whether to keep, remove, or correct them. Ask the following questions:

- **Is the outlier due to a measurement error?** Check for mistakes in data entry, sensor errors, or unit conversion problems.
- **Is the outlier due to sampling bias?** Consider whether the sample was representative of the overall population.
- **Does the outlier reflect a real and meaningful event?** Outliers can represent rare but significant events (e.g., breakthroughs in performance or unusual occurrences).
- **Is the outlier part of a naturally skewed distribution?** Some data, like income or sales figures, may naturally have extreme high or low values.

Step 3: Decide How to Handle Outliers

After determining the cause of the outliers, you can choose how to handle them. Here are common approaches:

1. Correct Errors

- If the outlier is due to a data entry, measurement, or processing error, correct the value. For example, if a typographical error caused the outlier, correct it to reflect the true value.

Example: If someone entered "1000" instead of "100" due to a typo, fix the data to reflect "100."

2. Exclude Outliers

- If the outlier is an anomaly that skews results (and is not relevant to the analysis), it may be appropriate to exclude it. This is especially important when outliers distort statistical measures like the mean.

When to exclude: - The outlier is a result of a mistake. - The outlier is not part of the population you're studying. - The outlier distorts the overall analysis and is irrelevant to the conclusions.

Example: In an analysis of employee salaries, if one data point represents a CEO's salary and the analysis is focused on mid-level employees, excluding the CEO's salary may make sense.

3. Transform the Data

- If outliers result from a skewed distribution, transformations like the **logarithmic** or **square root transformation** can make the data more normal (bell-shaped). This reduces the influence of extreme values without removing them.

Example: For a dataset where most values are clustered together but a few values are extremely high, applying a logarithmic transformation can compress the high values and make the data more manageable.

4. Apply Robust Statistical Methods

- **Robust statistical techniques** are less affected by outliers and provide a more accurate representation

of the data.
- **Median**: Unlike the mean, the median is not influenced by extreme values, making it a better measure of central tendency when outliers are present.
- **Trimmed mean**: This method involves removing a small percentage of the extreme values (both high and low) and then calculating the mean of the remaining data.

Example: In financial datasets with extreme values, using the median to represent average earnings rather than the mean might provide a clearer picture of the typical earnings.

5. Cap or Winsorize Outliers

- **Capping (Winsorizing)** involves replacing extreme outliers with the nearest non-outlier value or setting a threshold at which values are capped.
- This method is useful when you don't want to completely remove data but need to limit the effect of extreme values.

Example: In a customer spending dataset, you might set a cap on the maximum spending value at the 95th percentile, replacing all values beyond this point with the 95th percentile value.

6. Retain and Analyze Outliers

- In some cases, outliers are meaningful and should not be removed or altered. If they represent important information (such as a breakthrough performance or rare event), it may be necessary to retain them and explore why they occurred.

Example: In a scientific experiment, if one test subject responds exceptionally well to a treatment, the outlier should be retained to investigate why that subject had a different outcome from the rest.

Step 4: Analyze the Impact of Outliers

Once outliers have been addressed, it's essential to evaluate how they affect your analysis. Here are steps to ensure their impact is well-understood:

- **Re-run analysis with and without outliers**: Compare the results of your analysis before and after handling the outliers to assess how much they influence the outcomes.
- **Check the stability of your model**: For predictive models, evaluate whether the presence of outliers affects the model's performance or whether it remains robust after removing or adjusting for outliers.

Step 5: Document Decisions and Methods

When working with outliers, it's important to document the decisions made and the methods used for handling them. This ensures that future analyses are transparent and reproducible. Key points to document:

- The method used to identify outliers.
- The decision process for keeping, correcting, or excluding outliers.
- The specific actions taken (e.g., transformation, exclusion, capping).
- Any changes in results after handling the outliers.

Practical Example of Handling Outliers

Scenario: A company is analyzing the monthly sales performance of its employees. The dataset includes one unusually high sales figure for a new product launch that distorts the overall analysis.

- **Step 1**: The outlier is identified using a box and whisker plot, which shows the extreme value far above the rest of the data.
- **Step 2**: Investigation reveals that the outlier is due to a one-time event: the employee made an unusually large sale during the product launch.
- **Step 3**: The company decides to exclude the outlier from the analysis of regular sales performance but retains it for a separate analysis on product launches.
- **Step 4**: After excluding the outlier, the mean and median sales figures return to normal, providing a clearer picture of regular performance.
- **Step 5**: The decision to exclude the outlier is documented, and the findings from the separate product launch analysis are used to improve future sales strategies.

Conclusion

Handling outliers is a crucial part of data analysis that requires careful consideration. Whether the outlier is an error, a rare event, or part of a skewed distribution, understanding its cause and effect allows you to choose the most appropriate method to deal with it. By identifying, investigating, and carefully deciding how to handle outliers, you can improve the quality of your analysis and make better-informed decisions based on the data.

Box Plot vs. Histogram:

A Detailed Comparison

Both box plots and histograms are graphical methods used to represent data distributions, but they serve different purposes and provide distinct insights. Here's a comparison to help understand the strengths, weaknesses, and best use cases for each.

1. Purpose and Visualization

Box Plot (Box-and-Whisker Plot)

- **Purpose**: A box plot summarizes the distribution of a dataset, highlighting key statistics like the median, quartiles, and potential outliers. It is ideal for comparing distributions between different datasets.

- **Visualization**: The box plot is a simple rectangular box representing the interquartile range (IQR) and "whiskers" extending to the minimum and maximum non-outlier values. Outliers are often displayed as individual points outside the whiskers.

Key Components:

   - **Median (Q2)**: A line inside the box showing the middle value.
   - **Quartiles (Q1 and Q3)**: The edges of the box, representing the 25th and 75th percentiles.
   - **Whiskers**: Lines extending from the quartiles to the smallest and largest values within 1.5 times the IQR.
   - **Outliers**: Values that fall beyond the whiskers, displayed as individual points.

Example: A box plot comparing test scores between different classrooms might reveal the median score, variability, and any extreme performances in each group.

Histogram

- **Purpose**: A histogram displays the frequency distribution of a dataset by showing how often data points fall within specific ranges (bins). It is ideal for visualizing the shape of the data distribution, such as whether it is skewed or normally distributed.
- **Visualization**: The histogram consists of bars where the height of each bar represents the frequency (or count) of data points within a specified bin or range of values.

Key Components:

  - **Bins**: Ranges of values grouped together (e.g., 10-20, 20-30).
  - **Frequency**: The height of each bar shows how many data points fall within each bin.

Example: A histogram of customer wait times at a restaurant might show the frequency of wait times falling between specific intervals (e.g., 5-10 minutes, 10-15 minutes).

2. Key Insights Provided

Box Plot Insights:

- **Summary statistics**: Box plots offer a quick summary of the central tendency (median), variability (IQR), and spread of data (whiskers).
- **Outliers**: Box plots highlight outliers explicitly, making them useful for detecting extreme values.
- **Comparison across categories**: Box plots are great for comparing the distribution of different datasets (e.g.,

performance across departments, test scores across classrooms).

Example: In a dataset of employee salaries across departments, a box plot can quickly show which department has higher median salaries, which has more variability, and if any departments have extreme outliers (e.g., CEOs).

Histogram Insights:

- **Shape of the distribution**: A histogram visually shows the distribution shape (normal, skewed, bimodal, etc.) and provides more detail on where data points cluster.
- **Frequency**: Histograms are particularly effective at showing how frequently data points fall within specific ranges, making it easier to spot trends and patterns (e.g., most common age ranges of customers).
- **Spread and skewness**: Histograms can illustrate whether data is skewed left or right, or if it has multiple peaks (bimodal distributions).

Example: A histogram of house prices might reveal that most houses are priced within the $200,000-$300,000 range but with a long tail extending to higher prices (right skew).

3. Strengths and Weaknesses

Box Plot Strengths:

- **Concise summary**: Box plots provide a compact view of the data's key statistics in a single visualization.
- **Comparisons**: They make it easy to compare multiple datasets side by side without overwhelming detail.
- **Outliers**: Box plots clearly identify outliers, which are crucial for understanding extreme values.

Box Plot Weaknesses:

- **Lack of detail**: While box plots show summaries, they do not show the full shape or frequency distribution of the data.

- **Not good for small datasets**: With small datasets, box plots may not provide much additional value since individual points are more meaningful than summary statistics.

Histogram Strengths:

- **Detailed frequency distribution**: Histograms show exactly how data is distributed across the range, making them great for understanding the shape of the data.

- **Skewness and modality**: They are ideal for spotting skewness and multimodal distributions (more than one peak).

Histogram Weaknesses:

- **No outlier identification**: Histograms do not explicitly highlight outliers; extreme values might simply extend the bar length.

- **No summary statistics**: Unlike box plots, histograms do not show the median, quartiles, or specific statistical values, so additional interpretation is needed for central tendency and spread.

- **Bin size sensitivity**: The appearance of the histogram can change significantly depending on the choice of bin width. Too many bins may create a fragmented appearance, while too few may oversimplify the data.

4. When to Use Box Plots vs. Histograms

Use Box Plots When:

- You need to quickly summarize key statistics (median, quartiles, spread, and outliers).
- You want to compare the distributions of multiple datasets side by side.
- Outliers are of particular interest, and you want to easily identify them.

Example: Comparing the test scores of students across several schools, where outliers (exceptionally high or low scores) are important to identify.

Use Histograms When:

- You need to understand the shape and frequency distribution of the data.
- The goal is to visualize how data points are spread across different ranges.
- You are interested in seeing patterns such as skewness, modality, or clustering of values.

Example: Analyzing the distribution of response times in a customer service center, where understanding the most frequent response time ranges is important.

---

5. Example: Comparing Test Scores

Imagine you're analyzing test scores from three different classrooms:

- **Box Plot**:
    - Each classroom's scores are represented as a box, with the median score and interquartile range clearly visible.
    - You can easily compare the median score,

variability (spread), and identify which classroom has outliers (e.g., extremely low or high scores).

Insight: Classroom A has the highest median score, Classroom B has a large spread, and Classroom C has an outlier of an extremely low score.

- **Histogram**:
    - A histogram would show how frequently scores fall into specific ranges (bins). For example, you might see that most scores in Classroom A fall between 70 and 80, while Classroom B has a more spread-out distribution, and Classroom C has a high concentration of scores around 90.

Insight: You can see the overall shape of the score distribution, whether it is skewed, and where the scores cluster within each classroom.

Conclusion: Box Plot vs. Histogram

- **Box plots** are ideal for summarizing key statistics and comparing multiple datasets. They are especially useful when outliers are a concern.
- **Histograms** are best for understanding the shape and distribution of a single dataset, showing frequency, skewness, and modality in detail.

Choosing between a box plot and a histogram depends on the specific questions you're asking about the data. For comparisons between groups or datasets, box plots are often more efficient. For exploring the overall shape of the data and frequency distribution, histograms are more informative.

How to Read Whiskers

in a Box Plot

In a box-and-whisker plot (or box plot), the **whiskers** provide visual cues about the spread of data and help identify any outliers. Understanding how to read and interpret whiskers is crucial for gaining insights into the distribution of the dataset.

Key Components of a Box Plot

Before diving into whiskers, it's essential to understand the basic components of a box plot:

1. **Median (Q2):** The middle value of the dataset, represented by a line inside the box.
2. **First Quartile (Q1):** The 25th percentile, where 25% of the data falls below this value.
3. **Third Quartile (Q3):** The 75th percentile, where 75% of the data falls below this value.
4. **Interquartile Range (IQR):** The range between Q1 and Q3 (IQR = Q3 - Q1). This range represents the middle 50% of the data.
5. **Whiskers:** These are lines extending from the edges of the box (Q1 and Q3) to the smallest and largest values in the dataset that are not considered outliers.
6. **Outliers:** Data points that fall outside the whiskers, often represented as dots or asterisks.

Understanding Whiskers

The **whiskers** on a box plot extend from the edges of the box (the first and third quartiles) to the minimum and maximum values within the dataset, excluding any outliers. The whiskers help you understand the **spread of the data** beyond the interquartile range (IQR).

1. How Whiskers Are Drawn

- **Lower Whisker**: Extends from the lower quartile (Q1) to the smallest data point that is not considered an outlier. The length of this whisker shows how spread out the lower 25% of the data is.
- **Upper Whisker**: Extends from the upper quartile (Q3) to the largest data point that is not considered an outlier. The length of this whisker shows the spread of the upper 25% of the data.

The whiskers generally reach the **smallest and largest values** in the dataset **within 1.5 times the IQR**. Any points beyond this threshold are classified as **outliers**.

2. How to Interpret Whiskers

- **Short whiskers**: If the whiskers are short, it suggests that the data is tightly clustered around the quartiles, indicating low variability outside the IQR.
- **Long whiskers**: Long whiskers suggest that the data is more spread out and that there is greater variability beyond the quartiles.

3. Whiskers and Outliers

Outliers are values that lie significantly outside the general spread of the data. They are typically identified as data points that fall beyond **1.5 times the IQR** from the quartiles:

- **Lower outliers**: Values below Q1 − 1.5 * IQR.
- **Upper outliers**: Values above Q3 + 1.5 * IQR.

In a box plot, outliers are represented as individual dots or symbols outside the whiskers.

4. Symmetry and Skewness in Whiskers

- **Symmetrical Whiskers**: If the whiskers are of approximately equal length, it suggests that the data is symmetrically distributed.

Example: If the data follows a normal distribution, the whiskers are likely to be balanced, showing even spread on both sides.

- **Asymmetrical Whiskers**: If one whisker is much longer than the other, it indicates **skewness** in the data.
    - **Right-skewed data**: If the upper whisker is much longer than the lower whisker, it indicates that the data is skewed to the right (i.e., there are larger values stretching the upper end of the dataset).
    - **Left-skewed data**: If the lower whisker is longer, it means the data is skewed to the left (i.e., there are smaller values stretching the lower end of the dataset).

Example: Reading Whiskers in a Box Plot

Consider a box plot for the heights of students in two different classrooms:

Classroom A	Classroom B
Median height: 150 cm	**Median height**: 148 cm
Lower whisker: 135 cm	**Lower whisker**: 140 cm
Upper whisker: 160 cm	**Upper whisker**: 155 cm

- **Classroom A**:
    - The **lower whisker** extends to 135 cm, and the **upper whisker** extends to 160 cm, indicating that the data points between 135 cm and 160 cm are within the expected range.
    - The data seems more spread out, with taller students as outliers, as indicated by the longer upper whisker.

- **Classroom B:**
  - The **lower whisker** extends to 140 cm, and the **upper whisker** extends to 155 cm, showing a smaller spread compared to Classroom A.
  - The short whiskers suggest that heights are more tightly clustered in Classroom B, indicating less variability.

Summary of How to Read Whiskers

- **Length of whiskers**: Indicates the spread of data outside the interquartile range (IQR).
- **Symmetry of whiskers**: Helps identify skewness in the data.
- **Presence of outliers**: Data points outside the whiskers are flagged as outliers and indicate extreme values that deviate from the rest of the dataset.

By understanding whiskers in a box plot, you can quickly grasp the variability, spread, and outliers in your data set, allowing for effective comparisons and insights.

CHAPTER – 7
Cause & Effect {Fishbone} Diagram

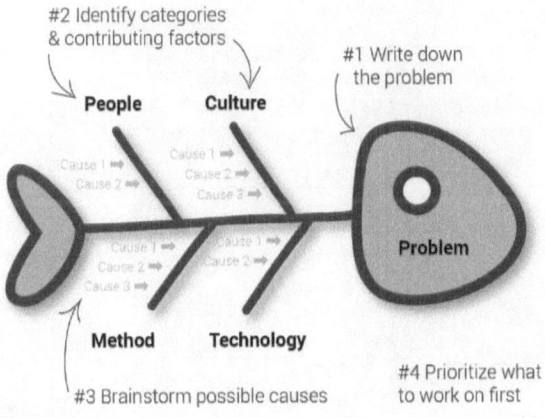

In the realm of Lean Six Sigma, one of the most widely used and effective tools for identifying the root cause of a problem is the **Fishbone Diagram**. Also known as the **Ishikawa**

Diagram or **Cause-and-Effect Diagram**, it is a critical tool in the Continuous Improvement and Operational Excellence toolbox, particularly in retail and e-commerce industries. By systematically breaking down potential causes of an issue, it allows teams to approach problem-solving with clarity and structure.

In this chapter, we will explore the Fishbone Diagram in depth, its variations, when to use it, and how to create one effectively. We'll also include a real-world retail example to illustrate how the Fishbone Diagram can be applied in practice.

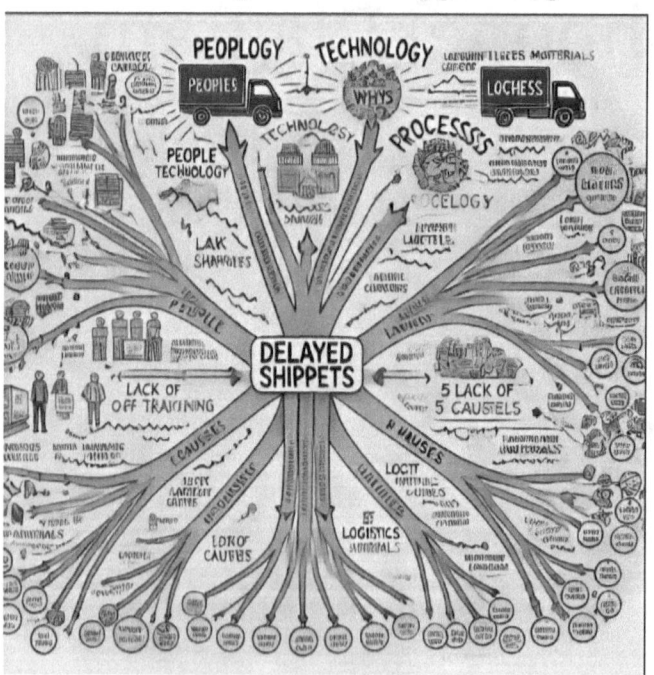

What is a Fishbone Diagram?

The Fishbone Diagram visually displays the relationship between a problem (or effect) and its potential causes. By mapping out the possible contributors to an issue, it helps teams pinpoint the root causes of problems in processes, operations, or systems.

The name "Fishbone" comes from its shape; it resembles the

skeleton of a fish, with the problem as the "head" and the categories of causes branching out like the "bones."

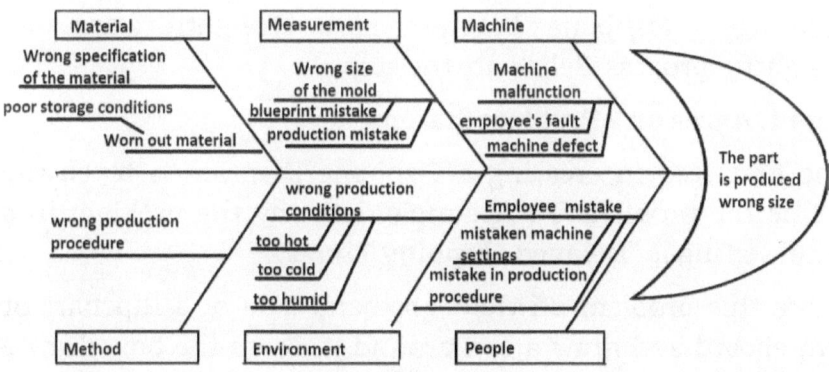

Common Names:

- Cause-and-effect diagram
- Ishikawa diagram (named after its inventor, Dr. Kaoru Ishikawa)
- Cause enumeration diagram
- Reverse fishbone diagram

When to Use a Fishbone Diagram

1. **Identifying potential causes**: When a process or system isn't performing as expected, the Fishbone Diagram helps identify all the possible reasons for the problem.

2. **Breaking away from limited thinking**: Teams often focus on the most obvious causes, but the Fishbone Diagram forces a more thorough exploration of possible contributors.

Example of when it's useful in Retail:

Let's say a retail store is struggling with customer complaints about delayed shipping. The root cause isn't immediately apparent, so the team decides to create a Fishbone Diagram to systematically investigate all possible reasons.

Fishbone Diagram Procedure

Creating a Fishbone Diagram is a straightforward, yet insightful process. Below are the steps:

Step 1: Agree on a Problem Statement

The first step in creating a Fishbone Diagram is to clearly define the problem. For example, let's say the problem in a retail setting is **"Delayed Shipping Times."**

Write this problem on the right-hand side of a flipchart or whiteboard and draw a box around it. From the box, draw a horizontal line extending to the left — this is the "spine" of the fish.

Step 2: Identify Major Categories of Causes

Next, brainstorm the major categories of causes that could contribute to the problem. If this is challenging, use generic categories commonly referred to as the "6Ms":

- **Methods**: How the process is being carried out.
- **Machines (Equipment)**: The tools, technology, or machinery used in the process.
- **People (Manpower)**: The individuals involved in the process.
- **Materials**: The raw materials or products.
- **Measurement**: How performance or quality is being measured.
- **Environment**: External factors such as physical or digital environment.

In our retail example, the categories might include:

- **Processes**: Shipping procedures.

- **Technology**: Warehouse management systems.
- **Suppliers**: Quality and timeliness of supplier deliveries.
- **Human Resources**: Employee errors in order picking or packing.
- **Logistics**: Transportation issues.
- **External Factors**: Weather or traffic conditions affecting delivery.

Step 3: Brainstorm Possible Causes

Once the categories are identified, the next step is brainstorming all the potential causes within each category. Ask the question **"Why does this happen?"** for each category to drill deeper into the root causes.

For example:

- Under **Processes**, you might identify "inefficient packaging procedures."
- Under **Technology**, you might list "warehouse management system glitches."
- Under **Logistics**, "insufficient carrier capacity" could be a cause.

Step 4: Drill Down into Sub-Causes

As you ask "Why?" for each cause, you may uncover additional layers of sub-causes. For instance:

- The cause "inefficient packaging procedures" under **Processes** may have sub-causes like "lack of standard operating procedures" or "inadequate employee training."
- For the cause "warehouse system glitches" under **Technology**, the sub-cause could be "outdated software."

Step 5: Highlight Gaps or Areas of Opportunity

After brainstorming all possible causes and sub-causes, it's important to identify areas where the chart appears sparse. This often signals potential gaps in the team's thinking or areas where more investigation is needed.

Fishbone Diagram Example in Retail: Delayed Shipping Times

Here's an example of a Fishbone Diagram applied to the issue of delayed shipping in a retail business.

Problem: Delayed Shipping Times

Categories and Causes:

Processes

- Inefficient packaging procedures
- Lack of standardized processes
- Inadequate training for new hires

Technology

- Warehouse management system glitches
- Outdated software
- Poor internet connectivity

Human Resources

- Employee errors in order picking
- Insufficient training
- High turnover rate leading to inexperienced staff

Suppliers

- Delayed receipt of goods
- Poor communication with suppliers
- International shipping delays

Logistics

- Insufficient carrier capacity
- Overloaded transport schedules
- Unreliable third-party logistics providers

External Factors
- Traffic or weather disruptions
- Seasonal weather patterns affecting delivery times
- Unforeseen events like strikes or accidents

Illustration

To create a Fishbone Diagram:

1. Draw the "spine" with the problem ("Delayed Shipping Times") at the right end.
2. Add branches for the categories (Processes, Technology, etc.).
3. Under each category, add potential causes and sub-causes.

By visualizing these causes, the retail team can start to see which areas require immediate attention, whether it's better employee training, upgrading the warehouse management system, or improving communication with suppliers.

Variations of the Fishbone Diagram

Depending on the problem and the level of detail needed, there are several variations of the Fishbone Diagram:

- **Time-delay fishbone**: Focuses on causes of delays in processes.
- **CEDAC**: Adds cards to the diagram for possible countermeasures or solutions.
- **Desired-result fishbone**: Starts with a desired outcome and works backward to identify enablers or barriers.

The Fishbone Diagram is a powerful tool for identifying the root causes of problems in any industry, including retail and e-commerce. By organizing potential causes into categories and drilling down into sub-causes, teams can systematically identify the root cause of an issue. This structured approach allows for targeted improvement strategies, which are critical for achieving continuous improvement and operational excellence.

we explored how the **Fishbone Diagram** (also known as the Ishikawa or Cause-and-Effect Diagram) helps teams map out potential causes of problems by organizing them into categories. While the Fishbone Diagram is an excellent tool for identifying a broad range of potential causes, it can be even more powerful when combined with another problem-solving technique: the **5 Whys**.

The **5 Whys methodology** focuses on repeatedly asking "Why?" for each identified cause until the true root cause of a problem is uncovered. By merging these two approaches, retail and e-commerce teams can dive deep into understanding issues and implement effective, sustainable solutions.

In this chapter, we'll explain how to use the Fishbone Diagram in tandem with the 5 Whys technique, offering practical steps, examples, and illustrations tailored to retail operations.

The Power of Combining the Fishbone Diagram with the 5 Whys

While the Fishbone Diagram provides a broad view of potential causes for a problem, the 5 Whys technique digs deeper into each cause to uncover the root cause. This combination results in a thorough, multi-layered analysis that allows teams to:

- **Identify all possible causes**: The Fishbone Diagram helps brainstorm all possible causes within different categories.

- **Pinpoint the root cause**: The 5 Whys method narrows down the most important contributors by probing each potential cause in greater depth.

In the context of **retail operations**, where challenges like delayed shipping, stockouts, or poor customer service can arise, this approach enables teams to move from symptom-based solutions to addressing the root of the problem, leading to better long-term results.

Step-by-Step Process: Using the Fishbone Diagram with the 5 Whys

Step 1: Define the Problem Clearly

As with any problem-solving tool, start by clearly defining the issue. This is typically the "effect" or the main issue your team is experiencing.

Example (Retail Context):

Problem: Orders are consistently shipped late, resulting in customer complaints.

Write this problem on the right-hand side of the board and draw the "spine" of the Fishbone Diagram, with an arrow pointing toward the problem.

Step 2: Identify Categories of Potential Causes

Next, use the Fishbone Diagram to brainstorm the main categories where the potential causes might fall. For retail, these could be based on the **6 Ms** or tailored to the specifics of the situation.

Common Categories for Retail Problems:

- **Processes**: The workflow of picking, packing, and shipping.

- **Technology**: Software or systems like inventory or warehouse management.
- **People**: Staff responsible for fulfilling orders.
- **Materials**: Packaging supplies, products, and inventory management.
- **Logistics**: Third-party delivery services and transportation methods.
- **External Factors**: Weather, traffic, or supplier-related issues.

For our shipping delay example, the categories might look like this:

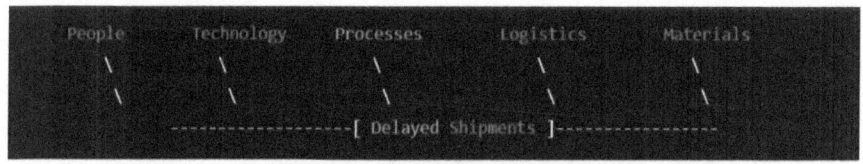

Step 3: Brainstorm Possible Causes Within Each Category

Once the categories are established, start brainstorming the potential causes within each one.

Example (Retail Context):

- **People**: Lack of training for new warehouse employees.
- **Technology**: Warehouse management system is outdated and prone to glitches.
- **Processes**: Inefficient order picking procedures.
- **Logistics**: Insufficient carrier capacity for peak periods.
- **Materials**: Stockouts of popular items causing delays in order fulfillment.

Here's a simplified diagram to illustrate:

```
People        Technology      Processes      Logistics        Materials
   \              \              \               \                \
[Lack of       [System         [Order         [Insufficient    [Stockouts]
Training]      Glitches]       Picking]       Carrier]
```

Step 4: Apply the 5 Whys to Each Cause

Now, apply the 5 Whys technique to drill deeper into each identified cause. For each cause on the Fishbone Diagram, ask "Why does this happen?" five times (or more if needed), until you reach the root cause.

Example: Drilling Down "Lack of Training" in People

1. **Why are new employees not adequately trained?**
2. **Why is there no structured onboarding process?**
3. **Why hasn't the company documented standard operating procedures?**
4. **Why does management believe on-the-job training is sufficient?**
5. **Why is there a high turnover rate?**

Root Cause:

The high turnover rate, driven by non-competitive pay and poor working conditions, is leading to insufficient training and delayed shipments.

Step 5: Repeat for Other Causes

For each cause on the Fishbone Diagram, repeat the 5 Whys. Here's how you might tackle **Technology (System Glitches)**:

1. **Why does the warehouse management system experience glitches?**
2. **Why hasn't the software been updated?**

3. **Why were IT budgets cut?**
4. **Why was the warehouse not seen as a priority?**

Root Cause:

The outdated system stems from budget cuts, driven by a lack of attention to warehouse efficiency as a key performance area.

Step 6: Take Action Based on Root Causes

Once you have drilled down into the root causes of the problem, the next step is to take actionable steps. Solutions should directly address the root causes uncovered by the 5 Whys analysis, ensuring that you are targeting the true underlying issues, not just the symptoms.

Example (Solutions for Delayed Shipping):

- **For People**: Revise hiring practices to offer competitive wages and improve working conditions to reduce turnover. Establish structured onboarding and training programs.
- **For Technology**: Reallocate budget to prioritize upgrading the warehouse management system.
- **For Logistics**: Work with carriers to adjust contracts or explore additional partnerships to increase capacity during peak periods.

Real-World Retail Example: Combining Fishbone and 5 Whys to Reduce Stockouts

In a real-world retail setting, stockouts were causing customer dissatisfaction and lost sales. The company used a Fishbone Diagram to categorize potential causes and then applied the 5 Whys to drill down into each issue. Here's how it unfolded:

- **Problem**: Frequent stockouts of popular items.

Fishbone Categories:

1. **Processes**: Inaccurate demand forecasting.
2. **Technology**: Inventory management software errors.
3. **People**: Delays in updating inventory levels.
4. **Suppliers**: Late or incomplete deliveries.
5. **Logistics**: Poor coordination between warehouses.

Applying 5 Whys to "Inaccurate Demand Forecasting":

1. **Why is demand forecasting inaccurate?** Because sales data is not integrated with the forecasting system.
2. **Why is sales data not integrated?** Because the system upgrade to integrate sales data was delayed.
3. **Why was the system upgrade delayed?** Because the IT team was focused on implementing other priorities.
4. **Why were other priorities deemed more important?** Because management underestimated the impact of stockouts on revenue.

Solution:

Reprioritize the system upgrade to integrate real-time sales data with the demand forecasting system.

Conclusion

By combining the Fishbone Diagram with the 5 Whys, retail and e-commerce teams can enhance their problem-solving abilities, moving from surface-level solutions to addressing root causes. This approach provides structure to brainstorming and offers a path to deeper insights, ultimately leading to more sustainable improvements.

CHAPTER – 8
Chaku-Chaku

Chaku-Chaku (Japanese for "load-load") is a **Lean manufacturing technique** designed to facilitate fast and efficient production by minimizing operator idle time. In Chaku-Chaku, an operator **loads parts sequentially into multiple machines** arranged in a logical flow, with each machine automatically ejecting the processed part. The goal is to create **continuous, one-piece flow** with minimal waste, ensuring that operators remain engaged while eliminating non-value-adding activities.

This chapter explores the principles, benefits, and applications of Chaku-Chaku, along with real-world illustrations and guidance on how to implement it effectively.

What is Chaku-Chaku?

Chaku-Chaku refers to a **high-efficiency production method** in which a single operator works across multiple machines, loading parts into each machine in sequence. Instead of waiting for machines to finish their cycle, the operator **loads a part, moves to the next machine, and repeats the process**, allowing the machines to work autonomously. The focus is on **automation and simplicity**, where each machine can autonomously unload the finished product and prepare for the next operation.

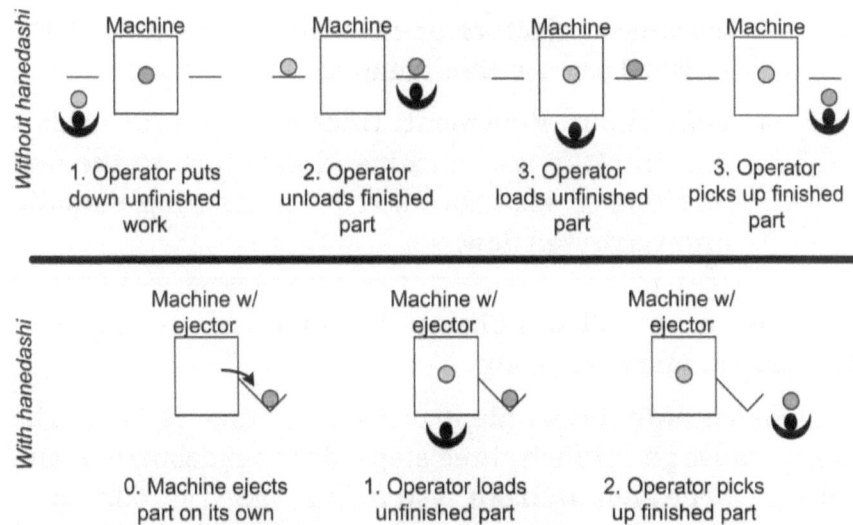

Key Characteristics of Chaku-Chaku:

1. **One-Piece Flow:** Only one part is processed at a time, reducing lead time and work-in-progress (WIP) inventory.

2. **Autonomous Machines:** Machines are designed or modified to perform operations independently after loading.

3. **Minimized Waste:** Operators focus only on loading parts, eliminating waiting time and unnecessary movement.

How Chaku-Chaku Works

1. **Machine Setup:** Each machine in the production line is **arranged in sequence** according to the required process flow (e.g., drilling, milling, polishing).

2. **Operator Activity:** The operator moves along the sequence, **loading raw or semi-finished parts** into each machine.

3. **Autonomous Unloading:** Machines are fitted with

automatic ejectors or mechanisms to unload the finished parts without manual intervention.

4. **Continuous Movement:** Once the operator loads a part into the last machine, they return to the first machine to load the next part, ensuring **smooth, uninterrupted flow.**

Illustration of Chaku-Chaku in Practice: Automotive Component Manufacturing

Imagine an **automotive plant** producing brake calipers. The caliper must go through three steps: drilling, deburring, and polishing. The **Chaku-Chaku system** is designed as follows:

1. **Step 1: Drilling Station** – The operator loads a raw caliper into the first machine for drilling. Once loaded, the machine starts automatically.

2. **Step 2: Deburring Station** – The operator moves to the next machine and loads a caliper for deburring while the drilling machine continues working.

3. **Step 3: Polishing Station** – At the final station, the operator loads another caliper for polishing. Once complete, the machines eject the finished parts.

4. **Repeat Process** – The operator returns to the first machine to start the next cycle.

This arrangement ensures **one-piece flow**, prevents idle time, and improves efficiency, resulting in faster throughput and higher productivity.

Chaku-Chaku vs. Traditional Batch Production

Aspect	Chaku-Chaku	Batch Production
Flow	One-piece flow, continuous movement	Parts processed in batches
Inventory	Minimal WIP	High WIP between processes

Cycle Time	Shorter lead time	Longer lead time
Operator Engagement	Continuous operator involvement	Operators may wait between steps
Flexibility	Adaptable to small lot sizes and changes	Suited for larger batch sizes

Benefits of Chaku-Chaku Production

1. **Increased Efficiency:** Operators remain active by continuously loading machines, minimizing downtime.

2. **Reduced WIP Inventory:** One-piece flow eliminates large stockpiles between processes, resulting in **lower storage costs**.

3. **Improved Quality Control:** Defects are identified earlier because only one piece is processed at a time.

4. **Shorter Lead Times:** Products move smoothly from one process to the next, speeding up delivery to customers.

5. **Operator Flexibility:** Operators can manage multiple machines without complex skills, increasing their versatility.

Applications of Chaku-Chaku in Lean and Six Sigma

Chaku-Chaku is most effective in **environments with repetitive tasks** where machine automation can support operator activity. It finds applications in industries such as:

- **Automotive:** For assembling or machining car parts, such as engine components or transmission systems.
- **Electronics:** In the production of small parts (e.g., circuit boards) where quick loading and unloading improve efficiency.
- **Medical Devices:** In the assembly of precision

instruments to ensure fast, defect-free production.

Example of Chaku-Chaku in Electronics Manufacturing

A **printed circuit board (PCB) manufacturer** implements Chaku-Chaku to streamline its production. The operator:

1. **Loads a PCB panel** into the solder paste printer machine.
2. Moves to the **pick-and-place machine** to load the next part.
3. Returns to the **reflow oven** to load the previous part for heating.
   Once a panel is processed, it is automatically ejected, and the operator cycles back to the beginning.

This Chaku-Chaku setup ensures **seamless coordination**, reducing production time and preventing bottlenecks.

Challenges in Implementing Chaku-Chaku

1. **Initial Machine Setup:** Machines must be equipped with **automatic loaders/unloaders**, which may require upfront investment.
2. **Operator Training:** Employees need **training in operating multiple machines** and maintaining the workflow.
3. **Layout Optimization:** Machines must be arranged efficiently to minimize unnecessary movement between them.
4. **Limited Applicability:** Some processes may not support Chaku-Chaku due to **long machine cycle times** or complex manual interventions.

How to Implement Chaku-Chaku: A Step-by-Step Guide

1. **Analyze Process Flow:** Identify tasks suitable for

Chaku-Chaku by focusing on **repetitive activities with low complexity**.

2. **Modify Machines:** Equip machines with **automated unloading mechanisms** to ensure smooth operation.
3. **Arrange Workstations Efficiently:** Place machines in sequence to **minimize movement** between steps.
4. **Train Operators:** Ensure operators are comfortable managing multiple machines and following the production flow.
5. **Monitor and Improve:** Use data from the production process to **identify bottlenecks** and make continuous improvements.

Chaku-Chaku and Its Role in Lean and Six Sigma

1. **Lean Principles:** Chaku-Chaku eliminates waste by reducing **waiting time and excess inventory**, promoting **continuous flow and efficiency**.
2. **Six Sigma Integration:** By creating a **one-piece flow**, Chaku-Chaku ensures that defects are identified immediately, supporting **quality improvement** and reducing variability in the process.
3. **Continuous Improvement:** The feedback loop created by Chaku-Chaku enables **real-time problem solving**, fostering a culture of **Kaizen (continuous improvement)**.

Conclusion

Chaku-Chaku is a powerful tool in **Lean production**, helping organizations achieve **higher productivity and operational efficiency** by minimizing idle time and facilitating one-piece flow. By empowering operators to manage multiple machines and automating repetitive tasks, Chaku-Chaku ensures **consistent quality and faster delivery times**.

Though it requires careful planning and training to implement, the **benefits of reduced waste, lower inventory, and improved responsiveness** make Chaku-Chaku a valuable method for **streamlining processes in manufacturing and service industries** alike. When combined with other Lean tools such as **Andon, Jidoka, and Kanban**, Chaku-Chaku becomes a cornerstone of operational excellence and continuous improvement.

CHAPTER – 9
Critical Incident Technique (CIT)

The **Critical Incident Technique** (CIT) is an advanced and highly effective root cause analysis tool used to understand the causes of unanticipated events. Unlike more basic tools like the Fishbone Diagram or brainstorming, which categorize possible causes, CIT goes deeper by gathering firsthand information through interviews with individuals involved in the incident. This approach allows for a more nuanced understanding of both the problem and the broader environment in which it occurred.

In this chapter, we will explore how the Critical Incident Technique works, when to use it, and how it can be applied in the context of **retail and ecommerce operations** to address operational challenges, improve processes, and reduce risk. We will provide practical steps, real-world examples, and illustrations to clarify the technique's implementation.

Overview of the Critical Incident Technique

The Critical Incident Technique is a qualitative method for collecting specific and detailed information about an event, with the goal of identifying patterns that point to root causes. This technique relies on **interviews** with key participants who were involved in or affected by the incident. These interviews allow you to dig deeper into the incident, asking about challenges, workarounds, and difficulties not immediately visible from process charts or reports.

Key Features of the CIT:

- **Structured Interviews**: The heart of the CIT lies in conducting structured, open-ended interviews with people directly involved in the process, as well as those who have knowledge of it.
- **Focus on Events**: Rather than a continuous process analysis, the CIT zooms in on **specific events or incidents** that represent failures or deviations.
- **Trust and Openness**: This technique requires an atmosphere of trust, encouraging participants to be honest and open about errors, workarounds, and failures without fear of retribution.
- **Comprehensive Perspective**: Unlike narrow investigative tools, CIT offers a comprehensive understanding of the situation by involving multiple stakeholders.

When to Use the Critical Incident Technique:

- **Post-incident Analysis**: Use CIT after a significant event, such as a customer complaint spike, warehouse accidents, or major delivery delays.
- **Identifying Root Causes**: When simpler tools fail to uncover the root causes, CIT helps by diving into the complexities of the process through firsthand experiences.
- **Complex Processes**: Ideal for analyzing complex processes where numerous factors or departments are involved, such as in retail supply chain

management or ecommerce fulfillment operations.

Steps to Implement the Critical Incident Technique

Step 1: Select Participants for the Interview Process

Start by identifying all individuals directly or indirectly involved in the event. Consider participants from different **departments or functional areas** involved in the incident, as they can offer unique perspectives. This ensures that you capture a comprehensive picture of the situation.

Example (Retail Context):

Imagine a scenario where an ecommerce company experiences a series of **order fulfillment delays**, causing dissatisfaction among customers. The participants might include:

- **Warehouse personnel**: Responsible for picking and packing orders.
- **Delivery drivers**: Involved in transporting packages.
- **Customer service representatives**: Who handled the customer complaints.
- **IT personnel**: Who manage the inventory system.

By interviewing people across these areas, you gain insight into not only what happened but also why the delays occurred.

Step 2: Conduct Structured Interviews

Each participant is asked a series of structured, open-ended questions. The aim is to uncover not just what went wrong in the recent incident but also identify any broader patterns that might have contributed.

Sample Questions:

- **What processes or tasks do you find the most difficult?**

- **What factors create delays in your work?**
- **Have you encountered similar problems before? If so, when and why?**
- **Do you employ workarounds to get things done? If yes, what are they and why do you use them?**
- **Are there any gaps in your training or tools that hinder your performance?**

These questions aim to explore both specific incidents and broader **systemic issues** that could be affecting performance.

Step 3: Sort and Analyze Responses

After the interviews are completed, collect and analyze the responses. Look for patterns in the responses, such as common complaints or recurring issues. Group similar answers to identify **critical incidents**, or points where the process frequently breaks down.

Example (Retail Context):

In the case of delayed orders, let's assume the interviews reveal the following recurring incidents:

- **Warehouse delays** due to inadequate staff training on new software.
- **Delivery route inefficiencies** causing long transportation times.
- **IT system errors** leading to mismatches between inventory and actual stock levels.

Create a matrix, like the one below, to organize the findings:

Critical Incident	Frequency of Occurrence	Category
Warehouse staff struggling with new software	High	Training
Delivery drivers taking inefficient routes	Medium	Logistics
IT system errors causing inventory mismatches	High	Technology

This table helps pinpoint **high-priority areas** for further investigation.

Step 4: Drill Down into the Most Frequent Incidents

Now that you've identified the critical incidents, it's time to dig deeper. Focus on the most frequent or impactful issues first. Use follow-up interviews or root cause analysis techniques (such as the **5 Whys**) to uncover deeper causes.

Example (Retail Context):

Let's focus on the **IT system errors**:

1. **Why is the IT system frequently showing mismatched inventory?**
    - Because it hasn't been updated to reflect the new product database.
2. **Why wasn't the system updated?**
    - Because there's no dedicated IT team overseeing warehouse software.

This analysis helps identify the root cause: the lack of a dedicated IT resource for warehouse management.

Step 5: Take Action Based on the Findings

Once the analysis is complete, create an action plan that addresses the root causes of the incident. Ensure that solutions are not just temporary fixes but **long-term improvements** designed to prevent the same issues from recurring.

Example (Solutions for the IT System Errors):

- **Hire dedicated IT personnel** for warehouse systems.
- Implement an **automatic system update schedule** to avoid discrepancies.
- Provide additional training to warehouse staff on using the updated software.

Critical Incident Example: Delayed Ambulance Arrival

To further illustrate the CIT in action, consider the case of an **ambulance service company** where a patient died due to late arrival. Multiple factors were involved, from dispatch errors to traffic delays. By interviewing dispatchers, drivers, and hospital staff, the investigation uncovered several critical incidents, such as:

- **Dispatch delays** due to manual data entry errors.
- **Drivers choosing slower routes** due to outdated GPS systems.
- **Communication gaps** between dispatch and hospital staff.

By sorting and analyzing these incidents, the company pinpointed the root causes, including the need for a **modern GPS system** and better **dispatcher training**.

Illustration of Critical Incident Analysis for Ecommerce

Below is an illustration of the Critical Incident Matrix for an ecommerce company dealing with **late order deliveries**:

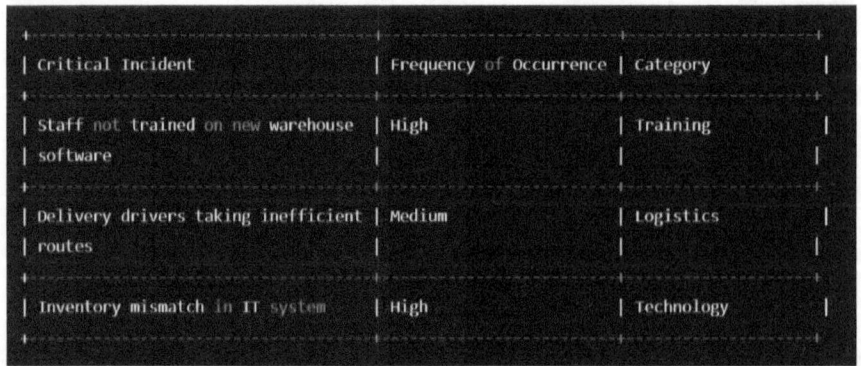

Critical Incident	Frequency of Occurrence	Category
Staff not trained on new warehouse software	High	Training
Delivery drivers taking inefficient routes	Medium	Logistics
Inventory mismatch in IT system	High	Technology

This matrix highlights the **areas requiring immediate attention**, such as warehouse training and IT system improvements, to resolve the delays.

The **Critical Incident Technique** is a powerful tool for diving deep into the root causes of problems in retail and ecommerce operations. By interviewing individuals involved in the incident and collecting qualitative data, CIT allows teams to identify and address the true underlying issues, ensuring that improvements are meaningful and long-lasting.

Real-time data monitoring has become an essential element in today's fast-paced retail and ecommerce environments. By integrating it into the **Critical Incident Technique** (CIT) process, companies can enhance their ability to quickly identify, analyze, and resolve issues. Real-time data provides immediate, actionable insights that can help detect anomalies, track performance, and predict problems before they escalate into full-blown critical incidents.

In this section, we will explore how real-time data monitoring can complement the CIT and drive operational excellence.

The Role of Real-Time Data Monitoring in Critical Incident Management

Real-time data monitoring involves continuously collecting and analyzing data from various sources to identify potential problems as they happen. When combined with the CIT, real-time monitoring can enhance problem identification, speed up response times, and provide a more comprehensive understanding of issues.

Key Benefits of Real-Time Monitoring:

1. **Early Detection**: Detect operational issues or anomalies early, reducing the time between identifying and addressing critical incidents.
2. **Data-Driven Decision Making**: Provides data-backed insights that eliminate guesswork and improve the accuracy of root cause analysis.

3. **Improved Response Time**: Real-time alerts enable immediate actions to resolve issues before they escalate.

4. **Pattern Recognition**: Helps identify recurring incidents by analyzing data trends over time.

5. **Enhanced Accountability**: Teams can track performance metrics and quickly assign responsibility when incidents occur.

How Real-Time Data Enhances the Critical Incident Technique

Real-time data can enhance various stages of the **CIT process**, allowing organizations to:

- **Identify Critical Incidents Faster**: Instead of relying solely on interviews after an incident occurs, real-time data can alert teams when key performance indicators (KPIs) deviate from the norm. For example, if order fulfillment times suddenly spike, the system can flag this as a critical incident before customers even experience delays.

- **Enrich Interviews with Data**: During CIT interviews, having access to real-time performance data allows participants to better understand the context of incidents. Data-backed insights can shed light on specific factors (e.g., peak times, staffing levels, or equipment downtime) that may not be immediately visible to workers.

- **Targeted Root Cause Analysis**: Real-time data helps zero in on critical issues by providing metrics such as processing times, equipment utilization rates, or system downtimes. This allows teams to focus their interviews and investigations on the areas where the data suggests problems exist.

Example of Real-Time Data in Action:

Let's consider a **retail warehouse** that's experiencing delays in order fulfillment. Real-time data might highlight specific choke points, such as:

- **Increased pick and pack times** during peak hours.
- **Inventory discrepancies** due to a system lag.
- **High volume of returns** for certain SKUs, creating bottlenecks in the return process.

The CIT can then use this data to guide interviews and further investigate root causes, such as training deficiencies or inventory system malfunctions.

Implementing Real-Time Data Monitoring: Key Metrics

For real-time data monitoring to work effectively alongside CIT, it's important to track the right metrics. In retail and ecommerce, common metrics that can feed into critical incident analysis include:

1. Order Fulfillment Metrics:

- **Order cycle time**: The total time it takes to process and ship an order. Spikes in cycle time can indicate bottlenecks.
- **Backorder rates**: A rise in backorders could signal inventory management or supplier issues.

2. Warehouse Efficiency Metrics:

- **Pick and pack times**: Slow pick times may indicate problems with warehouse layout, technology, or staffing.
- **Order accuracy**: An increase in order errors can lead to customer complaints and operational disruptions.

3. Customer Experience Metrics:

- **Delivery delays**: Real-time data on delivery times allows for quick adjustments when deliveries fall behind schedule.
- **Customer service response time**: Monitoring customer complaints in real-time can alert teams to potential systemic issues before they become critical incidents.

4. Inventory Management Metrics:

- **Stockout frequency**: High frequency of stockouts suggests supply chain issues that need investigation.
- **Inventory accuracy**: Discrepancies between system stock levels and actual stock can lead to delayed shipments and customer dissatisfaction.

By continuously tracking these metrics, you can pinpoint areas where the **CIT interviews** should focus, as well as address problems before they cause significant harm.

Real-World Example: Enhancing CIT with Real-Time Data in Ecommerce

Imagine an ecommerce company facing a spike in customer complaints related to **late deliveries**. Traditionally, this would be addressed after the fact using the CIT, with interviews conducted across departments like customer service, warehousing, and logistics.

However, with **real-time data monitoring**, the company's system sends an alert that average delivery times have exceeded the target for the past two days. On further analysis, the data reveals:

- **Unusual delays** in the **picking process** at the warehouse.

- **A high number of backorders** for a certain product category.
- **Congestion** in a key shipping route due to temporary road closures.

With this data in hand, the CIT process can begin **immediately** and focus on specific areas like warehouse staffing, inventory management, and alternative shipping routes, saving precious time and avoiding further customer dissatisfaction.

Integrating Real-Time Data and CIT: A Continuous Feedback Loop

The most powerful way to use real-time data in combination with CIT is by creating a **continuous feedback loop**:

1. **Monitor real-time data**: Continuously track operational metrics like fulfillment times, customer complaints, and inventory levels.
2. **Trigger critical incident analysis**: When key metrics fall below thresholds, immediately initiate a CIT process to investigate the issue.
3. **Implement solutions**: Based on the findings from the CIT and real-time data analysis, implement process improvements.
4. **Track improvements**: Use real-time data to monitor the effectiveness of the implemented solutions, ensuring sustained operational excellence.

Conclusion

By integrating **real-time data monitoring** into the **Critical Incident Technique**, retail and ecommerce operations can significantly enhance their problem-solving capabilities. Real-time insights allow companies to identify critical incidents early, drive targeted investigations, and create a culture of continuous improvement.

In the next chapter, we will explore **Predictive Analytics** and how it can further revolutionize retail operations by predicting incidents before they occur, enabling even more proactive management of processes.

Example: Enhancing Critical Incident Technique with Real-Time Data in Retail Operations

Let's take the scenario of a **large retail warehouse** that is responsible for fulfilling ecommerce orders. The company has recently experienced an increase in **late deliveries**, leading to customer complaints and negative reviews. To solve the issue, the company combines **real-time data monitoring** with the **Critical Incident Technique** to identify and address the root cause.

Step 1: Monitoring Real-Time Data

The company's real-time data dashboard tracks key metrics related to their warehouse and fulfillment operations. They regularly monitor the following metrics:

- **Order fulfillment time** (target: 48 hours)
- **Pick and pack time** (target: 30 minutes per order)
- **Inventory accuracy** (target: 99%)
- **Backorder rate** (target: <2%)
- **Customer complaints related to delivery** (target: <50 per week)

Recently, the dashboard has shown some alarming trends:

- **Order fulfillment times** have spiked to an average of **72 hours**.
- **Backorder rates** have risen to **5%**.
- **Customer complaints** have jumped to **150 per week**.

Step 2: Triggering a Critical Incident Analysis

When these metrics breach the thresholds, the system triggers an automatic alert, prompting the management team to initiate a **Critical Incident Technique (CIT)** analysis.

The team selects participants from different departments:

- **Warehouse supervisors** (to understand picking and packing inefficiencies)
- **Inventory managers** (to check stock accuracy issues)
- **Customer service representatives** (to identify patterns in customer complaints)
- **Delivery partners** (to investigate logistics bottlenecks)

Step 3: Conducting Structured Interviews with Data-Backed Insights

During CIT interviews, real-time data helps narrow down the specific areas of concern.

Interview Questions (with data insights):

- **Warehouse Supervisor**: "We've seen that pick and pack times have increased by 30%. What operational changes or challenges have occurred in the past week that could explain this?"
    - Response: "We introduced a new order management system last week, and staff are struggling to adjust. Many have not completed their training yet, which has slowed down order processing."
- **Inventory Manager**: "Real-time data shows a rise in backorder rates for electronics products. What's causing the delay in inventory restocking?"
    - Response: "Our supplier is facing shipping delays, and we have yet to integrate their inventory system with ours, leading to

miscommunication and stockouts."

- **Customer Service Representative**: "Customer complaints have increased by 200% in the past two weeks, primarily due to late deliveries. Have you noticed any patterns in these complaints?"
  - Response: "Many complaints are related to orders placed for out-of-stock items. Customers are frustrated by delays and unclear communication about their orders."

Step 4: Analyzing Responses and Data to Pinpoint Root Causes

By correlating real-time data with interview insights, the company identifies several critical incidents that have contributed to the delays:

1. **Lack of Training**: Warehouse staff is not fully trained on the new order management system, leading to delays in order processing.
2. **Inventory Management Gaps**: The failure to integrate the supplier's system with the company's inventory system has caused backorders and stockouts, especially for high-demand items.
3. **Communication Gaps**: Customers are not being informed about out-of-stock items in real-time, leading to increased complaints.

Step 5: Implementing Solutions and Monitoring Improvements

With the root causes identified, the company implements the following solutions:

- **Training sessions** are immediately scheduled for warehouse staff to speed up the adoption of the new order management system.

- The IT department fast-tracks the **integration of the supplier's system** with the inventory system to reduce backorders and improve stock accuracy.
- **Automated customer notifications** are introduced to inform buyers in real-time when an item is out of stock, reducing the number of complaints.

The real-time data dashboard is continuously monitored to track improvements:

- **Pick and pack times** return to the target of **30 minutes** within a week.
- **Backorder rates** fall back to **1.5%** after the supplier integration is completed.
- **Customer complaints** drop to **40 per week** as transparency in communication improves.

Visual Example: Real-Time Data and CIT Integration

Metric	Threshold	Current Value	Issue Identified	Solution Implemented
Order Fulfillment Time	48 hours	72 hours	Delays in picking due to new system	Staff training on the new system
Pick and Pack Time	30 minutes	45 minutes	Slow processing due to untrained staff	Increased training sessions
Backorder Rate	<2%	5%	Supplier delays, inventory system gaps	Integration of supplier's inventory
Customer Complaints (Late Delivery)	<50/week	150/week	Out-of-stock items not communicated	Automated real-time customer notifications

This example demonstrates how **real-time data monitoring** combined with **Critical Incident Technique** can lead to faster identification and resolution of operational issues. By using real-time data to guide the CIT process, the company was able to quickly pinpoint the root causes of delivery delays, implement solutions, and monitor improvements over time.

Real-time monitoring not only enhances CIT's effectiveness but also creates a proactive approach to managing operational performance, reducing future incidents, and improving customer satisfaction.

CHAPTER – 10
Design of Experiments (DOE)

What Is Design of Experiments (DOE)?

Design of Experiments (DOE) is a powerful **applied statistical method** used to systematically plan, conduct, and analyze experiments to understand the relationship between multiple input factors and their effects on an output. Unlike traditional approaches that manipulate **one factor at a time (OFAT)**, DOE allows multiple inputs to be altered simultaneously, helping organizations **detect interactions** between variables and optimize processes efficiently.

DOE plays a crucial role in **Lean Six Sigma** initiatives, as it helps in identifying key factors that influence **product or process quality**. It provides data-driven insights that lead to process optimization and continuous improvement, reducing defects and enhancing operational performance. This chapter explores the principles, types, and applications of DOE, especially in industrial and business environments.

Why Is DOE Important?

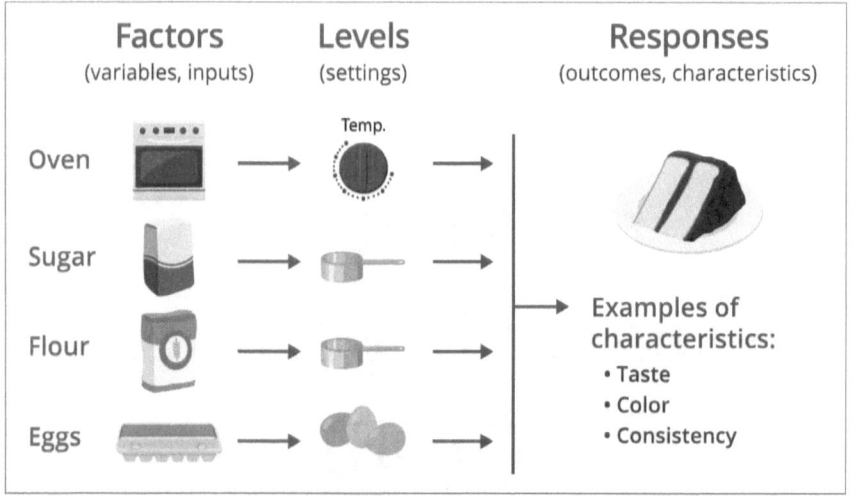

DOE addresses key questions that arise in process optimization:

- **What are the key factors influencing output?**
- **What settings will ensure consistent performance?**
- **Which interactions between factors drive variation?**
- **How can we achieve optimal outcomes with minimal variability?**

When applied effectively, DOE helps businesses **understand, predict, and improve** processes by making better use of available resources and minimizing experimentation time.

Fundamental Concepts of DOE

Several core principles underpin DOE to ensure the reliability and robustness of experimental results:

1. **Blocking**:
   In situations where randomizing a factor is not possible (e.g., due to costs or time constraints), blocking helps manage variability by grouping trials

with similar characteristics.
- **Example:** In a food packaging plant, experiments are blocked based on machine shifts (morning vs. evening) to account for variability in machine settings.

2. **Randomization:**
Randomization refers to conducting experiments in a **random order** to minimize the effects of **uncontrolled variables**. This ensures that any variations caused by environmental factors do not bias the results.
- **Example:** When testing different glue types for adhesion strength, randomizing the order of trials ensures that external factors like humidity are evenly distributed across all tests.

3. **Replication**:
Replication involves repeating the entire experiment to improve the **reliability** of results and measure variability across trials. This increases the confidence in statistical conclusions.
- **Example:** If pressure and temperature are tested as inputs in a plastic molding process, replicating the tests across different batches ensures consistency.

Types of DOE: Full Factorial vs. Fractional Factorial

1. **Full Factorial Design**
A full factorial design tests **all possible combinations** of factors at different levels. This approach ensures a complete understanding of main and interaction effects, but it may require a large number of trials.
- **Example:** For two input factors (e.g., temperature and pressure), each with two

levels (high and low), there will be 22=42^2 = 422=4 experimental runs. With three factors, the number of experiments rises to 23=82^3 = 823=8.

Factor 1 (Temperature)	Factor 2 (Pressure)	Output (Strength)
+1 (High)	+1 (High)	85
+1 (High)	-1 (Low)	78
-1 (Low)	+1 (High)	65
-1 (Low)	-1 (Low)	60

2. **Fractional Factorial Design**
   In cases with many factors, testing all possible combinations can become impractical. A **fractional factorial design** tests only a subset of the combinations to gain useful insights while reducing the number of experiments.
   - **Example:** Instead of running 16 trials for 4 factors, a fractional factorial design may require only 8 carefully selected trials.

Key Steps in Designing a DOE

The success of any DOE depends on proper planning. The following steps outline how to design and execute a DOE:

1. **Understand the Process and Define Variables**
   Create a **process flowchart or map** to identify inputs and outputs, consulting subject matter experts as needed.
   - **Example:** In a coffee production line, temperature, grind size, and water volume may affect the taste profile of coffee.

2. **Select the Output Measure (Response Variable)**
   Choose an output variable that is easy to measure and provides meaningful data. **Continuous data** is

preferable to attribute data (pass/fail).
    - **Example:** Measuring the tensile strength of a material (continuous) is more informative than pass/fail assessments.
3. **Create a Design Matrix**
   The **design matrix** is a structured table showing combinations of input factors and their levels. Use **+1** for high levels and **-1** for low levels.

2-Factor Design Matrix Example:

Factor 1: Temperature	Factor 2: Pressure	Output (Glue Strength)
+1 (High)	+1 (High)	85
+1 (High)	-1 (Low)	80
-1 (Low)	+1 (High)	70
-1 (Low)	-1 (Low)	65

DOE in Lean Six Sigma: A Practical Example

Imagine a manufacturing plant is producing **plastic containers**, and the goal is to optimize the production process by identifying how temperature and pressure impact **wall thickness consistency**. The factors under consideration are:

- **Temperature (°C):** Low (190°C), High (210°C)
- **Pressure (psi):** Low (50 psi), High (80 psi)
- **Output (Response):** Wall thickness deviation (in mm)

Using a **full factorial DOE**, the experiment will have four trials (2 factors × 2 levels = 4 runs). The results are as follows:

Temperature (°C)	Pressure (psi)	Thickness Deviation (mm)
210 (High)	80 (High)	0.03

210 (High)	50 (Low)	0.05
190 (Low)	80 (High)	0.06
190 (Low)	50 (Low)	0.09

Findings

- **Interaction Effect:** High temperature and high pressure together result in minimal thickness deviation (0.03 mm).
- **Recommendation:** Set both temperature and pressure to high for optimal results.

When to Use DOE?

Use DOE when:

- **Multiple inputs** are believed to influence an output.
- You need to **optimize a process** or product performance.
- **Interactions** between variables might exist.
- Conducting a "what-if" analysis or **predicting future outcomes**.

Example: In a **cosmetic production line**, DOE can help determine the ideal combination of mixing speed, pH, and temperature to ensure product consistency and minimize defects.

Conclusion

DOE is an invaluable tool for organizations seeking **data-driven insights** into process optimization. It allows teams to test multiple variables efficiently, uncover interactions between inputs, and improve performance with minimal variability. When applied within a Lean Six Sigma framework, DOE fosters **continuous improvement** by identifying key factors and optimizing processes to meet high-quality standards.

By using the structured approach of DOE, businesses can reduce trial-and-error experimentation, save resources, and achieve **consistent, high-quality outcomes**.

DOE vs. OFAT: A Comparative Analysis

When conducting experiments to optimize processes or understand the relationships between variables, two main approaches come into play: **Design of Experiments (DOE)** and **One Factor at a Time (OFAT)**. Both methods aim to uncover how inputs affect outcomes, but they differ significantly in efficiency, depth of insights, and practicality. In this section, we explore the differences, advantages, and limitations of both approaches.

What is OFAT (One Factor at a Time)?

OFAT involves **changing one input variable at a time** while keeping all other variables constant. The goal is to measure how changes in that single factor influence the output. This approach is often straightforward but can be **time-consuming and limited** in detecting complex interactions between factors.

Example of OFAT:

- A coffee brewer tests the effect of **water temperature** on coffee taste by adjusting only the temperature while keeping grind size and water volume constant.
- First trial: 85°C, second trial: 90°C, third trial: 95°C.

While OFAT gives insights into the effect of individual factors, it **fails to reveal interactions**—such as how water temperature and grind size together might influence flavor.

What is DOE (Design of Experiments)?

In contrast to OFAT, DOE tests **multiple factors simultaneously** at different levels, making it possible to identify **both main effects and interaction effects**. DOE is structured, efficient, and statistically powerful. It provides deeper insights into how inputs work together to affect the output, enabling better optimization of processes.

Example of DOE:

- A coffee brewer tests three factors: water temperature, grind size, and brewing time, at **two levels each** (e.g., high and low). A **full factorial DOE** with 3 factors would require 8 runs, covering all possible combinations of these factors.

Temperature (°C)	Grind Size	Brewing Time (min)	Taste Score
85	Fine	4	7.0
85	Fine	6	6.5
85	Coarse	4	7.5
85	Coarse	6	8.0
95	Fine	4	8.5
95	Fine	6	9.0
95	Coarse	4	8.8
95	Coarse	6	9.5

This example illustrates how DOE can reveal both **main effects** (e.g., how temperature alone affects taste) and **interaction effects** (e.g., how temperature and grind size together influence the final flavor).

Key Differences Between DOE and OFAT

Criteria	DOE (Design of Experiments)	OFAT (One Factor at a Time)
Approach	Tests multiple factors simultaneously	Tests one factor at a time
Efficiency	Requires fewer runs to gain insights	Requires many trials for similar insights
Interaction Detection	Detects interactions between factors	Cannot detect interactions
Optimization Potential	Identifies optimal settings across factors	Only optimizes one factor at a time
Statistical Power	Statistically robust and precise	Limited statistical reliability
Time and Resources	More efficient for complex systems	Time-consuming and resource-heavy

Advantages of DOE over OFAT

1. **Interaction Detection:**
   DOE reveals **interaction effects** between variables, which OFAT often misses. For example, in a manufacturing process, increasing both pressure and temperature might improve product quality—an insight that OFAT might overlook.

2. **Fewer Trials:**
   DOE is more **efficient** for experiments with multiple factors. Instead of testing each factor independently (as in OFAT), DOE uses a design matrix to minimize the number of experiments while still gaining meaningful insights.

3. **Comprehensive Optimization:**
   DOE allows researchers to identify the **best combination of factor settings**, leading to optimal results. In contrast, OFAT may only improve one parameter while missing the overall process potential.

4. **Statistical Precision:**
   DOE ensures **statistical rigor**, increasing the confidence in results and reducing the chance of misleading conclusions caused by variability or randomness.

When to Use OFAT?

While DOE offers superior insights, there are cases where **OFAT** may still be appropriate:

- **Preliminary exploration:** If little is known about the process, OFAT can provide initial insights.
- **Simple systems:** When only one factor is suspected of having a dominant effect on the output, OFAT may suffice.
- **Resource constraints:** In cases where budget or time limitations prevent the use of DOE, OFAT can offer a basic, albeit less efficient, alternative.

When to Use DOE?

Use **DOE** when:

- **Multiple factors** influence the output, and interactions are likely.
- You need to **optimize** a process or product.
- Time and resources are available for planning a more comprehensive experiment.
- **Predictive modeling** or "what-if" scenarios are required for future decision-making.

Numerical Example: OFAT vs. DOE in Practice

Imagine a factory wants to optimize the yield of a chemical process. Three factors—temperature, pressure, and pH—are under consideration, each with two levels (high and low).

- **OFAT Approach:**
  The factory tests each factor separately, requiring **6 trials** (2 levels × 3 factors). However, this approach misses the combined effect of **temperature and pressure** on the reaction yield.

- **DOE Approach:**
  A **full factorial design** tests all combinations of the three factors, requiring **8 trials** ($2^3 = 8$). DOE uncovers that the interaction between **temperature and pressure** leads to a 20% increase in yield—an insight OFAT could not provide.

Conclusion: Why DOE is Superior for Complex Experiments

While OFAT is simple and easy to use for initial exploration, **DOE offers a more efficient, insightful, and statistically sound approach** for process optimization. DOE's ability to detect **interactions** between multiple variables makes it indispensable for complex systems, particularly in industries like manufacturing, pharmaceuticals, and engineering.

Organizations adopting DOE gain a **competitive edge** by optimizing processes quickly, reducing variability, and making data-driven decisions. For long-term success, DOE should be the preferred method whenever multiple factors are suspected of influencing performance.

CHAPTER – 11
Five S's (5S) of Lean

What is 5S?

The **5S methodology** is a core tool within the **Lean philosophy**, designed to create a clean, organized, and safe workplace, which in turn helps reduce **waste, improve productivity**, and foster a positive work environment. Originating from Japan, the term "5S" refers to **five principles**—each beginning with the letter "S"—that together establish the foundation for **visual management, continuous improvement, and operational excellence**.

The 5S approach can be applied to **any work environment**, from manufacturing floors to offices, warehouses, retail stores, and even digital spaces. This methodology not only improves **physical organization** but also promotes mental clarity, discipline, and morale among employees.

The Five S's of Lean

Japanese Term	Translation	English Term	Definition
Seiri	Organize	**Sort**	Separate needed tools, parts, and materials from unneeded ones, and remove what is unnecessary.
Seiton	Orderliness	**Set in Order**	Neatly arrange and label tools, materials,

			and equipment to ensure everything is easy to find and use.
Seiso	Cleanliness	**Shine**	Conduct regular cleaning to keep the workspace spotless, identifying any maintenance issues in the process.
Seiketsu	Standardize	**Standardize**	Create schedules and practices for regular maintenance and cleaning to ensure consistency.
Shitsuke	Discipline	**Sustain**	Instill discipline by making 5S practices a habit and part of the organizational culture.

Understanding Each of the Five S's

1. Sort (Seiri)

The first step focuses on **decluttering** the workspace by removing unnecessary items. Employees must distinguish between what is essential for daily operations and what is not. Anything that is no longer useful is discarded or stored elsewhere.

- **Example:** A retail stockroom eliminates outdated or damaged inventory to free up space for new stock.
- **Benefit:** Reduces clutter, improves focus, and ensures only the necessary tools are available when needed.

2. Set in Order (Seiton)

Once the sorting process is complete, the remaining tools and materials are **organized** systematically for easy access. Everything should have a designated place, with labels or visual cues to promote efficiency.

- **Example:** In a manufacturing plant, all tools are placed on shadow boards with outlines showing where each tool belongs.
- **Benefit:** Saves time searching for tools or materials, minimizing downtime.

3. Shine (Seiso)

This step emphasizes **cleanliness** by making it everyone's responsibility to clean the work area regularly. Cleaning not only improves aesthetics but also reveals **potential maintenance issues** like leaks, wear, or damage.

- **Example:** Employees at a car repair workshop conduct daily inspections, cleaning tools and machines to prevent malfunctions.
- **Benefit:** Ensures a safer and more efficient work environment.

4. Standardize (Seiketsu)

Standardization ensures that the first three steps—**Sort, Set in Order, and Shine**—become routine practices. Checklists, schedules, and visual controls are created to maintain consistency.

- **Example:** A restaurant kitchen sets a daily cleaning schedule with specific tasks assigned to each shift.
- **Benefit:** Increases consistency, reduces errors, and prevents backsliding into old habits.

5. Sustain (Shitsuke)

The final step, **Sustain**, focuses on creating a culture of **discipline and continuous improvement**. The goal is to make 5S a natural part of the organization's work habits, ensuring long-term success.

- **Example:** A company conducts monthly 5S audits to ensure that employees continue following the 5S

principles.
- **Benefit:** Promotes accountability and fosters a culture of continuous improvement.

The Benefits of 5S in Lean Operations

Implementing 5S offers a wide range of advantages that directly contribute to operational excellence. These benefits include:

- **Improved Safety:** Organized spaces reduce the risk of accidents.
- **Higher Equipment Availability:** Regular cleaning helps identify and resolve equipment issues early.
- **Lower Defect Rates:** A well-organized environment minimizes errors.
- **Reduced Costs:** Eliminating unnecessary tools and materials reduces storage and maintenance expenses.
- **Increased Agility and Flexibility:** Employees can work more efficiently when everything is in order.
- **Improved Morale:** A clean, organized workspace promotes employee well-being.
- **Enhanced Brand Image:** A well-maintained workspace makes a positive impression on customers, suppliers, and auditors.

5S Example: Kaiser Permanente Colorado's Medicaid Enrollment Project

The Medicaid Enrollment Project Team at **Kaiser Permanente Colorado** applied the 5S methodology to optimize their enrollment process. The team achieved the following:

1. **Sort:** Eliminated unnecessary fields in the

enrollment template.

2. **Set in Order:** Rearranged fields based on stakeholder feedback for better flow.
3. **Shine:** Created a Microsoft Access database to prevent duplicate entries.
4. **Standardize:** Protected the template and ensured data accuracy through Excel controls.
5. **Sustain:** Developed a self-sustaining system using Access and Excel to ensure long-term consistency.

This example illustrates how 5S principles can be applied beyond physical workspaces to improve **digital workflows and processes**.

5S Diagnostic Checklist Example

To ensure effective implementation of 5S, organizations often conduct regular **workplace scans** using a diagnostic checklist. Below is a sample 5S checklist for an office environment:

5S Principle	Checklist Item	Status
Sort	Are all unnecessary documents removed?	☐ Yes / ☐ No
Set in Order	Are all supplies labeled and easy to find?	☐ Yes / ☐ No
Shine	Is the work area clean and free of clutter?	☐ Yes / ☐ No
Standardize	Is there a cleaning schedule in place?	☐ Yes / ☐ No
Sustain	Are employees following the 5S principles?	☐ Yes / ☐ No

---

How 5S Supports Lean and Continuous Improvement

The 5S methodology is integral to **Lean manufacturing** and **continuous improvement** efforts. By **reducing waste** in the form of clutter, lost time, and unnecessary movements, 5S promotes efficiency and productivity. Regular application of 5S also supports **Kaizen**, the practice of continuous improvement, ensuring that small, incremental changes become part of everyday work routines.

In digital work environments, 5S can improve **information flow** by organizing files and databases systematically, reducing errors, and ensuring smooth operations.

The **5S methodology** is more than just a cleaning exercise—it is a framework for creating a well-organized, efficient, and safe workplace. Whether applied in manufacturing, retail, healthcare, or digital operations, 5S promotes **order, discipline, and continuous improvement**. Organizations that embrace 5S benefit from improved productivity, reduced costs, enhanced safety, and a positive work culture.

By making 5S a habit and part of the organizational mindset, companies can achieve **long-term operational excellence**, ensuring sustainable growth and customer satisfaction.

How to Implement 5S: A Step-by-Step Guide

Implementing **5S** successfully requires a structured approach to ensure it becomes ingrained in the workplace culture. Below is a practical step-by-step guide to **rolling out 5S** within any organization, whether in manufacturing, office environments, or digital settings.

Step 1: Plan and Prepare for 5S Implementation

Before starting, it's essential to lay the groundwork to ensure smooth adoption and sustained success.

- **Assemble a 5S Team:** Include employees from different levels and departments to encourage buy-in.
- **Set Goals:** Define specific objectives, such as reducing clutter, improving efficiency, or enhancing safety.
- **Conduct a Baseline Assessment:** Perform a **workplace audit** to understand the current state and identify key problem areas.
- **Secure Management Support:** Leadership must visibly support the 5S program to encourage participation and allocate necessary resources.

Step 2: Implement the Five S's in Order

1. Sort (Seiri): Remove Unnecessary Items

The goal is to eliminate items that are not essential to the job. Ask: *What do we need, and what can we discard or store elsewhere?*

- **Action Steps:**
    - Walk through the workspace and tag unnecessary items with **red tags** for removal.
    - Categorize items: **Keep, Store, Dispose, or Recycle**.
    - For tools or materials used infrequently, move them to **secondary storage areas**.
- **Example:** A factory removes old machine parts and broken tools to free up floor space.

2. Set in Order (Seiton): Organize Tools and Materials

Arrange everything logically so it's easy to access and return.

"A place for everything, and everything in its place."
- **Action Steps:**
    - Label shelves, cabinets, and containers to make items easy to find.
    - Use **shadow boards** or **tool outlines** to show where equipment belongs.
    - Position frequently used items near workstations to reduce movement.
- **Example:** In a hospital, medical supplies are labeled and stored in clearly marked bins to reduce search time during emergencies.

3. Shine (Seiso): Clean and Inspect the Workspace Regularly

Cleaning not only makes the workplace more pleasant but also helps identify potential issues like wear and leaks.
- **Action Steps:**
    - Develop a **cleaning schedule** assigning specific tasks to individuals or teams.
    - Inspect equipment during cleaning to catch maintenance needs early.
    - Involve everyone in the cleanup process to foster ownership.
- **Example:** An office conducts a daily five-minute cleanup to keep desks clear and shared areas neat.

4. Standardize (Seiketsu): Develop Procedures for Consistency

Create systems to ensure the first three S's—**Sort, Set in Order, and Shine**—are followed regularly.
- **Action Steps:**
    - Use **visual controls** such as charts, signs, and checklists.
    - Develop **standard operating procedures (SOPs)** to define how tasks should be

performed.
- Assign responsibilities to maintain accountability.
- **Example:** A manufacturing plant posts a checklist at each workstation outlining daily cleanup tasks and tool inspections.

5. Sustain (Shitsuke): Maintain Discipline and Continuous Improvement

The final step focuses on making 5S a habit and embedding it into the organizational culture.

- **Action Steps:**
    - Conduct **regular audits** and track progress with 5S metrics.
    - Recognize and reward employees who consistently follow 5S practices.
    - Continuously look for ways to improve the system through **Kaizen (continuous improvement)**.
- **Example:** A company holds monthly 5S audits and shares the results in team meetings, encouraging employees to suggest improvements.

Step 3: Measure Progress and Adjust as Needed

It's important to monitor the effectiveness of your 5S program and make adjustments where necessary.

- **Establish Key Performance Indicators (KPIs):** Examples include reduced search time, improved productivity, or fewer safety incidents.
- **Conduct 5S Audits:** Use **diagnostic checklists** to assess compliance with 5S principles.
- **Collect Feedback:** Encourage employees to suggest

improvements and report issues they encounter.
- **Example KPI:** A warehouse reduces the average time spent searching for inventory from **15 minutes to 5 minutes**.

Step 4: Address Challenges and Sustain Long-Term Success

5S implementation may face challenges, including resistance to change or lapses in discipline. Overcoming these challenges is key to long-term success.

- **Common Challenges:**
    - **Employee Resistance:** Some employees may see 5S as extra work.
    - **Sustaining Effort:** Without regular reinforcement, 5S efforts may fade over time.
    - **Lack of Leadership Commitment:** Inconsistent leadership support can demotivate employees.
- **Solutions:**
    - **Training and Communication:** Help employees understand the benefits of 5S.
    - **Celebrate Successes:** Recognize teams that excel in implementing 5S.
    - **Continuous Improvement:** Regularly review and update processes to ensure 5S evolves with the organization's needs.

Real-World Example: Implementing 5S in a Manufacturing Plant

A **metal fabrication plant** adopted 5S to improve efficiency and reduce waste.

- **Sort:** The team removed obsolete tools and equipment, freeing up 30% of workspace.

- **Set in Order:** They reorganized tools on shadow boards near workstations, reducing the time to retrieve tools by 50%.
- **Shine:** Regular cleaning uncovered a hydraulic leak, preventing a costly breakdown.
- **Standardize:** The plant introduced daily checklists and SOPs for machine maintenance.
- **Sustain:** Monthly audits and team rewards kept employees engaged and committed to 5S practices.
  Result: The plant achieved a 20% increase in productivity and a 15% reduction in downtime within six months.

Checklist for 5S Implementation Success

Task	Completed?
Assemble a cross-functional 5S team	☐ Yes / ☐ No
Conduct a baseline workplace audit	☐ Yes / ☐ No
Remove unnecessary items (Sort)	☐ Yes / ☐ No
Organize tools and materials (Set in Order)	☐ Yes / ☐ No
Develop a cleaning schedule (Shine)	☐ Yes / ☐ No
Create SOPs and visual controls (Standardize)	☐ Yes / ☐ No
Conduct regular audits and track progress	☐ Yes / ☐ No
Reward employees for 5S participation (Sustain)	☐ Yes / ☐ No

Conclusion

Implementing 5S is a **step-by-step journey** toward creating a clean, organized, and efficient work environment. By following the principles of **Sort, Set in Order, Shine, Standardize, and Sustain**, organizations can reduce waste, enhance productivity, and foster a culture of continuous improvement. The key to success lies in **consistent application, leadership support, and employee involvement**. When done right, 5S not only improves physical workspaces but also promotes better morale, safety, and customer satisfaction, driving long-term operational excellence.

CHAPTER – 12
Gemba

The Power of Being Where the Work Happens

Gemba (現場) is a Japanese term meaning "the actual place" or "where the real work happens." In Lean and Six Sigma, Gemba refers to **the physical location where value is created**—whether it's a manufacturing floor, a retail store, a customer service center, or an operational process.

The essence of Gemba lies in **firsthand observation**. Managers, leaders, and employees engage in **Gemba Walks** to observe processes directly, identify inefficiencies, and connect with employees who carry out day-to-day activities. The goal is **continuous improvement (Kaizen)** through direct involvement and feedback from the front line.

This chapter explores the importance of Gemba in Lean Six Sigma, practical methods for conducting effective Gemba Walks, and real-world examples of its application across industries.

What Is Gemba?

In Lean thinking, Gemba represents **the heart of operations**. It's where products are made, services are delivered, and processes are executed. Visiting Gemba ensures that decisions are based on **real observations** rather than assumptions or secondhand reports.

Gemba is **not limited to manufacturing**—it applies equally well to service industries, healthcare, IT, and logistics. For instance, in retail, Gemba is the shop floor; in healthcare, it's the hospital ward; in IT, it could be the development floor or helpdesk.

Key Principle:

- "Go and See" – Direct observation is critical to uncover inefficiencies, engage employees, and solve problems.

The Gemba Walk: How to Observe for Continuous Improvement

A **Gemba Walk** involves managers or team leaders **visiting the work site** to observe operations, talk to employees, and assess processes for improvement opportunities. Unlike traditional audits or inspections, Gemba Walks emphasize **collaboration and problem-solving** rather than assigning blame.

Steps to Conduct a Gemba Walk:

1. **Define the Purpose:** Clearly identify the focus of the walk—such as improving workflow, addressing quality issues, or understanding customer experience.
2. **Plan the Route:** Choose the areas, processes, or operations to observe.
3. **Engage Employees:** Interact with workers to gain insights about daily challenges and inefficiencies.
4. **Observe and Take Notes:** Focus on **waste, bottlenecks, safety concerns, and quality issues**.
5. **Ask Why (Root Cause Analysis):** Use the **5 Whys** technique to explore the root cause of observed problems.
6. **Identify Opportunities for Improvement:** Collect

ideas from employees for process improvements.

7. **Follow Up:** After the Gemba Walk, take action on findings and communicate progress to the team.

The 3 Realms of Gemba

Gemba insights often fall into three categories:

1. **Gemba of Product (Materials & Inventory):**
   Focuses on the flow of products through the value stream to reduce **waste and bottlenecks**.
   - *Example:* In manufacturing, Gemba might reveal that workers frequently search for missing tools, indicating the need for better tool organization.

2. **Gemba of Process (Workflows & Operations):**
   Involves observing daily activities to **identify inefficient steps** or unnecessary tasks.
   - *Example:* In an office setting, Gemba may reveal that approvals are delayed due to outdated paper-based processes.

3. **Gemba of Customer (Customer Interactions):**
   Focuses on **customer experience and satisfaction**. Observing customer interactions reveals pain points and areas for improvement.
   - *Example:* In retail, managers might notice that long checkout lines frustrate customers, highlighting the need for self-service kiosks.

Example of Gemba in Retail

A manager at a retail chain conducts a Gemba Walk to investigate why **checkout times are increasing**. During the visit, the manager observes the following:

- Cashiers spend extra time scanning barcodes on

bulky items.
- Employees frequently pause to retrieve price tags or missing product details.
- Customers often leave the queue due to delays.

After gathering feedback from cashiers and customers, the manager identifies solutions:
- Implementing **mobile scanning devices** for bulky items.
- Training employees to handle common product issues.
- Installing **express checkout counters** for small purchases.

This Gemba Walk not only resolves the checkout issue but also improves **customer satisfaction and employee efficiency**.

Gemba in Lean and Six Sigma

Gemba is a fundamental element of both **Lean and Six Sigma methodologies**, serving as a foundation for process improvement through **direct observation and problem-solving**.

1. **Lean Applications of Gemba:**
    - **Identify Waste:** Gemba uncovers the 8 wastes of Lean (defects, overproduction, waiting, non-utilized talent, transportation, inventory, motion, and extra processing).
    - **Foster Kaizen:** Observations lead to small, incremental improvements across the workflow.
2. **Six Sigma Applications of Gemba:**
    - **Data-Driven Decisions:** Gemba Walks provide **firsthand insights** for identifying

process variations that need statistical analysis.
- **Identify Root Causes:** In the DMAIC (Define, Measure, Analyze, Improve, Control) framework, Gemba Walks play a key role in the **Analyze phase** to pinpoint issues directly at the source.

Benefits of Gemba

1. **Improved Problem Solving:** Decisions are based on **observations of real processes** rather than reports or assumptions.
2. **Employee Engagement:** Employees feel valued when their insights are heard, fostering a **culture of continuous improvement**.
3. **Reduced Waste:** Gemba identifies inefficiencies, bottlenecks, and non-value-adding activities.
4. **Better Customer Experience:** Observing customer interactions reveals pain points that need to be addressed.
5. **Faster Response to Issues:** Managers can **quickly identify problems** and take corrective action.

Challenges of Gemba Walks

1. **Resistance from Employees:** Employees may initially feel uncomfortable with managers observing their work.
2. **Lack of Focus:** Gemba Walks without a clear purpose can waste time and lead to vague results.
3. **Limited Follow-Up:** Without proper action on identified issues, the Gemba Walk becomes meaningless.

How to Implement Gemba Effectively

1. **Build Trust with Employees:** Make it clear that Gemba Walks are meant for **improvement, not judgment**.
2. **Start Small:** Begin with **targeted areas** to address specific issues.
3. **Collaborate with Employees:** Encourage employees to share their insights during the walk.
4. **Document Findings:** Take notes and photos for easy reference later.
5. **Act on Feedback:** Show employees that their input leads to real improvements.

Example: Gemba in Healthcare

At a hospital, a Gemba Walk revealed that nurses spend significant time searching for missing patient charts, which delays patient care. The hospital's Lean team implemented a **centralized electronic record system**, saving nurses time and improving patient care quality.

Conclusion

Gemba is a powerful tool in both **Lean and Six Sigma methodologies**, emphasizing the importance of direct observation for continuous improvement. By visiting the actual place where value is created, managers and team leaders can **identify waste, engage employees, and drive meaningful change**.

A **well-conducted Gemba Walk** provides deep insights into processes, fosters collaboration, and ensures that decisions are grounded in reality. Whether applied in manufacturing, service, or retail industries, Gemba helps organizations achieve **operational excellence and sustained improvement**.

When combined with other Lean tools such as **Kaizen,**

Kanban, and Chaku-Chaku, Gemba plays a vital role in creating an environment where **waste is minimized, and value is maximized**.

CHAPTER – 13
Hansei

The Art of Reflection for Continuous Improvement

Hansei (反省) is a Japanese term meaning **self-reflection** or introspection. It is a crucial element in both **Lean** and **Six Sigma** methodologies, promoting a mindset of **continuous learning and improvement**. Hansei encourages individuals and teams to **pause, reflect on their actions, identify gaps**, and take responsibility for mistakes, even when things seem to be going well.

In Lean thinking, **Hansei drives continuous improvement (Kaizen)** by recognizing not just successes, but also areas that could be improved, ensuring complacency does not set in. This chapter explores the meaning of Hansei, how to integrate it into business practices, and how it fosters a culture of accountability and growth.

What is Hansei?

At its core, Hansei is **self-awareness through reflection**, a practice used to evaluate **what went well, what didn't, and what can be improved**. Unlike performance reviews focused only on external feedback, Hansei requires individuals and teams to **look inward** and **accept responsibility** for shortcomings. It emphasizes that even successful outcomes may contain lessons for future improvement.

Key principles of Hansei:

1. **Honesty:** Acknowledge both strengths and weaknesses without rationalization.
2. **Humility:** Accept personal responsibility and avoid assigning blame to others.
3. **Learning from Success and Failure:** Recognize that even successes can reveal areas for growth.

Hansei is a reminder that **perfection is never achieved**, and there is always room for **Kaizen (continuous improvement)**.

The Role of Hansei in Lean and Six Sigma

Hansei plays a pivotal role in **Lean** by encouraging a mindset of **non-stop progress**. It promotes the principle of **learning from the past**—whether the outcome is positive or negative—and integrates those lessons into future actions. This aligns perfectly with Six Sigma's **DMAIC (Define, Measure, Analyze, Improve, Control)** framework, particularly in the **Analyze and Control phases**, where process variations and missed opportunities must be identified and addressed.

How to Practice Hansei: Steps for Structured Reflection

1. **Define the Objective:** Choose a specific project, task, or process to reflect upon.
    - *Example:* Reflecting on a product launch that met revenue targets but resulted in high operational costs.
2. **Ask Key Questions:**
    - *What went well?* Identify positive outcomes and strengths.
    - *What didn't go well?* Recognize issues, bottlenecks, or missed opportunities.
    - *What could we have done better?* Explore actions that could have prevented failures or

improved performance.

3. **Involve All Stakeholders:** Gather input from everyone involved in the process to gain diverse perspectives.
   - *Example:* Conducting a Hansei meeting with sales, operations, and finance teams after a promotional campaign to get well-rounded feedback.

4. **Document Insights:** Create a record of lessons learned for future reference and continuous improvement.
   - *Example:* Use a **Lessons Learned Log** that teams can revisit before future projects.

5. **Plan Future Actions:** Translate insights into **specific, measurable actions** for improvement.

6. **Repeat the Process:** Hansei is not a one-time exercise—it should become a **habit** integrated into regular operations.

Example: Hansei in a Manufacturing Plant

A manufacturing plant conducts a **Hansei meeting** after delivering a major order to a key client. Although the order was fulfilled on time, the team reflects on several areas for improvement:

- **What went well?:** The production process was efficient, and the client was satisfied with the delivery.
- **What didn't go well?:** Several machines experienced downtime, and the overtime cost exceeded the budget.
- **What can be improved?:** Implement preventive maintenance to avoid downtime and streamline

labor planning to reduce overtime costs.

The insights gathered from this Hansei session become **action items** for future production cycles, ensuring fewer disruptions and cost overruns.

Hansei in Action: Case Study in Toyota

Toyota, one of the pioneers of Lean manufacturing, **integrates Hansei into its culture** at all levels. After every major milestone, Toyota conducts a **Hansei meeting** where both successes and failures are examined. Even when a project is successful, employees are required to **identify potential improvements** and **lessons learned**.

By embedding Hansei into its daily practices, Toyota ensures that **even the smallest improvements are identified** and applied to future projects, maintaining its commitment to **continuous improvement and operational excellence**.

Hansei in Service Industries

Hansei is not limited to manufacturing. In **customer service**, for instance, it can be used to reflect on service interactions.

Example: A customer support team reflects on a day with unusually high complaint resolution times.

- **What went well?** The team maintained composure despite the high volume of calls.
- **What didn't go well?** Several cases were escalated due to incomplete issue tracking.
- **What can be improved?** Introduce **automated ticket tracking** to reduce escalations and provide faster resolutions.

How Hansei Fosters a Culture of Accountability and Growth

1. **Promotes Learning from Failures:** Mistakes are

treated as **learning opportunities** rather than reasons for blame.

2. **Prevents Complacency:** Even successful outcomes are scrutinized for further improvements.

3. **Increases Engagement:** Employees feel empowered when they are involved in **reflecting on and improving processes**.

4. **Strengthens Collaboration:** Hansei encourages **open communication** and teamwork by involving everyone in the reflection process.

5. **Supports Continuous Improvement:** Lessons learned through Hansei feed directly into **Kaizen initiatives** and **process improvements**.

Challenges in Implementing Hansei

1. **Resistance to Self-Criticism:** Employees and leaders may be reluctant to **acknowledge mistakes** openly.

2. **Blame Culture:** If not handled correctly, Hansei can devolve into a **blame game** rather than a constructive reflection.

3. **Lack of Follow-Through:** Without actionable insights and follow-ups, Hansei can become a **pointless exercise**.

Solution:

- Build a **safe environment** where employees feel comfortable sharing insights.

- Focus on **constructive feedback** and solutions rather than pointing fingers.

- Ensure **insights lead to concrete actions** to demonstrate the value of Hansei.

Conclusion

Hansei is a critical practice in Lean and Six Sigma methodologies that fosters **continuous learning, accountability, and improvement**. By promoting **self-reflection and responsibility**, it ensures that both successes and failures provide valuable lessons for future actions. Organizations that adopt Hansei cultivate a **growth mindset**, where **improvement is a continuous journey** rather than a destination.

When combined with other Lean tools like **Kaizen, Gemba, and Andon**, Hansei plays a crucial role in creating a **culture of excellence**, where teams constantly strive to **reflect, learn, and improve**. Whether applied in manufacturing, service industries, or business operations, Hansei ensures that **every experience—whether good or bad—contributes to a better future**.

CHAPTER - 14
Heijunka

Heijunka (pronounced hey-june-kah) is a Japanese term meaning "production leveling" or "production smoothing." It is a key concept in **Lean manufacturing** that focuses on distributing production evenly over time to reduce fluctuations and increase efficiency. Rather than responding to customer demand in peaks and troughs, Heijunka enables businesses to **produce at a consistent pace**—minimizing waste, avoiding bottlenecks, and maintaining stable workflows.

This chapter delves into the concept of Heijunka, its importance in **Lean and Six Sigma methodologies**, and practical ways to apply it for optimal results.

What is Heijunka?

At its core, **Heijunka aims to level the quantity and type of production** to align better with fluctuating demand. The practice shifts the focus from high-volume batch production to a more **even and predictable flow**. By doing so, Heijunka prevents spikes in workload that may lead to overproduction, excessive inventory, worker fatigue, or idle time.

Traditional manufacturing often reacts directly to customer orders in an on-demand way (which can be chaotic). However, Heijunka spreads out production to **ensure consistent output**

—avoiding both overburden (Muri) and inefficiencies (Muda).

How Heijunka Works: Two Types of Production Leveling

1. **Leveling by Quantity:**
   - This method ensures that the **same amount of products** is produced daily or during a defined period.
   - **Example:** Instead of producing 100 units in one day and 300 units the next, the factory levels production at **200 units per day**. This stabilizes workloads and avoids operational spikes.

2. **Leveling by Product Mix:**
   - In this approach, different types of products are scheduled in small quantities across time, ensuring a **variety of products** is produced without long lead times.
   - **Example:** Rather than producing 1,000 units of Product A in one week and 1,000 units of Product B the next, the factory mixes both products evenly into daily production schedules—producing **500 units of A and 500 of B** each week.

Heijunka in Lean and Six Sigma Applications

Heijunka aligns with **Lean principles** of continuous flow, minimizing waste, and improving efficiency. **In Six Sigma**, it complements efforts to **reduce process variation** and maintain consistent quality.

1. **Reducing Waste (Muda):**
   By smoothing production, Heijunka eliminates unnecessary waiting times, avoids overproduction, and reduces inventory. These wastes are often major problems in manufacturing and service processes.

2. **Lowering Variation (Six Sigma):**
   Uneven workflows introduce **variability** that can degrade product quality. Heijunka minimizes fluctuations in the production schedule, helping organizations achieve **stable processes with lower defects**—a key Six Sigma goal.

3. **Improving Customer Satisfaction:**
   Customers benefit from **shorter and predictable lead times** since product availability is maintained at an optimal level, even when demand fluctuates. This consistency improves customer loyalty and reduces stockouts.

4. **Sustaining Workforce Morale:**
   Heijunka ensures that employees are not overburdened during peak times and underutilized during low-demand periods. This **balances workloads**, preventing burnout and idle time.

Heijunka Board: A Visual Control Tool

A **Heijunka board** is a practical tool used to visualize and manage leveled production. It allows teams to track production schedules and workloads in real-time, ensuring adherence to the leveled plan.

- **Example Setup of a Heijunka Board:**
  Imagine a factory producing three product types: **A, B, and C**.
  - **Daily Plan:**
    - 50 units of A
    - 30 units of B
    - 20 units of C

Heijunka Board Example:

Time Slot	Product Type	Units to Produce

Time	Product	Quantity
8:00 AM - 10:00 AM	A	25
10:00 AM - 12:00 PM	B	15
12:00 PM - 2:00 PM	C	10
2:00 PM - 4:00 PM	A	25
4:00 PM - 6:00 PM	B	15
6:00 PM - 8:00 PM	C	10

This board helps visualize both **production leveling by quantity and by product mix**, ensuring that production stays on track throughout the day.

Practical Illustration: Heijunka in an E-commerce Warehouse

Let's explore a practical example of **Heijunka in an e-commerce setting**:

Scenario:
An online retailer experiences fluctuating demand, with peak orders on Mondays and Fridays. Instead of waiting until the last minute to fulfill these large orders, the warehouse applies Heijunka to level its order-picking process over the week.

- **Without Heijunka:**
    - Mondays and Fridays: 500 orders to fulfill, leading to overtime and errors.
    - Other days: 100 orders with idle workers and underutilized equipment.
- **With Heijunka:**
    - Orders are leveled to **200 per day** throughout the week.
    - Workers operate at a **steady pace**, leading to fewer errors and no need for overtime.
    - Customers receive their orders faster since **shipments are prepared continuously**

instead of waiting for peak days.

By applying **Heijunka in the warehouse**, the retailer balances its operations and improves **efficiency, customer satisfaction, and workforce morale**.

Challenges of Implementing Heijunka

Implementing Heijunka is not without its challenges. Some key hurdles include:

1. **Inconsistent Customer Demand:**
   Achieving a perfectly leveled production schedule can be difficult when demand is highly volatile.

2. **Change Resistance:**
   Employees and management may resist changes from batch production to leveled production, requiring effective change management strategies.

3. **Inventory Risks:**
   If not carefully managed, leveled production can lead to **excess inventory** for products with low demand, which contradicts Lean principles.

4. **Complex Scheduling:**
   Heijunka requires advanced **planning and scheduling tools**, especially in multi-product environments. Automated scheduling systems may be needed to manage production smoothly.

Best Practices for Heijunka Implementation

To ensure the successful application of Heijunka, consider the following best practices:

- **Use Historical Data:** Analyze past demand trends to create realistic and achievable production schedules.
- **Introduce Small Production Lots:** Move from large batch production to smaller, more frequent runs to

align with customer needs.

- **Monitor Progress with KPIs:** Use metrics such as **lead time, on-time delivery rate, and production cycle time** to measure the impact of Heijunka.
- **Train Employees:** Conduct workshops and training sessions to familiarize workers with the new leveled production processes.
- **Pilot the System:** Test Heijunka with a small product line or area before scaling it across the entire organization.

Heijunka is a powerful tool for **leveling production and maintaining stable workflows** in Lean and Six Sigma environments. It aligns operations with customer demand by ensuring a consistent pace of production—minimizing waste, reducing variability, and improving customer satisfaction. While challenges exist, organizations that successfully implement Heijunka enjoy **smoother operations, happier employees, and better resource utilization**.

By **balancing workloads and leveling production**, Heijunka helps businesses achieve operational excellence—making it an essential strategy for organizations striving for sustainable growth in today's dynamic markets.

Heijunka vs Kanban: A Comparative Analysis

Both **Heijunka** and **Kanban** are integral tools within the **Lean manufacturing** framework, designed to enhance efficiency, reduce waste, and align operations with customer demand. However, they address different aspects of production control and complement each other when applied effectively. This chapter compares **Heijunka and Kanban**, their differences, roles, and how they work together to optimize production processes.

Understanding Heijunka and Kanban

1. **Heijunka: Production Leveling**
   - **Objective:** Smooth out fluctuations in demand and ensure a consistent production pace over time.
   - **Core Function:** It spreads production evenly across time to prevent bottlenecks and overproduction.
   - **Scope:** Focuses on **long-term scheduling and stability** by determining what to produce, in what quantity, and in what sequence.
   - **Example:** A bakery producing an equal number of pastries daily, instead of increasing production on weekends based on demand spikes.

2. **Kanban: Visual Workflow Management**
   - **Objective:** Control and manage workflows in real time to avoid overburdening any process step.

- **Core Function:** It uses **visual signals (cards or boards)** to ensure just-in-time (JIT) production, triggering the replenishment of inventory or movement of items.
- **Scope:** Kanban controls **work-in-progress (WIP)**, ensuring that the production or service flow matches the current capacity and demand.
- **Example:** A car manufacturing plant uses Kanban cards to signal when more engine parts are needed on the assembly line.

Key Differences between Heijunka and Kanban

Aspect	Heijunka	Kanban
Focus	Long-term production leveling	Real-time workflow and inventory control
Objective	Stabilize production to reduce variability	Manage WIP and ensure smooth flow of operations
Application	Production planning and scheduling	Execution and movement of tasks or materials
Time Horizon	Medium to long-term (weekly, monthly)	Immediate, real-time operations
Signal Mechanism	No direct signaling mechanism (pre-planned)	Uses Kanban cards or boards as visual triggers
Primary Benefit	Reduces demand fluctuations and bottlenecks	Prevents overproduction and streamlines WIP
Usage Scenario	Effective for managing product mix and demand spikes	Ideal for managing parts replenishment and task limits
Lean Principle	Production leveling (smoothing)	Just-in-time (JIT) manufacturing

How Heijunka and Kanban Complement Each Other

While **Heijunka** smooths production over time, **Kanban** ensures the real-time execution of tasks within that leveled schedule. In **complex operations**, both tools can work together effectively:

- **Heijunka creates a stable production schedule**, and **Kanban signals execution** within the leveled plan to prevent bottlenecks or inventory shortages.
- For example, in a **mixed-product factory**, Heijunka might schedule the production of **100 units of Product A, 150 units of Product B, and 50 units of Product C** daily, while Kanban cards control the **flow of raw materials and parts** needed to maintain this schedule without stockpiling.

Practical Illustration: Heijunka vs Kanban in an Auto Parts Plant

Scenario:

An auto parts manufacturer produces different types of car engines, with fluctuating demand over the month. It wants to maintain a stable output and reduce inventory costs.

1. **Heijunka Application:**
   - The plant uses **Heijunka to spread production evenly**—producing 100 engines per day, including a mix of 40 diesel engines, 40 gasoline engines, and 20 hybrid engines.
   - This plan ensures a balanced production across the month, avoiding sudden peaks.
2. **Kanban Application:**
   - On the assembly line, workers use **Kanban cards to trigger replenishment** whenever engine parts, like pistons or crankshafts, fall

below a specific threshold.
- This ensures that **only the needed parts are delivered to the line**, preventing overstock and maintaining smooth production without delays.

When to Use Heijunka vs. Kanban

- **Use Heijunka** if:
    - Your business faces **high variability in customer demand**.
    - You need to stabilize production across **multiple product types**.
    - You want to plan production in advance to **reduce stress on operations**.
- **Use Kanban** if:
    - You aim to **control WIP and limit inventory** in real-time.
    - Your focus is on **workflow management** and avoiding bottlenecks.
    - You need **flexibility** to adjust processes dynamically in response to changing conditions.

Heijunka and Kanban in a Service Industry Example

In a **call center**, customer inquiries peak at certain times of the day.

- **Heijunka:**
    - The call center schedules shifts and staffing levels evenly throughout the day to **smooth out workloads**. This ensures that agents are not overwhelmed during peak times and idle during off-peak hours.
- **Kanban:**

- Each agent's **task queue is managed using Kanban principles**. When an agent completes a call, the system assigns the next available inquiry, ensuring no agent is overloaded while maintaining smooth call flow.

Conclusion: Heijunka vs. Kanban – Two Sides of the Same Coin

Heijunka and Kanban, while distinct, are highly complementary tools in **Lean and Six Sigma methodologies**. **Heijunka** addresses the strategic level of production by leveling outputs over time, while **Kanban** manages the tactical aspect, ensuring smooth execution and just-in-time delivery within the leveled schedule.

Together, they **reduce waste, increase efficiency, and stabilize processes**, making them essential tools for businesses that aim to align operations with demand while minimizing variability. In today's fast-paced markets, organizations that master both Heijunka and Kanban will enjoy **higher productivity, better customer satisfaction, and sustainable growth.**

CHAPTER – 15
Hoshin Kanri

Strategic Alignment for Organizational Excellence

Hoshin Kanri (方針管理), also known as **policy deployment**, is a **strategic planning method** used to align a company's goals with its operational activities. It ensures that every level of the organization is working toward a **common vision** through well-defined objectives and measurable actions. In Lean and Six Sigma frameworks, Hoshin Kanri plays a crucial role by aligning **continuous improvement initiatives** with the organization's **long-term strategy**. This chapter explores the core principles, benefits, and practical implementation of Hoshin Kanri.

What is Hoshin Kanri?

The term **Hoshin Kanri** translates as:

- **Hoshin** (方針) – Direction or strategy
- **Kanri** (管理) – Management or control

Thus, Hoshin Kanri can be understood as a system for **managing strategic direction**. It is a **structured approach** for ensuring that an organization's **long-term goals** cascade down into **departmental objectives and daily activities**.

Hoshin Kanri combines **top-down strategy** (long-term goals) with **bottom-up execution** (day-to-day processes), ensuring alignment across every level of the organization. The method emphasizes **continuous review and adjustment** to keep the organization on track toward achieving its key objectives.

Core Principles of Hoshin Kanri

1. **Alignment and Focus:** Ensure that every action, from the CEO's desk to the shop floor, aligns with the company's strategic goals.
2. **Catchball Process:** Encourage **collaboration and feedback** between different levels of the organization to refine objectives and action plans.
3. **PDCA (Plan-Do-Check-Act) Cycle:** Use **continuous review** to monitor progress and make course corrections.
4. **Measurable Outcomes:** Set specific and **quantifiable objectives** (KPIs) to track progress.
5. **Continuous Improvement:** Promote **Kaizen** by integrating improvements into the strategy and operations.

Hoshin Kanri vs Traditional Strategic Planning

Hoshin Kanri	Traditional Strategic Planning
Strategy aligned with **daily activities**	Strategy often disconnected from execution
Emphasizes **cross-functional collaboration**	Often top-down with limited feedback
Uses the **PDCA cycle** for continuous adjustments	Plans reviewed annually or bi-annually
Bottom-up feedback ensures practicality	Top management creates the plan alone

The 7 Steps of Hoshin Kanri Implementation

1. **Establish the Vision and Breakthrough Objectives**
    - Define the company's **long-term vision** (3 to 5 years) and identify breakthrough objectives critical to achieving that vision.
    - *Example:* A company aims to become a **market leader in sustainable packaging** within five years.

2. **Set Annual Objectives**
    - Break down the breakthrough objectives into **one-year targets**. These must be **specific, measurable, and achievable**.
    - *Example:* Reduce plastic packaging by **30%** in one year.

3. **Deploy Objectives Using the Catchball Process**
    - The **catchball process** involves **communication and feedback** between different levels of the organization. Managers share objectives with their teams and **refine goals collaboratively** to ensure alignment.
    - *Example:* The sustainability department collaborates with production and marketing teams to set realistic goals for packaging reduction.

4. **Create Action Plans at All Levels**
    - Each department creates **action plans** to achieve their assigned objectives. This ensures that every function contributes to the **company's overall vision**.
    - *Example:* The production team plans to switch to biodegradable materials, while the marketing team promotes eco-friendly

packaging to customers.

5. **Implement the Action Plans (Do)**
    - Execute the planned activities and **ensure everyone understands their role** in achieving the objectives.
    - *Example:* Train employees on using new packaging materials and track early production metrics.

6. **Monitor Progress Using the PDCA Cycle (Check)**
    - Conduct **regular reviews** to assess progress toward objectives. Identify bottlenecks and make **course corrections** where necessary.
    - *Example:* Monthly performance reviews reveal that the new material is causing production delays, prompting adjustments to the process.

7. **Reflect and Adjust (Act)**
    - At the end of the year, conduct a **Hansei (reflection)** session to review the outcomes, learn from mistakes, and **integrate improvements** into the next year's plan.
    - *Example:* Based on insights from the first year, the company sources higher-quality biodegradable materials for future production runs.

Hoshin Kanri X-Matrix: A Key Tool for Alignment

A **Hoshin Kanri X-Matrix** is a visual tool used to map out the **relationships between strategic goals, annual objectives, key actions, and KPIs**. The X-Matrix provides a **comprehensive view of the entire strategy** on a single page.

Example Structure of the X-Matrix:

1. **Top Row:** Breakthrough objectives (long-term goals)

2. **Right Column:** Annual objectives (aligned with breakthrough goals)
3. **Bottom Row:** Key actions or initiatives to achieve annual objectives
4. **Left Column:** Metrics/KPIs to track performance

This structured layout ensures that **every objective and action is linked to measurable outcomes**, promoting alignment and focus.

Applications of Hoshin Kanri in Lean and Six Sigma

1. **Lean Manufacturing:**
   Hoshin Kanri aligns **Lean initiatives**, such as **reducing waste** and **improving flow**, with strategic business goals.
   - *Example:* A company aiming to reduce production costs by 15% aligns Lean efforts like **Just-in-Time (JIT) delivery** and **Gemba walks** with this target.

2. **Six Sigma Projects:**
   Six Sigma projects can be integrated into the Hoshin Kanri framework by aligning **DMAIC (Define, Measure, Analyze, Improve, Control)** initiatives with strategic objectives.
   - *Example:* A Six Sigma project aimed at reducing defect rates contributes to the broader company goal of achieving **customer satisfaction** targets.

3. **Cross-Functional Collaboration:**
   Hoshin Kanri ensures that improvement projects are **coordinated across departments**, preventing siloed efforts and **enhancing efficiency**.
   - *Example:* Production, quality, and supply chain teams align their activities to meet a **leaner inventory management** goal.

Benefits of Hoshin Kanri

1. **Strategic Alignment:** Ensures that everyone in the organization works toward the **same long-term goals**.
2. **Engagement and Ownership:** The **catchball process** fosters collaboration and creates **buy-in** from employees.
3. **Continuous Improvement:** The **PDCA cycle** promotes regular reviews and **course corrections**.
4. **Improved Communication:** Clear objectives and shared goals improve **cross-departmental collaboration**.
5. **Measurable Results:** Objectives are tied to specific **KPIs**, enabling **data-driven decision-making**.

Example: Hoshin Kanri in Action – Toyota's Strategic Deployment

Toyota, a pioneer of Lean, uses **Hoshin Kanri to align its operations with its long-term vision**. For example, when Toyota set a goal to become a leader in **electric vehicles**, it used Hoshin Kanri to deploy this strategy across multiple functions.

- **Annual objectives** were set for engineering to develop EV models, manufacturing to adopt greener practices, and marketing to position Toyota as an eco-friendly brand.
- **Monthly reviews** ensured the teams stayed on track, and insights from these reviews were integrated into **future planning cycles**.

Challenges in Implementing Hoshin Kanri

1. **Resistance to Change:** Employees may resist adopting new planning and review processes.
2. **Complexity:** Managing the X-Matrix and multiple KPIs can become **overwhelming**.
3. **Lack of Alignment:** Without proper communication, departmental objectives may **drift away from strategic goals**.

Solution:

- Provide **training** to employees and managers on the Hoshin Kanri process.
- Use **simplified visual tools** like the X-Matrix to maintain clarity.
- **Ensure regular reviews** to keep goals aligned across the organization.

Conclusion

Hoshin Kanri is a powerful framework for aligning **strategy with operations**, ensuring that every action taken by employees contributes to the organization's **long-term vision**. Through **collaboration, continuous feedback, and measurable outcomes**, it promotes a **culture of excellence** where goals are not only set but also achieved through **focused, collective effort**.

By integrating **Hoshin Kanri with Lean and Six Sigma practices**, organizations can unlock new levels of efficiency, quality, and growth, ensuring that **strategic intent becomes operational reality**.

CHAPTER – 16
Jidoka

Jidoka: Empowering Lean Six Sigma in Technology-Driven Global Businesses

In an era where businesses are increasingly digital and interconnected, Lean Six Sigma (LSS) frameworks are evolving to meet the unique challenges of the 21st-century landscape. One of the fundamental pillars of Lean, **Jidoka**—often translated as "automation with a human touch"—plays a pivotal role in enhancing operational excellence. This article delves into the concept of Jidoka and explores its relevance and implementation in **technology-based global business platforms**.

What is Jidoka?

Jidoka, originally introduced by Toyota, emphasizes **intelligent automation** where machines or processes autonomously detect abnormalities and immediately halt to prevent defective output from progressing downstream. This empowers workers and systems to focus not just on speed but also on quality at every step of the process.

The core elements of Jidoka are:

1. **Autonomous Defect Detection** – Machines or software stop automatically when anomalies occur.
2. **Immediate Action and Response** – Processes halt,

and alerts are sent.
3. **Root Cause Analysis** – Investigating the issue before restarting to ensure it doesn't recur.
4. **Empowering Employees** – Operators or engineers have the autonomy to intervene and correct processes as needed.

The Essence of Jidoka in Lean Six Sigma

In Lean Six Sigma, Jidoka aligns with the DMAIC (Define, Measure, Analyze, Improve, Control) methodology. Jidoka strengthens the **Control** phase by ensuring that defects are detected and eliminated at the earliest stage, thereby reducing rework, waste (muda), and downtime. It reinforces **continuous improvement (Kaizen)** by systematically driving the resolution of process bottlenecks.

Jidoka in Technology-Driven Global Platforms: An Evolutionary Necessity

With the shift toward digital and AI-enabled platforms, businesses must ensure operational resilience and customer satisfaction at scale. Global platforms such as **eCommerce, SaaS platforms, and cloud infrastructure** providers rely heavily on fast, accurate, and reliable processes. For them, Jidoka extends beyond physical machinery into **software-driven quality assurance**, **AI-powered monitoring systems**, and **real-time anomaly detection**. Let's explore how this concept applies across technology-driven industries.

Practical Applications and Use Cases

1. Ecommerce Platforms: Order Fulfillment and Quality Control

Large eCommerce platforms like **Amazon** handle millions of orders daily. Automating defect detection in warehouse operations ensures that incorrect or damaged products are identified before dispatch.

- **Example:**
  A robotic arm picks products from inventory bins for shipment. If a product is not aligned correctly or matches a damaged SKU, the system halts, triggering an alert for a manual check.

Numerical Impact:

- **Time saved:** 3 minutes per order inspection across 1 million orders = 50,000 labor hours saved weekly.
- **Defect reduction:** Identifying misaligned shipments can reduce returns by 15%, resulting in **$2M saved annually** for a mid-sized eCommerce operation.

Jidoka ensures operational precision and helps platforms build **customer loyalty** by reducing order errors.

---

2. SaaS Platforms: Monitoring Software Reliability and User Experience

For SaaS companies, uninterrupted service delivery is paramount. Jidoka is implemented in the form of **real-time monitoring systems** that autonomously detect errors, outages, or breaches, and trigger alerts or self-healing actions.

- **Example:**
  A SaaS provider offering HR software monitors login failures and abnormal server behavior. If the system detects a sudden spike in failed login attempts, it halts the login service, notifies the engineering team, and initiates a **temporary block on IP addresses** until the issue is resolved.

Numerical Impact:

- Reducing downtime by **10 minutes per incident** across 100 outages saves **$500,000 annually** in lost revenue.

- **Customer churn** decreases by 5% due to proactive issue management and enhanced reliability.

Jidoka here supports **Continuous Improvement (CI)**, feeding root cause analysis data into Six Sigma improvement cycles.

---

3. Cloud Infrastructure: Self-Healing Systems

Cloud providers like **AWS and Azure** deploy intelligent algorithms that monitor infrastructure performance. If a server exceeds a temperature threshold or a workload exceeds safe limits, the system either spins up new virtual machines or shuts down the faulty server to prevent cascading failures.

- **Example:**
  AWS's **Auto-Scaling Groups** autonomously detect abnormal loads. If CPU utilization exceeds 80% for more than 5 minutes, it deploys additional resources to maintain stability and alert the operations team for further investigation.

Numerical Impact:

- Scaling proactively improves SLA compliance, reducing penalties from **$50,000 per SLA breach**.
- Operational costs decrease by 10% due to **optimal resource allocation** from automated monitoring systems.

Jidoka ensures high uptime and fosters customer trust through predictive resource management.

Jidoka through AI and IoT Integration: The New Frontier

Jidoka is no longer limited to isolated factory floors or basic automation processes. **AI-driven analytics** and **Internet of Things (IoT)** devices are taking Jidoka to the next level in technology-based industries:

- **Predictive Maintenance**: Sensors on machines predict failures before they occur and automatically trigger maintenance schedules.
- **AI Monitoring in Data Centers**: Machine learning algorithms predict cooling system failures and halt non-critical workloads to prevent overheating.
- **Autonomous Customer Support Systems**: Chatbots pause and escalate complex customer issues to human agents when they detect emotional distress or unusual patterns.

Challenges and How to Overcome Them

While Jidoka offers clear advantages, implementing it in global, technology-based platforms is not without challenges:

1. **System Complexity**: Managing interconnected systems can make identifying root causes difficult.
   - **Solution:** Use Six Sigma tools like Fishbone Diagrams to trace issues effectively.
2. **Alert Fatigue**: Frequent alerts can overwhelm teams.
   - **Solution:** Employ AI-powered monitoring to filter and prioritize critical incidents.
3. **Cultural Resistance**: Employees may be reluctant to rely on automated systems.
   - **Solution:** Invest in **training programs** to empower staff and build trust in the new processes.

Conclusion: Jidoka as a Catalyst for Continuous Improvement

In a world where speed, quality, and customer experience are paramount, **Jidoka plays a crucial role in bridging the gap between automation and human oversight.** It ensures that technology-based global platforms remain agile and customer-centric, all while driving efficiency and reducing operational risks. When integrated with Lean Six Sigma, Jidoka becomes a powerful enabler of **operational excellence** by transforming real-time problem detection into structured improvement opportunities.

Whether in **eCommerce fulfillment**, **SaaS reliability management**, or **cloud infrastructure monitoring**, the principle of Jidoka fosters a culture of accountability, enabling businesses to stay competitive in a fast-paced, digital world.

CHAPTER – 17
Kaikaku

Driving Radical Change for Transformational Improvement

In Lean thinking, **Kaikaku** (改革) refers to **radical, transformational change** that challenges the status quo, redesigns processes, and significantly alters the way an organization operates. While **Kaizen** focuses on incremental, continuous improvement, Kaikaku brings about **drastic shifts** —addressing situations where small improvements are no longer enough to meet competitive demands. It often leads to **breakthrough performance** in areas such as **cost reduction, productivity, quality, and efficiency**.

This chapter explores the concept of Kaikaku, compares it with **Kaizen**, and discusses **practical applications, benefits, and challenges** with real-world examples to highlight its relevance.

What is Kaikaku?

The Japanese term **Kaikaku** means **reform, transformation, or innovation**. In a business context, it signifies a complete rethinking of processes, practices, or workflows to achieve **large-scale improvement**. Unlike Kaizen, which involves minor, continuous adjustments, Kaikaku is a **step-change** that can involve:

- **New technology adoption**
- **Process re-engineering**
- **Structural or cultural shifts**
- **Product or service redesign**

It is typically **top-down** in nature, initiated by leadership to **leapfrog** competitors or address fundamental inefficiencies. Kaikaku aligns well with **strategic changes** that organizations need to survive or thrive in dynamic markets.

Kaikaku vs. Kaizen: Key Differences

Aspect	Kaikaku	Kaizen
Definition	Radical change or transformation	Continuous, incremental improvement
Scale of Change	Large-scale, disruptive	Small, gradual improvements
Initiator	Top management-led	Bottom-up from employees
Timeline	Short-term implementation	Ongoing, long-term effort
Impact	High, transformational results	Steady, incremental gains
Risk	Higher risk due to scope of change	Lower risk with smaller adjustments

Example:

- **Kaizen:** Improving assembly-line efficiency by reducing motion waste.
- **Kaikaku:** Completely redesigning the production line by introducing **automation technology**.

When to Implement Kaikaku

Organizations may choose Kaikaku when:

1. **Current Processes Are Obsolete:** Small

improvements are no longer sufficient to keep up with market trends.

2. **Major Technological Advancements:** New tools, systems, or automation can drastically improve efficiency.

3. **Competitive Pressure:** There is an urgent need to **reduce costs** or **improve quality** to stay competitive.

4. **Strategic Shift:** The business changes its focus, such as shifting from **traditional retail** to **e-commerce platforms**.

5. **Crisis or Turnaround Situations:** When the organization is in financial distress and needs drastic reforms to survive.

Steps to Implement Kaikaku

1. **Identify the Need for Transformation**
   - Recognize areas where small improvements are insufficient, and **major change** is required.
   - *Example:* A factory struggling with high defect rates despite numerous Kaizen efforts may opt for **process automation**.

2. **Define the Objectives**
   - Set clear, measurable goals for the transformation. Objectives could include **reducing lead time by 50%**, achieving **zero defects**, or **cutting costs by 30%**.

3. **Conduct a Gap Analysis**
   - Assess the gap between the current state and the desired future state.
   - *Example:* A manufacturing company identifies that its outdated equipment is the main reason for slow production.

4. **Develop a Transformation Plan**
   - Create a detailed **roadmap** for implementing Kaikaku, including timelines, resource allocation, and responsibilities.
5. **Communicate and Engage Stakeholders**
   - Since Kaikaku is disruptive, **employee buy-in** and proper communication are essential.
   - Use the **catchball method** to gather feedback from middle managers and employees during the planning phase.
6. **Execute the Plan**
   - Implement the change quickly to minimize disruption. Ensure proper **training** for employees to adapt to new processes or technologies.
7. **Monitor and Evaluate Results**
   - Use the **PDCA cycle** to monitor performance after implementation and make adjustments as needed.

Illustrations and Practical Examples of Kaikaku

1. **Case Study: Toyota's Introduction of Hybrid Cars**
   Toyota's decision to develop the **Prius hybrid** vehicle is a prime example of Kaikaku. The transition from traditional combustion engines to hybrid technology required **significant R&D investments**, a new production approach, and **supplier re-alignment**. It resulted in Toyota becoming a **market leader in fuel-efficient vehicles**.

2. **Example: E-commerce Shift in Retail**
   A traditional retailer struggling with declining in-store sales decides to **transform its business model** by shifting entirely to **e-commerce**. The company implements **new digital infrastructure**, automates

order fulfillment, and retrains staff for customer support roles. This radical change allows the business to **adapt to changing consumer behavior**.

3. **Manufacturing Example: Transition to Automation**
A factory producing consumer electronics faces increasing labor costs. After small improvements fail to meet productivity targets, the company implements **fully automated robotic assembly lines**. This Kaikaku transformation reduces **cycle times by 40%** and **production costs by 25%** within six months.

Benefits of Kaikaku

1. **Dramatic Improvement in Performance**
   - Kaikaku can result in **immediate and significant gains** in productivity, cost-efficiency, or quality.
   - *Example:* A company cuts production time in half by switching to **Just-in-Time (JIT)** manufacturing.

2. **Competitive Advantage**
   - Radical changes can position the business **ahead of competitors** by adopting new technologies or processes.

3. **Alignment with Long-Term Strategy**
   - Kaikaku allows organizations to **pivot** toward new business models, markets, or technologies in line with strategic objectives.

4. **Improved Employee Morale**
   - Although initially disruptive, the long-term benefits of Kaikaku—such as **better tools or streamlined workflows**—can boost employee satisfaction.

Challenges of Kaikaku

1. **Resistance to Change**
   - Employees may resist drastic changes, especially if it involves **new technology** or **job roles**.
   - *Solution:* Provide **training and communication** to ease the transition.

2. **High Costs and Risks**
   - Kaikaku often involves significant investments, and if not properly executed, it can lead to **financial losses**.
   - *Solution:* Conduct a **thorough cost-benefit analysis** before initiating radical change.

3. **Disruption to Operations**
   - Major transformations may temporarily disrupt **normal business operations**.
   - *Solution:* Use a **phased implementation** approach where possible to minimize disruptions.

Kaikaku and Lean Six Sigma Applications

1. **Lean Manufacturing**
   - Kaikaku aligns with Lean principles by eliminating waste and improving **flow** through radical process redesign.
   - *Example:* A company replaces batch production with **cellular manufacturing** to reduce lead times and inventory.

2. **Six Sigma**
   - Kaikaku can address **systemic issues** by introducing new processes that drastically reduce **defect rates**.

- *Example:* A pharmaceutical company introduces automated quality control systems, leading to a **99.9% reduction in defects**.

3. **Technology Integration**
   - Kaikaku is often used to **integrate new technologies** that enhance productivity.
   - *Example:* Introducing an **ERP (Enterprise Resource Planning)** system to streamline operations across departments.

Conclusion

Kaikaku is a powerful tool for organizations that need to **rethink their operations** and **embrace change** on a large scale. While it requires significant investment, effort, and leadership, the potential rewards include **transformational improvements** in efficiency, cost savings, and customer satisfaction. Kaikaku complements **Kaizen** by addressing areas where incremental improvements are no longer enough. When implemented correctly, Kaikaku helps organizations **adapt to market shifts, leverage new technologies**, and **achieve sustainable growth**.

By balancing **radical transformation** with continuous improvement, businesses can ensure they remain **resilient, competitive, and innovative** in today's fast-changing landscape.

CHAPTER – 18
Kaizen

The Philosophy of Continuous Improvement

Introduction to Kaizen

The term **Kaizen (改善)** means **"continuous improvement"** in Japanese. It reflects a **philosophy of ongoing efforts** to improve processes, products, services, and workplace environments. Unlike radical change approaches such as **Kaikaku**, Kaizen emphasizes **small, incremental improvements** that accumulate over time to create **substantial progress**. It is a **people-centered approach**, involving employees at all levels—from executives to front-line workers—in the pursuit of **operational excellence**.

Kaizen serves as the **foundation of Lean thinking**, and it plays a critical role in **waste elimination, problem-solving**, and **process optimization**. This chapter explores Kaizen's principles, methodologies, applications, and examples, illustrating how businesses can foster a culture of continuous improvement.

Key Principles of Kaizen

1. **Continuous Improvement**
    - Improvement is not a one-time event but an ongoing process.
    - Small, incremental changes add up to

significant progress over time.

2. **People-Oriented Approach**
   - Kaizen empowers all employees to identify and implement improvements.
   - Collaboration and teamwork are key to Kaizen's success.

3. **Elimination of Waste (Muda)**
   - The focus is on identifying and eliminating **waste** in processes, including time, effort, and materials.

4. **Process-Focused Thinking**
   - Kaizen emphasizes improving the **process** rather than only focusing on the outcomes.

5. **Standardization and Sustainability**
   - Improvements must be **standardized** to maintain gains over time and avoid reverting to old practices.

How Kaizen Works

Kaizen is implemented through **small, manageable changes** that can be quickly adopted and refined. It encourages every individual to think about how **"today can be better than yesterday"** and **"tomorrow better than today."** The process follows the **PDCA (Plan-Do-Check-Act) cycle** to continuously evaluate and refine improvements.

PDCA Cycle in Kaizen

1. **Plan:**
   - Identify the problem or area for improvement.
   - Set measurable goals.
   - Develop an action plan.

2. **Do:**

- Implement the changes on a small scale.

3. **Check:**
    - Monitor and evaluate the results.
    - Compare outcomes to the goals set in the planning phase.

4. **Act:**
    - Standardize successful improvements.
    - If the results are unsatisfactory, refine and reimplement the changes.

Kaizen vs. Kaikaku: A Complementary Relationship

Aspect	Kaizen	Kaikaku
Definition	Continuous small improvements	Radical, large-scale change
Approach	Incremental, gradual	Drastic, disruptive
Timeline	Ongoing, long-term	Short-term, focused
Risk	Low risk	High risk
Initiator	Bottom-up from employees	Top-down from leadership
Impact	Steady gains over time	Breakthrough improvements

While **Kaizen** drives **incremental progress**, **Kaikaku** is used when a business needs to undergo **radical transformation**. Both approaches are essential and complement each other in Lean management.

Practical Applications of Kaizen

1. Manufacturing Example: Reducing Setup Time

A car manufacturer applies Kaizen to reduce the time required to set up machines between production runs.

- **Plan:** Identify the bottleneck in setup time.

- **Do:** Introduce quick-change tools and optimize setup steps.
- **Check:** Measure the reduction in setup time.
- **Act:** Standardize the new setup process to maintain improvements.
  Result: Setup time is reduced from 45 minutes to 10 minutes, increasing productivity and reducing downtime.

2. Kaizen in Service Industry: Improving Customer Experience

A retail company uses Kaizen to reduce customer wait times at checkout.

- **Plan:** Study the checkout process to identify bottlenecks.
- **Do:** Implement a second queue and self-checkout systems.
- **Check:** Compare the new system with the original process.
- **Act:** Roll out the improvements to all stores.
  Result: Customer wait times decrease by 30%, enhancing customer satisfaction.

3. Office Kaizen: Reducing Paperwork

A company applies Kaizen to reduce excessive paperwork in internal processes.

- **Plan:** Identify forms and reports that add no value.
- **Do:** Eliminate unnecessary forms and automate recurring tasks.
- **Check:** Monitor the reduction in processing time.
- **Act:** Standardize the new workflow to sustain improvements.

Result: Paperwork is reduced by 40%, freeing employees to focus on higher-value activities.

Benefits of Kaizen

1. **Improved Efficiency**
   - Streamlining processes reduces waste and improves productivity.
2. **Employee Empowerment and Engagement**
   - Involving employees in decision-making fosters a sense of **ownership** and motivation.
3. **Cost Savings**
   - Small improvements result in cumulative cost savings over time.
4. **Higher Quality**
   - Continuous improvements lead to **better product or service quality** and fewer defects.
5. **Cultural Shift Toward Innovation**
   - Kaizen creates a **culture of continuous learning and improvement**.
6. **Customer Satisfaction**
   - Improved processes lead to faster delivery times and higher-quality products, enhancing the **customer experience**.

Challenges of Kaizen

1. **Resistance to Change**
   - Some employees may resist even small changes, fearing disruptions to their routines.
   - *Solution:* Encourage open communication and emphasize the benefits of

improvements.

2. **Maintaining Momentum**
   - Continuous improvement requires sustained effort and can lose momentum over time.
   - *Solution:* Use **Kaizen events** and recognize employee contributions to keep motivation high.

3. **Difficulty in Measuring Impact**
   - Small changes may have subtle effects that are hard to quantify.
   - *Solution:* Track key metrics and focus on **cumulative improvements**.

Kaizen Events (Kaizen Blitz)

A **Kaizen event** or **Kaizen blitz** is a focused, short-term effort (usually 2-5 days) to achieve rapid improvements in a specific area or process.

- Example: A team conducts a **Kaizen blitz** to reorganize a storage area, reducing search time by 50%.

Kaizen events are **highly structured**, with clear objectives, timelines, and measurable outcomes. They can serve as a **catalyst** for longer-term improvement efforts.

Kaizen and Lean Six Sigma Integration

Kaizen integrates seamlessly with **Lean Six Sigma** principles:

- **Lean:** Kaizen focuses on **eliminating waste** (Muda), which aligns with Lean's goal of improving flow and reducing non-value-adding activities.
- **Six Sigma:** Kaizen's continuous improvement approach aligns with **Six Sigma's focus on reducing**

variation and improving process quality.

- *Example:* A Six Sigma team uses Kaizen to make incremental changes that improve **customer complaint resolution times** by 20%.

Kaizen is more than just a set of practices; it is a **mindset and cultural philosophy** that encourages everyone in the organization to participate in continuous improvement. By focusing on **small, incremental changes**, Kaizen empowers businesses to **eliminate waste, enhance efficiency**, and **improve quality** sustainably. When embedded into the fabric of an organization, Kaizen fosters a **culture of innovation, collaboration, and excellence**—ensuring long-term success and adaptability in a competitive market.

Whether in manufacturing, services, or office environments, Kaizen serves as a **cornerstone of Lean thinking** and a reliable approach to achieving **ongoing operational excellence**.

Kaizen Tools: Essential Techniques for Continuous Improvement

Kaizen tools are critical instruments that help organizations implement and sustain continuous improvement effectively. These tools support problem-solving, waste elimination, process optimization, and employee engagement. In this chapter, we explore some of the most widely used **Kaizen tools** with practical illustrations and examples.

1. 5S: Organize the Workplace for Efficiency

The **5S methodology** ensures a clean, organized, and efficient workspace. It stands for:

1. **Seiri** (Sort) – Remove unnecessary items.
2. **Seiton** (Set in Order) – Organize needed items for easy access.

3. **Seiso** (Shine) – Clean the workspace regularly.
4. **Seiketsu** (Standardize) – Maintain consistent processes.
5. **Shitsuke** (Sustain) – Build a habit of following the first four steps.

Example:
A production line uses 5S to organize tools by type and frequency of use, reducing search time by 30%.

2. PDCA Cycle (Plan-Do-Check-Act)

The **PDCA cycle** is a continuous loop of planning, executing, evaluating, and acting upon improvements.

- **Plan:** Identify areas for improvement.
- **Do:** Implement a small change or test solution.
- **Check:** Monitor the results.
- **Act:** If successful, standardize the change; if not, refine and try again.

Example:
A call center uses PDCA to reduce average customer call waiting times by testing different scheduling patterns.

3. Value Stream Mapping (VSM)

VSM is a tool to **visualize and analyze the flow of materials and information** throughout a process. It helps identify bottlenecks, waste, and improvement opportunities.

Example:
A food manufacturer uses VSM to map the time from raw material receipt to product delivery. By eliminating delays, the lead time is reduced by 20%.

4. Fishbone Diagram (Ishikawa Diagram)

The **fishbone diagram** helps teams identify the **root causes of a problem**. It organizes potential causes into categories such as **People, Process, Materials, Machine, Environment, and Methods**.

Example:
A manufacturing team uses the fishbone diagram to explore the root causes of high defect rates, identifying outdated equipment as the main issue.

---

5. Gemba Walks

In a **Gemba walk**, managers and team leaders visit the workplace to **observe processes and engage with employees**. The goal is to identify real issues and encourage direct communication.

Example:
A hospital director conducts Gemba walks to understand the challenges faced by nurses during patient handovers, leading to improvements in shift change protocols.

---

6. Kaizen Blitz (Kaizen Event)

A **Kaizen Blitz** is an **intensive, short-term event** aimed at achieving rapid improvements in a focused area. These events typically last 2-5 days and involve cross-functional teams.

Example:
A logistics company uses a Kaizen Blitz to reorganize its warehouse, reducing picking times by 25%.

---

7. Standard Work

Standard work involves documenting and formalizing the **best-known process for performing tasks**, ensuring consistency across operations.

Example:
A restaurant develops a standard recipe for its dishes to

maintain consistent taste and reduce errors.

8. 5 Whys Analysis

The **5 Whys** is a technique used to **drill down to the root cause** of a problem by repeatedly asking "Why?" until the underlying issue is uncovered.

Example:
Problem: A delivery is delayed.

- Why? The truck left late.
- Why? The goods were not packed on time.
- Why? The packaging machine broke down.
- Why? It was not maintained properly.
- Why? There is no preventive maintenance plan.
  Solution: Implement a maintenance schedule.

9. Kanban System

The **Kanban system** is a visual tool to **manage workflow** by signaling when to move items or tasks from one stage to the next. It ensures that processes run smoothly without bottlenecks.

Example:
A software development team uses a **Kanban board** with columns like "To Do," "In Progress," and "Done" to track work tasks.

10. Poka-Yoke (Error Proofing)

Poka-Yoke is a tool to **prevent mistakes** by designing processes that make it impossible to produce defects or errors.

Example:
A car manufacturer uses Poka-Yoke by installing fixtures that allow bolts to be fastened only in the correct orientation.

11. Continuous Flow (Chaku-Chaku)

Chaku-Chaku means "load-load" in Japanese. It refers to a continuous flow production system where machines are **arranged sequentially** to eliminate delays between steps. Operators move from one machine to the next, ensuring efficiency.

Example:
An electronics company applies Chaku-Chaku by aligning machines in sequence to speed up circuit board assembly.

12. Takt Time

Takt time is the rate at which a product needs to be completed to meet customer demand. It ensures that production aligns with market needs.

Formula:

$$\text{Takt Time} = \frac{\text{Available Time}}{\text{Customer Demand}}$$

Example:
If a shift has 7 hours of working time (25,200 seconds) and the demand is 600 units, the **Takt Time** is 42 seconds per unit.

13. SIPOC Diagram

A **SIPOC diagram** (Suppliers, Inputs, Process, Outputs, Customers) provides a **high-level overview** of a process and ensures alignment with customer expectations.

Example:
A bank uses a SIPOC diagram to map its loan approval process, ensuring that every step adds value to the customer.

14. One-Piece Flow

In **one-piece flow**, products move through a production line one at a time, reducing inventory and lead time.

Example:
A furniture manufacturer switches from batch production to one-piece flow, cutting lead times from 10 days to 2 days.

15. Visual Management

Visual management uses **color codes, charts, and signage** to make processes transparent and easy to understand at a glance.

Example:
A factory installs **color-coded bins** for different materials to avoid confusion and minimize material-handling errors.

Conclusion

Kaizen tools provide practical methods to **analyze, improve, and standardize processes** while engaging employees at all levels. From **problem-solving frameworks** like the Fishbone diagram and 5 Whys to **workplace organization tools** like 5S, these tools empower organizations to **eliminate waste, improve quality**, and **boost productivity**. When consistently applied, Kaizen tools foster a culture of **continuous improvement** that ensures organizations remain agile and competitive in changing markets.

CHAPTER – 19
Kanban

A Visual System for Managing Workflow and Production

Kanban, meaning "signboard" or "visual signal" in Japanese, is a **lean management tool** designed to manage the flow of materials, tasks, or information within a production process. It serves as a powerful technique to help organizations **eliminate waste, minimize inventory**, and **optimize workflow** by ensuring that work is only pulled when needed. Kanban aligns production directly with real-time demand, preventing overproduction and bottlenecks.

In this chapter, we explore the **concept of Kanban**, how it works, its key principles, and how it applies in both manufacturing and service industries.

---

1. How Kanban Works: The Core Concept

The Kanban system is **based on visual signals, such as cards, boards, or containers**, to regulate and streamline production. Each signal (typically a **Kanban card**) indicates that new materials or tasks are required to replenish or advance the flow to the next stage.

It helps manage **"pull production"**—a system where downstream activities dictate what is produced upstream, ensuring that work-in-process (WIP) inventory stays low.

Example:

In a car assembly line, a **Kanban card** is placed in a bin for steering wheels. When a worker pulls the last wheel from the bin, the empty bin and its card act as a signal to the warehouse team to supply more wheels.

2. Kanban in Action: Key Elements

Kanban Cards

- **Kanban cards** represent a specific task, product, or batch that needs replenishment or processing.
- Each card contains essential information such as the part number, quantity required, and production instructions.

Kanban Board

A **Kanban board** is a visual tool used to track work progress through various stages. It is divided into columns representing different phases (e.g., **"To Do," "In Progress," "Done"**).

Example:
A software development team may use a Kanban board to track feature development. Tasks move across columns as they progress through different phases, ensuring visibility and balance.

3. The Six Core Rules of Kanban

1. **Visualize Workflow:**
   Use a Kanban board to make the status of work transparent.

2. **Limit Work in Progress (WIP):**
   Set limits on the number of tasks in progress at each stage to avoid bottlenecks.

3. **Manage Flow:**
   Track how tasks move through the system to identify delays or inefficiencies.

4. **Make Process Policies Explicit:**
   Define clear rules for moving tasks from one stage to the next.

5. **Implement Feedback Loops:**
   Regularly review and improve processes based on feedback.

6. **Improve Collaboratively:**
   Continuously optimize workflows with input from the team.

4. Kanban vs. Push Systems: Why Kanban is Better

In **push systems**, production is driven by forecasts, often leading to overproduction or stockpiling. In contrast, **Kanban is a pull system**, where production happens only when there is demand.

Example:

A traditional **push system** bakery may bake 1,000 loaves of bread based on a forecast but end up wasting unsold inventory. A **Kanban-based bakery**, however, bakes batches of bread based on real-time customer demand, reducing waste.

5. Types of Kanban Systems

1. **Single-Card Kanban**
   In this system, only one card is used to trigger replenishment. This is typical in simpler processes with fewer production stages.

2. **Two-Card Kanban**
   This system uses two cards:
   - **Production Kanban:** Signals that more products need to be made.
   - **Withdrawal Kanban:** Authorizes the movement of materials from storage to production.

3. **Electronic Kanban (E-Kanban)**
   In modern systems, **Kanban cards are digitized**, allowing for automated tracking and alerts. This is widely used in industries like IT and logistics.

6. Practical Examples of Kanban Implementation

Manufacturing Example: Automotive Industry

Toyota, the pioneer of the Kanban system, uses it in production lines to ensure **just-in-time (JIT)** manufacturing. Kanban cards are attached to bins containing parts like tires and bolts. When a bin is emptied, the Kanban card signals suppliers to refill it.

IT and Software Development Example

In software development, **Kanban boards** are used to manage tasks in Agile workflows. A team may create a board with columns labeled "Backlog," "In Progress," and "Completed." As developers work on tasks, the cards move across the columns, making the flow of work visible.

7. Key Benefits of Kanban

1. **Reduces Waste:**
   Only what is needed is produced, eliminating overproduction and excess inventory.

2. **Improves Efficiency:**
   Kanban limits WIP, reducing bottlenecks and improving task flow.

3. **Increases Flexibility:**
   Teams can quickly adapt to changing customer needs or priorities.

4. **Enhances Transparency:**
   Visual boards make it easy to see what work is in progress and where delays might occur.

5. **Boosts Collaboration:**

Kanban encourages open communication across departments or teams.

8. How to Implement Kanban: A Step-by-Step Guide

1. **Identify the Process:**
   Map out your workflow and determine key stages (e.g., "Planning," "Development," "Testing").

2. **Create a Kanban Board:**
   Set up a physical or digital board with columns representing each stage.

3. **Set WIP Limits:**
   Decide how many tasks can be in each stage at once to avoid overloading.

4. **Visualize Tasks:**
   Add Kanban cards for each task or product, including relevant details.

5. **Track Progress:**
   Move cards through the columns as tasks advance.

6. **Analyze and Improve:**
   Regularly review workflow and identify areas for improvement.

9. Challenges in Kanban Implementation

- **Resistance to Change:** Employees may resist adopting new processes.
- **Overcomplication:** Too many columns or complex rules can make the system inefficient.
- **Ignoring WIP Limits:** If limits are not respected, the system can become overloaded.
- **Lack of Engagement:** Teams must actively participate to make Kanban effective.

10. Kanban Metrics: How to Measure Success

1. **Lead Time:**
   The time it takes for a task to move from start to finish.

2. **Cycle Time:**
   The time a task spends in a specific stage.

3. **Throughput:**
   The number of tasks completed in a given period.

4. **Cumulative Flow Diagram (CFD):**
   A graph that shows the number of tasks in each stage over time, helping to identify bottlenecks.

Conclusion

Kanban is a **versatile tool** for managing workflow, balancing production, and aligning supply with demand. Its **visual nature and simplicity** make it easy to implement in various industries, from manufacturing to software development. By **limiting WIP, promoting transparency**, and ensuring tasks move smoothly through each stage, Kanban helps organizations achieve **lean operations** and **continuous improvement**.

When applied correctly, Kanban not only **improves efficiency** but also **boosts team morale** by making work visible and manageable. Whether you're in manufacturing, IT, or service industries, Kanban can play a pivotal role in helping your organization stay **agile, responsive, and customer-focused**.

Kanban Metrics: Key Examples and How to Use Them

Kanban metrics help teams track performance, identify bottlenecks, and continuously improve their workflows. These metrics provide insights into **how work flows through a process, how long tasks take**, and **where inefficiencies may occur**. Below are key Kanban metrics, their purpose, and examples to illustrate how they can be applied.

1. Lead Time

Definition:

Lead time refers to the **total time taken for a task or work item to move from the moment it is requested (or entered into the system) to its completion**.

Why It Matters:

- Helps teams understand how quickly they can deliver value to customers.
- Measures the time customers or stakeholders have to wait for results.

Example:

A customer service team tracks the **lead time** for handling support tickets. If a ticket is logged at 9:00 AM and resolved at 3:00 PM, the lead time is 6 hours. Monitoring lead time allows the team to spot trends (e.g., increasing response times), prompting process improvements.

2. Cycle Time

Definition:

Cycle time is the **time it takes for a task to move from "In Progress" to "Done"**—the amount of time work is actively being done on it.

Why It Matters:

- Helps identify how long tasks take within specific stages of a process.
- Shorter cycle times reflect smoother and more efficient workflows.

Example:

A software development team has a task in the "Development" stage that stays there for 3 days before being moved to "Completed." The **cycle time for this task** is 3 days. If other tasks take longer than expected in this phase, the team can investigate the cause (e.g., waiting on external approvals or testing delays).

3. Throughput

Definition:

Throughput measures **the number of tasks or work items completed in a specific period** (e.g., daily, weekly, or monthly).

Why It Matters:

- Throughput helps gauge the productivity of a team.
- It provides insight into whether the team can handle increased workloads.

Example:

A Kanban team completes 50 tasks over a two-week sprint. If the goal was 45 tasks, the team exceeded its throughput expectations. If throughput drops in the next sprint, it might indicate an issue such as team fatigue, overwork, or blockers.

4. Cumulative Flow Diagram (CFD)

Definition:

A **Cumulative Flow Diagram** is a graphical representation of how tasks are distributed across different stages of the Kanban workflow over time. It shows **how many tasks are in the backlog, in progress, and completed at any given time**.

Why It Matters:

- Helps identify bottlenecks and track overall process stability.
- Visualizes the balance between work-in-progress

(WIP) and throughput.

Example:

In a CFD, the "In Progress" section shows a sudden buildup of tasks that are not moving forward. This indicates a bottleneck that needs investigation (e.g., a dependency delay or insufficient resources).

---

5. Work-in-Progress (WIP) Limits

Definition:

WIP limits define the **maximum number of tasks allowed in a particular phase or stage**. Monitoring WIP helps avoid bottlenecks and ensures the team stays focused.

Why It Matters:

- Prevents overloading team members or stages.
- Ensures work moves smoothly through the system.

Example:

A team sets a **WIP limit** of 5 for the "In Progress" column on their Kanban board. If the limit is reached, no new tasks can be started until one is completed. This encourages the team to complete tasks before taking on new work, preventing unfinished work from piling up.

---

6. Blocker Clustering

Definition:

This metric tracks **how often tasks are blocked and for how long**. Blocked tasks are those that cannot progress due to dependencies, external approvals, or other constraints.

Why It Matters:

- Helps identify recurring issues causing delays.
- Teams can focus on removing systemic blockers to improve efficiency.

Example:

A marketing team logs all tasks that get blocked. Over the past month, **40% of tasks in the "Approval" stage were delayed due to management sign-off**. By identifying this as a bottleneck, the team can streamline or automate the approval process to reduce delays.

7. Aging Work in Progress (Aging WIP)

Definition:

This metric tracks **how long tasks have been sitting in each stage**. It is especially useful for identifying work items that have stagnated or become stuck.

Why It Matters:

- Encourages teams to prioritize tasks that have been in progress for too long.
- Helps prevent hidden bottlenecks.

Example:

A logistics company notices that several orders in the "Dispatch" phase have been there for 10 days, whereas the average cycle time for this phase is 3 days. This aging WIP metric alerts the team to investigate the cause of the delay (e.g., equipment breakdown or supplier issues).

8. Queue Length

Definition:

Queue length measures the **number of tasks waiting to enter a stage** of the workflow.

Why It Matters:

- A long queue indicates that the downstream process is overburdened.
- Helps in identifying capacity issues or bottlenecks.

Example:

In a Kanban system managing customer orders, the **queue for packaging** contains 30 orders, whereas the packaging team can handle only 10 orders per day. The queue length signals the need to either increase packaging capacity or reduce incoming orders.

9. Flow Efficiency

Definition:

Flow efficiency is the **ratio of active working time to total lead time**. It measures how efficiently work flows through the system.

$$\text{Flow Efficiency} = \left(\frac{\text{Active Working Time}}{\text{Lead Time}}\right) \times 100$$

Why It Matters:

- Reveals how much of the time is spent actively working versus waiting.
- A low flow efficiency suggests significant delays in the process.

Example:

A team tracks that a task took 10 days to complete, but only 4 days were spent actively working on it.

Flow efficiency = $(4/10) \times 100 = 40\%$.

This low flow efficiency indicates that tasks are waiting too long between stages and the team should focus on reducing idle time.

10. Time to Market (TTM)

Definition:

Time to market measures **the total time it takes to deliver a product or service from the moment it is conceived to when it becomes available to customers**.

Why It Matters:

- Helps businesses remain competitive by tracking their responsiveness to market needs.

- Shorter TTM improves customer satisfaction and reduces lost opportunities.

Example:

A tech company developing a new app measures the time from idea generation to product launch. If the **TTM** is 6 months, but competitors release similar products in 4 months, the company must speed up its development cycle to stay competitive.

Kanban metrics provide **actionable insights** into workflow, productivity, and potential bottlenecks. By tracking metrics like **lead time, cycle time, throughput**, and **WIP limits**, teams can improve efficiency and ensure smooth production flow. Visual tools like **Cumulative Flow Diagrams** and **aging WIP tracking** help identify bottlenecks and highlight opportunities for continuous improvement.

Using these metrics consistently allows organizations to **enhance collaboration, reduce waste, and achieve lean operations**—whether in manufacturing, software development, logistics, or customer service.

Kanban vs Scrum: Key Differences and Practical Insights

Both **Kanban** and **Scrum** are popular frameworks in Agile project management, but they cater to different needs and environments. While **Kanban** focuses on continuous workflow and visual management, **Scrum** is based on structured iterations called sprints. Understanding the differences between these two frameworks can help organizations choose the right one—or even integrate them—to achieve better outcomes.

---

1. Overview: What Are Kanban and Scrum?

- **Kanban**: A visual system that manages the flow of tasks through a process. It emphasizes **continuous** delivery, limiting **work-in-progress (WIP)**, and incremental improvements.

- **Scrum**: A time-boxed framework that structures work into **fixed-length sprints** (usually 2-4 weeks). It follows defined roles and ceremonies to ensure predictable delivery of product increments.

2. Core Differences Between Kanban and Scrum

Aspect	Kanban	Scrum
Framework Type	Continuous flow-based	Iterative, sprint-based
Work Cadence	Continuous delivery; no time limits	Time-boxed sprints (2–4 weeks)
Roles and Responsibilities	No mandatory roles	Defined roles: Product Owner, Scrum Master, Team
Work Planning	Pull-based: Tasks are pulled as capacity allows	Push-based: Tasks planned before each sprint
Changes to Work	Changes allowed anytime	No changes mid-sprint
Meetings and Events	No required meetings	Daily Scrum, Sprint Planning, Sprint Review, Sprint Retrospective
Work-in-Progress (WIP)	WIP limits ensure focus and smooth flow	No strict WIP limits
Metrics	Lead time, cycle time, throughput	Velocity, sprint burndown, burnup charts
Best For	Support/operations teams, continuous delivery	Product development with predictable releases

3. Practical Use Cases: When to Use Kanban or Scrum

- **Kanban** works well when:
    - You need **continuous delivery** without specific deadlines.
    - The nature of work is **unpredictable**, like **support or maintenance** tasks.
    - The focus is on **workflow optimization** and reducing bottlenecks.
- **Scrum** is ideal when:
    - There is a need for **incremental product delivery** at regular intervals.
    - The team is working on **complex projects** with evolving requirements.
    - You prefer **structured planning** and clear milestones.

Example:

- **Kanban in IT Support**: An IT support team uses Kanban to manage tickets. As new requests arrive, team members pull tasks from the **"To-Do" column** and move them through **"In Progress"** to **"Completed."**
- **Scrum in Software Development**: A development team working on a mobile app divides the project into 2-week sprints. Each sprint delivers a new feature (e.g., user authentication or chat functionality).

4. Key Metrics: Kanban vs. Scrum

- **Kanban Metrics:**
    - **Lead Time**: The time it takes for a task to move from request to completion.
    - **Cycle Time**: Time spent actively working on

a task.
- **Throughput**: Number of tasks completed in a given period.

- **Scrum Metrics:**
  - **Velocity**: The amount of work completed in a sprint, often measured in story points.
  - **Sprint Burndown Chart**: Tracks remaining work in a sprint to ensure on-time delivery.
  - **Sprint Burnup Chart**: Shows progress toward the overall goal.

5. Flexibility and Adaptability

- **Kanban** allows for more **flexibility**. Work items can be added or changed at any time since there are no fixed-length iterations.
- **Scrum** provides more **structure**, ensuring that the team remains focused on the sprint goal without interruptions.

6. Integration: Using Kanban and Scrum Together (Scrumban)

Many teams **combine elements of both Kanban and Scrum** to create a hybrid approach known as **Scrumban**. This hybrid model allows teams to enjoy the flexibility of Kanban while maintaining the structure of Scrum where needed. For example:

- The team follows Scrum's sprint planning but uses **Kanban boards** to visualize work.
- WIP limits from Kanban help manage the team's workload within Scrum sprints.

7. Strengths and Challenges

Strengths of Kanban:

- **Visual Workflow Management**: Teams can see where tasks are getting stuck.
- **Flexible and Adaptive**: Changes can be made on the fly.
- **Better for Operational Teams**: Works well in dynamic environments like customer service or DevOps.

Challenges of Kanban:

- **Lack of Time Boxes**: No set deadlines might reduce a sense of urgency.
- **Less Structured Planning**: Teams may struggle with long-term planning.

Strengths of Scrum:

- **Predictable Delivery**: Sprints allow for steady, incremental progress.
- **Strong Collaboration**: Defined roles and regular meetings promote teamwork.
- **Ideal for Product Development**: Focused sprints keep teams aligned with product goals.

Challenges of Scrum:

- **Rigid Framework**: Fixed-length sprints can be limiting for unpredictable work.
- **Role Dependency**: Success depends heavily on the Scrum Master and Product Owner.
- **Harder to Adapt Mid-Sprint**: Teams cannot easily change tasks during a sprint.

---

8. Conclusion: Which Framework Is Right for You?

Choosing between **Kanban and Scrum** depends on the **nature of the work**, the **team's needs**, and **organizational goals**:

- Use **Kanban** if you need **continuous delivery, high flexibility**, or are working on **support/maintenance tasks**.
- Use **Scrum** if you are working on **product development projects** with clear objectives and want to **deliver in predictable increments**.

In some cases, **combining Kanban and Scrum** provides the best of both worlds, allowing teams to balance flexibility with structure. Whether you choose one framework or a hybrid approach, both Kanban and Scrum emphasize **collaboration, visibility, and continuous improvement**, making them powerful tools in Agile management.

CHAPTER – 20
Mizusumashi

The Water Beetle of Lean Manufacturing

In Lean manufacturing, **Mizusumashi** plays a critical role in ensuring smooth operations by **replenishing materials and supplies** to keep production flowing efficiently. The term **"Mizusumashi"** translates to **"water beetle"** in Japanese, inspired by the beetle's swift, tireless movements across the water surface. Similarly, a Mizusumashi worker moves across the factory floor with precision, ensuring that **the right materials are available at the right time, in the right place, and in the right quantity.**

This chapter explores the concept, responsibilities, benefits, and practical applications of Mizusumashi in Lean operations, highlighting how it contributes to reducing waste and increasing efficiency.

1. Role of Mizusumashi in Lean Manufacturing

The Mizusumashi serves as a **"material handler"** responsible for **replenishing workstations** with necessary components and materials, ensuring that production is not interrupted due to shortages. The goal is to **minimize waste**, both in terms of waiting time and unnecessary material movement, aligning with Lean principles such as **Just-in-Time (JIT)** delivery.

Key Responsibilities of a Mizusumashi:

- **Replenishing Supplies:** Moving required components and tools to workstations before they run out.
- **Monitoring Inventory Levels:** Keeping track of stock in real-time to avoid overstocking or stockouts.
- **Following a Predefined Route:** Operating on an efficient, scheduled route or "milk run" to minimize unnecessary movement.
- **Ensuring 5S Compliance:** Keeping workspaces organized by removing unused items and replenishing with the exact quantity required.
- **Collaborating with Production Teams:** Communicating with operators to understand material requirements and usage patterns.

2. Mizusumashi's Role in Preventing Waste (Muda)

Mizusumashi's actions directly contribute to the elimination of several types of waste—**muda**—in Lean:

Type of Waste	How Mizusumashi Helps Eliminate It
Waiting Time	Ensures materials are delivered just-in-time, preventing delays.
Inventory Waste	Provides only the required amount, avoiding excess inventory.
Motion Waste	Operators don't need to leave their workstations to find supplies.
Overproduction	Supplies are replenished based on real demand, preventing overproduction.

3. How Mizusumashi Supports Lean Concepts

Just-in-Time (JIT) Delivery

The Mizusumashi follows **JIT principles** by delivering materials and tools as they are needed, avoiding unnecessary inventory buildup. This aligns production to customer demand, ensuring efficiency without compromising quality.

Kanban System Integration

A Mizusumashi often works in tandem with a **Kanban system**. When operators signal low inventory using Kanban cards, the Mizusumashi ensures replenishment. This system helps balance supply and demand within the production process.

Milk Run Concept

The **milk run** concept refers to a **scheduled delivery route** where the Mizusumashi collects and delivers supplies in **multiple locations on a set schedule.** This prevents multiple back-and-forth trips, minimizing transportation waste.

---

4. Practical Example of Mizusumashi in Action

Scenario: Automotive Assembly Plant

In an automotive manufacturing plant, the production line has multiple workstations, each needing parts like nuts, bolts, and panels. If workers leave their stations to fetch these materials, production efficiency drops.

To address this, the plant assigns a Mizusumashi worker. They follow a pre-planned **route every 30 minutes** to replenish parts at each station.

- If a station is running low on bolts, the operator drops a **Kanban card** into a designated slot.
- The Mizusumashi collects these Kanban cards, retrieves the required materials, and delivers them back on their next route.
  This **keeps the assembly line moving smoothly**, reducing downtime and ensuring that no operator needs to leave their station.

5. Benefits of Mizusumashi in Lean Operations

Implementing the Mizusumashi role offers several benefits:

- **Reduced Production Downtime:** Ensures materials are always available, preventing disruptions.
- **Improved Efficiency:** Operators stay focused on their tasks instead of fetching supplies.
- **Inventory Optimization:** Delivers only what is needed, avoiding overstock or stockouts.
- **Enhanced Flow:** Aligns production with demand, ensuring smooth workflow.
- **Employee Morale:** Operators appreciate having necessary materials delivered on time, boosting productivity and satisfaction.

6. Challenges and Solutions

While the Mizusumashi system offers numerous advantages, there can be challenges:

Challenge	Solution
Missed Replenishment Signals	Use visual cues like Kanban cards or electronic systems to monitor inventory in real-time.
Inefficient Routes	Optimize routes using time studies and route planning tools to ensure the shortest paths.
Overburdening the Mizusumashi Worker	Divide the replenishment tasks among multiple workers or automate replenishment with AGVs (automated guided vehicles).

7. Automating Mizusumashi with Technology

In modern Lean operations, **automated guided vehicles (AGVs)** or **robotic systems** can perform some Mizusumashi tasks, further enhancing efficiency. AGVs follow predefined routes, delivering materials to workstations based on real-time data.

- Example: **Amazon warehouses** use robots to replenish inventory at picking stations, mirroring the Mizusumashi role.

8. Mizusumashi in Service and Retail Sectors

While the Mizusumashi role is primarily associated with manufacturing, the concept can be applied in other industries.

- **Retail:** In retail stores, replenishment staff ensure that shelves are stocked without disrupting customer experience.
- **Healthcare:** In hospitals, supply technicians replenish medical supplies in operating rooms and nursing stations, ensuring smooth operations.

Conclusion

Mizusumashi is a crucial role in **Lean manufacturing**, embodying the principles of **waste reduction, continuous flow, and JIT delivery**. By efficiently managing material replenishment, Mizusumashi ensures that production processes remain uninterrupted and that operators can focus on their tasks. Whether in traditional manufacturing or modern automated systems, the Mizusumashi role plays a pivotal part in maintaining **efficiency, quality, and customer satisfaction**. As Lean principles extend beyond manufacturing into other industries, the Mizusumashi concept offers valuable lessons in **workflow optimization and supply management**.

Implementing Mizusumashi in Lean Manufacturing: Step-by-Step Guide

Implementing the **Mizusumashi role** effectively requires thoughtful planning and alignment with Lean principles. The key is to ensure that materials are replenished **efficiently, without excess movement or delay**, while keeping operators focused on their tasks. Below are the key steps to implement a **Mizusumashi system**, supported by practical examples.

Step 1: Assess Current Material Flow and Production Process

Before introducing Mizusumashi, conduct a thorough assessment of your current material flow. This will help you **identify gaps, bottlenecks, and opportunities for improvement**.

Key Actions:

- Create a **process map** to visualize the flow of materials and identify where operators leave their stations to collect supplies.
- Assess **inventory levels** at workstations to determine how often materials run out.
- Identify **waste** in motion, waiting, and transportation using value stream mapping (VSM).

Example: In an electronics assembly plant, the operators spend 10% of their time retrieving tools and materials, leading to production delays. The plant's management identifies this as a bottleneck and a potential area for Mizusumashi implementation.

Step 2: Define Replenishment Requirements

To set up an effective replenishment system, define the **types of materials and tools** required at each workstation, and establish appropriate quantities and timing for delivery.

Key Actions:

- Identify **critical components** needed at each station.
- Determine **minimum and maximum stock levels** to avoid both stockouts and overstocking.
- Work with operators to **prioritize replenishment schedules** (e.g., parts that run out fastest get top priority).

Example: A packaging station requires rolls of labels every two hours. Based on past usage data, the Mizusumashi will replenish one roll at a time to prevent excess inventory.

Step 3: Design the Replenishment Routes (Milk Runs)

Create **efficient replenishment routes** to minimize travel time. The Mizusumashi should follow a **"milk run" schedule**—a standardized route that covers multiple workstations in one trip.

Key Actions:

- Group nearby workstations to form a **logical route** that avoids unnecessary backtracking.
- Set **time intervals** for the Mizusumashi (e.g., every 30 minutes, every hour) based on production needs.
- Use **route planning software** or time studies to optimize travel paths.

Example: In an automotive plant, the Mizusumashi completes a loop every 45 minutes, delivering parts like fasteners and trim pieces to six stations along the assembly line.

Step 4: Establish Visual Management Tools (Kanban Integration)

Integrate **visual management tools**, such as **Kanban cards** or bins, to signal when replenishment is required. This ensures that the Mizusumashi is informed when materials run low and can replenish them on the next route.

Key Actions:

- Place **Kanban bins or cards** at each workstation.
- Train operators to **trigger replenishment** by placing Kanban cards in designated slots when stock is low.
- Use **color-coded bins** to indicate priority levels (e.g., red = urgent, green = scheduled).

Example: A station that installs dashboard components uses a **two-bin Kanban system**. When one bin is empty, the operator places the Kanban card in a pickup box, and the Mizusumashi replaces the empty bin on their next round.

Step 5: Train Employees and Define Roles

Ensure that all relevant employees, including operators and Mizusumashi staff, are **trained on their roles** and how the system works. Collaboration between the Mizusumashi and production teams is crucial for seamless operation.

Key Actions:

- Train operators to use **Kanban cards or bins** correctly and avoid hoarding materials.
- Train Mizusumashi staff on **route schedules, replenishment protocols, and 5S principles**.
- Assign backup personnel to cover **Mizusumashi responsibilities** when needed.

Example: The electronics assembly plant trains the Mizusumashi to adhere to **5S principles**, ensuring that workstations are neatly arranged after every delivery.

Step 6: Monitor and Measure Performance

Once the system is operational, track key performance metrics to ensure that the Mizusumashi process is **meeting goals** and continuously improving.

Key Actions:

- Monitor **delivery accuracy**: Are materials delivered on time and in the right quantity?
- Track **downtime**: Are there fewer production delays caused by stockouts?
- Measure **travel time** and **route efficiency**: Can the milk runs be optimized further?

Example: After implementing the Mizusumashi system, the plant reduces operator downtime by 15%, resulting in a **10% increase in productivity**.

Step 7: Continuously Improve the System

Following **Kaizen principles**, regularly assess and improve the Mizusumashi system. Employee feedback and performance data should guide adjustments in routes, delivery schedules, or replenishment quantities.

Key Actions:

- Conduct **monthly reviews** to assess whether routes are still optimal.
- Hold **feedback sessions** with operators and Mizusumashi staff.
- Implement **improvements** as needed (e.g., introducing AGVs or adjusting replenishment intervals).

Example: Based on employee feedback, the automotive plant modifies the Mizusumashi route to **reduce travel time by 20%**, further boosting productivity.

Challenges and Solutions

Challenge	Solution
Missed Replenishment Signals	Use **digital Kanban systems** or IoT-enabled bins.
Overburdened Mizusumashi Worker	Divide tasks among **multiple workers or shifts**.
Inefficient Routes	Conduct **time studies** to optimize routes.
Operator Resistance to Change	Provide **training and communicate benefits**.

Benefits of Mizusumashi Implementation

- **Reduced Downtime:** Ensures production flow without interruptions.
- **Increased Productivity:** Operators focus on tasks without leaving their stations.
- **Reduced Inventory Waste:** Only required quantities are replenished.
- **Improved Flow and Efficiency:** Optimized material flow aligns with JIT principles.

Conclusion

Implementing Mizusumashi is an **effective way to streamline material handling**, reduce waste, and ensure smooth production flow in Lean operations. Following a structured implementation process—from assessing material flow to designing milk runs and training staff—ensures the system's success. When integrated with tools like **Kanban systems and 5S principles**, Mizusumashi not only prevents disruptions but also improves **productivity and efficiency** across the production floor. With continuous improvement through **Kaizen**, the Mizusumashi process evolves, further contributing to Lean success.

CHAPTER – 21
Muda

Identifying and Eliminating Waste in Lean Manufacturing

Introduction to Muda

In Lean philosophy, **Muda** (無駄) is a Japanese term that refers to **waste**—any activity, process, or resource usage that does not add value to the final product or service from the customer's perspective. The presence of Muda is considered a primary cause of inefficiencies within manufacturing, service industries, and business operations. Eliminating or reducing Muda helps **streamline workflows, lower costs, improve quality**, and achieve **operational excellence**.

Muda is one of the three types of waste identified by Lean, alongside **Mura (unevenness)** and **Muri (overburden)**. While Mura and Muri often contribute to inefficiencies, Muda focuses directly on **non-value-adding activities**.

The Seven Types of Muda

The Lean methodology identifies **seven categories of Muda** that occur across production processes. In recent years, an eighth waste—**unused talent**—has also been recognized. Below is an overview of each type of Muda with practical illustrations.

1. Overproduction

Producing more than what is required or earlier than

necessary. This leads to excess inventory, increased storage costs, and potential product obsolescence.

- **Example:** A factory produces 1,000 units of a product even though only 600 are needed that month, resulting in unsold stock.

2. Waiting

Idle time when work is not being performed due to delays or dependencies.

- **Example:** Machine operators wait for parts to arrive or for a previous process to finish, leading to lost productivity.

3. Excess Inventory

Maintaining more raw materials, work-in-progress (WIP), or finished goods than necessary ties up capital and increases storage costs.

- **Example:** An automotive plant stocks six months' worth of tires, which occupy valuable warehouse space and increase carrying costs.

4. Transportation

Unnecessary movement of products or materials within or between facilities, leading to delays and damage risks.

- **Example:** Products are moved back and forth between departments due to poor layout design.

5. Overprocessing

Using more resources or steps than needed to accomplish a task, often due to outdated methods or redundant checks.

- **Example:** Sanding a surface multiple times beyond what is required for quality standards.

6. Defects

Products or processes that do not meet specifications, leading to rework, scrap, or customer dissatisfaction.

- **Example:** A batch of defective circuit boards is scrapped, resulting in material loss and increased labor costs for rework.

7. Unnecessary Motion

Unproductive movements by employees that do not add value, such as searching for tools or materials.

- **Example:** A worker has to walk across the shop floor multiple times a day to fetch parts due to poor workspace organization.

8. Unused Talent (Eighth Waste)

Failing to fully utilize the skills, knowledge, and creativity of employees.

- **Example:** A line worker with experience in process improvement is not involved in brainstorming sessions or Kaizen events.

How Muda Affects Business Performance

- **Higher Costs:** Waste leads to unnecessary expenses, including excess inventory, rework, and transportation.
- **Reduced Efficiency:** Processes slow down due to waiting times, overproduction, or defective products.
- **Lower Customer Satisfaction:** Defects and delays can result in poor customer experiences and lost business opportunities.
- **Decreased Employee Morale:** Unused talent and inefficient workflows can cause frustration and disengagement among employees.

Examples of Muda in Real-World Applications

- **Manufacturing:** In a car assembly line, overproduction results in parts lying idle, consuming space and creating bottlenecks.
- **Retail & E-commerce:** Excess inventory in warehouses leads to high storage costs and markdowns.
- **Healthcare:** Unnecessary motion occurs when nurses spend significant time locating equipment due to poor storage practices.
- **Software Development:** Overprocessing occurs when developers add features that were not part of the customer's original requirements, causing scope creep.

Tools to Identify and Eliminate Muda

Several Lean tools and methodologies help **identify and eliminate waste** in processes:

1. Value Stream Mapping (VSM)

A visual tool to map all steps in a process and distinguish value-adding activities from wasteful ones.

- **Example:** A manufacturing plant uses VSM to identify waiting times between processes and implements better scheduling to eliminate idle time.

2. 5S Methodology

A workplace organization tool that eliminates unnecessary motion and excess inventory.

- **Example:** A factory reorganizes workstations following the 5S principles, so tools are always within reach, reducing employee movement.

3. Kanban System

A visual tool that controls inventory levels and avoids overproduction by ensuring work is pulled only when needed.

- **Example:** In an electronics plant, Kanban cards are used to replenish components only when they are consumed.

4. Kaizen Events

Short, focused events to bring together employees to solve specific problems and eliminate waste in targeted areas.

- **Example:** A cross-functional team conducts a Kaizen event to reduce motion waste in the packaging area by rearranging workstations.

5. Poka-Yoke (Error Proofing)

Techniques used to eliminate defects by preventing errors before they occur.

- **Example:** A factory installs a sensor that stops the machine if parts are not aligned properly, reducing rework due to misalignment.

Steps to Reduce Muda

Step 1: Identify Waste

Use tools like Value Stream Mapping to uncover wasteful activities in the process.

Step 2: Analyze the Root Cause

Apply problem-solving tools like the **5 Whys** to find the underlying cause of the waste.

Step 3: Develop Countermeasures

Brainstorm and implement solutions to eliminate or reduce the identified waste.

Step 4: Monitor and Measure Improvements

Track key performance metrics (KPIs) to ensure the waste

reduction efforts are effective.

Step 5: Continuous Improvement (Kaizen)

Encourage ongoing efforts to seek out and address waste in everyday operations.

Case Study: Reducing Muda in an Automotive Plant

In an automotive plant, workers identified overproduction and excess inventory as major sources of waste. Using **Kanban and Value Stream Mapping**, they redesigned their workflow to ensure parts were produced just in time (JIT) rather than in large batches. As a result, they:

- Reduced **inventory levels by 30%**.
- Improved floor space utilization by **20%**.
- Cut transportation waste by **15%** by streamlining routes.

Conclusion

Muda is a critical concept in Lean manufacturing and business operations. It highlights the importance of **eliminating non-value-adding activities** to improve efficiency, reduce costs, and enhance customer satisfaction. Identifying and addressing Muda requires careful observation, the use of Lean tools like **VSM, Kanban, and 5S**, and a commitment to continuous improvement through **Kaizen**. When waste is systematically reduced, businesses can achieve **sustainable growth**, **higher quality**, and **operational excellence**.

CHAPTER – 22
Mura

Eliminating Inconsistencies for a Balanced Workflow

Introduction to Mura

In Lean manufacturing, **Mura (ムラ)** is a Japanese term that refers to **unevenness or inconsistency** in workflows, production rates, or demand. Mura creates **fluctuations in the system** that result in **bottlenecks, overproduction, idle time, and inefficiencies.** It is one of the three key types of waste in Lean, alongside **Muda (waste)** and **Muri (overburden).**

Achieving a smooth, consistent flow of operations is crucial to **meeting customer demands efficiently** without building up unnecessary inventory or adding strain on workers and equipment. Managing Mura helps companies **balance workloads** and eliminate disruptions in their production processes.

What Causes Mura?

Mura typically occurs when the pace of work is **unpredictable or uneven.** Various factors can contribute to this, including:

1. **Fluctuating Customer Demand:**
    - Example: An electronics company receives large orders during peak seasons but

struggles with low demand at other times.

2. **Inconsistent Production Schedules:**
   - Example: A factory produces more units in one shift and fewer in another, causing irregular inventory levels.

3. **Machine Downtime or Equipment Failures:**
   - Example: A critical machine breaks down unexpectedly, disrupting production.

4. **Uneven Workload Distribution:**
   - Example: Some workers are overloaded with tasks while others are idle.

5. **Poor Forecasting and Planning:**
   - Example: Inaccurate demand forecasts lead to either overproduction or stock shortages.

How Mura Affects Business Performance

1. Overproduction and Inventory Build-up

When production rates fluctuate, companies may **produce more than needed** during high-capacity periods to compensate for low-capacity periods. This leads to excess inventory, which increases storage costs and risks product obsolescence.

2. Bottlenecks and Idle Time

Uneven work distribution creates bottlenecks in certain areas, forcing **some processes to wait** while others rush to catch up. This **disrupts flow** and reduces efficiency.

3. Increased Defects and Errors

When production is rushed to meet sudden demand spikes, quality tends to suffer, resulting in defects and rework.

4. Worker Fatigue and Burnout

Inconsistent workloads place **undue stress on workers** during peak times and lead to disengagement during slower periods.

This inconsistency lowers morale and productivity.

How to Identify Mura: Practical Indicators

Mura is not always obvious, but some signs help identify unevenness in processes:

- **Varying Inventory Levels:** Frequent shifts between high and low inventory levels signal inconsistent production.
- **Uneven Worker Output:** Productivity fluctuates across shifts, teams, or departments.
- **Frequent Expediting of Orders:** Constantly rushing to meet deadlines indicates demand spikes are not handled well.
- **Delayed Deliveries:** Late shipments suggest that upstream processes are struggling with uneven workflows.

How to Eliminate Mura: Key Strategies

1. Heijunka: Production Leveling

Heijunka is the practice of **smoothing production schedules** to reduce fluctuations. It involves producing in smaller, consistent batches over time to align production with average customer demand.

- **Example:** An automobile manufacturer distributes production evenly across shifts by building different car models in small quantities rather than in large batches.

2. Just-in-Time (JIT) Production

JIT ensures that **materials and parts are only produced or ordered as needed** to meet current demand, reducing the risk of overproduction.

- **Example:** A printer manufacturer uses JIT to replenish cartridges only when they fall below a certain level, ensuring steady inventory.

3. Kanban System

Kanban helps **visualize and control workflows**, preventing excessive buildup of tasks or inventory. By signaling when more work should start, it balances work between different processes.

- **Example:** A manufacturing line uses Kanban cards to signal when components are needed, preventing bottlenecks from material shortages.

4. Load Balancing

Balancing workloads across teams and equipment prevents bottlenecks and idle time.

- **Example:** A call center rotates agents through tasks evenly throughout the day to avoid overload during peak hours.

5. Forecasting and Demand Management

Using **data analytics** to accurately forecast demand reduces fluctuations. Collaborating with customers to understand their needs can also help stabilize production.

- **Example:** An e-commerce retailer monitors seasonal trends and adjusts stock levels proactively to meet upcoming demand without overstocking.

Practical Example of Reducing Mura: Toyota Production System

Toyota's production system demonstrates how to **minimize Mura** through tools like **Heijunka** and **Just-in-Time (JIT)**. In Toyota plants, production is leveled to create a steady flow of cars rather than producing in large, uneven batches.

This approach ensures consistent utilization of workers and equipment, preventing bottlenecks and inventory build-up.

Case Study: Retail Supply Chain Optimization

A retail clothing brand experienced significant fluctuations in inventory due to inconsistent production and demand patterns. During peak seasons, excess stock filled the warehouse, while at other times, shortages led to backorders.

To eliminate Mura, the company:

1. **Implemented Heijunka:** Balanced production by distributing output evenly over weeks instead of concentrating production just before peak periods.
2. **Adopted JIT Inventory Management:** Coordinated with suppliers to replenish stock only when needed.
3. **Forecasted Demand with Machine Learning:** Improved forecasting accuracy to reduce production mismatches.

Results:

- Inventory levels reduced by **25%**, freeing up warehouse space.
- On-time delivery rate improved by **18%** due to smoother production schedules.

The Role of Technology in Reducing Mura

Modern technologies like **automation, IoT, and AI-based forecasting** play a crucial role in eliminating Mura:

- **IoT Sensors:** Track equipment performance in real time to prevent machine downtime.
- **AI Forecasting:** Analyzes sales trends to predict demand and smooth out production schedules.
- **Robotic Process Automation (RPA):** Automates

repetitive tasks, ensuring consistent output.

Mura vs Muda vs Muri

While Mura focuses on **unevenness in processes**, it is related to **Muda** and **Muri**:

- **Muda:** Waste resulting from non-value-adding activities (e.g., defects, waiting).
- **Muri:** Overburden caused by excessive workloads.
- **Mura:** Unevenness or inconsistencies in workloads or demand that cause disruptions and lead to both Muda and Muri.

Conclusion

Mura represents **inconsistencies and unevenness** in workflows that cause inefficiencies, bottlenecks, and excess inventory. Reducing Mura is essential to achieving **stable, predictable operations** and smooth flow. Tools such as **Heijunka, JIT, Kanban, and load balancing** help eliminate Mura and ensure a balanced workflow. Businesses that address Mura not only reduce waste and improve efficiency but also create a **more resilient and agile operation** capable of meeting customer demands smoothly and reliably.

CHAPTER – 23
Nagara

Achieving Smooth Continuous Flow in Lean Manufacturing

Introduction to Nagara

In the realm of Lean manufacturing, the term **Nagara** (流れ) translates to **"flow"** and represents the **smooth, continuous flow of work** through various processes. The concept emphasizes the importance of ensuring that each step in a production process is seamlessly connected to the next, thereby minimizing delays, reducing waste, and enhancing overall efficiency. The goal of implementing a Nagara system is to create a **responsive production environment** that can adapt quickly to changes in demand while maintaining high-quality standards.

The Importance of Continuous Flow

1. Waste Reduction

A fundamental principle of Lean is the elimination of **waste**. By achieving continuous flow, organizations can reduce waste related to:

- **Waiting:** Minimizing idle time between processes allows for quicker transitions.
- **Overproduction:** Producing only what is needed when it is needed prevents excess inventory.

- **Transportation:** Reducing unnecessary movement of materials and products streamlines operations.

2. Increased Throughput

A smooth flow increases the overall throughput of a system, enabling a higher volume of products to be completed in a given timeframe. This leads to improved profitability and customer satisfaction.

3. Minimized Inventory

By ensuring that work moves continuously from one stage to the next, companies can maintain lower levels of inventory, reducing holding costs and minimizing the risk of obsolescence.

4. Enhanced Flexibility and Responsiveness

A well-implemented Nagara system allows businesses to respond quickly to fluctuations in demand or unexpected challenges, maintaining operational efficiency.

Key Principles of Nagara

To successfully implement a Nagara system, several key principles must be adhered to:

1. Standardized Work

Establishing standardized procedures for each task ensures that every worker performs the task in the same way, creating a predictable and efficient flow.

- **Example:** In a packaging line, a company may standardize the steps for sealing boxes to ensure consistency and speed.

2. Balancing Workloads

Ensuring that each workstation has an equal amount of work prevents bottlenecks and enhances the overall flow.

- **Example:** In an automotive assembly line, tasks

can be redistributed among workers to balance the workload evenly.

3. Visual Management

Implementing visual cues and tools (such as Kanban boards) helps workers understand workflow status at a glance, allowing for quick identification of issues.

- **Example:** A color-coded board can signal which tasks are completed, in progress, or pending, enhancing communication.

4. Continuous Improvement (Kaizen)

Regularly seeking opportunities to improve processes contributes to a smoother flow.

- **Example:** A team conducts daily stand-up meetings to discuss challenges and brainstorm solutions to improve the flow.

Implementing Nagara: Practical Steps

Step 1: Map the Current Process

Create a process map to visualize the flow of work. This helps identify bottlenecks, delays, and areas for improvement.

- **Example:** A food processing plant maps out its production line, highlighting steps from ingredient preparation to packaging.

Step 2: Identify Waste

Analyze the process map to spot waste and inefficiencies.

- **Example:** Analyzing a map may reveal that materials are frequently transported long distances, indicating potential for better layout design.

Step 3: Redesign the Workflow

Modify the process layout and workflow based on insights

from the analysis, aiming for continuous flow.

- **Example:** Reorganizing a warehouse to place frequently used materials closer to the production area can enhance flow.

Step 4: Implement Visual Management Tools

Introduce tools that aid in visualizing the flow of work.

- **Example:** Use Kanban boards to track progress and visualize tasks in different stages of completion.

Step 5: Train Employees

Provide training to employees on the new processes and the importance of maintaining continuous flow.

- **Example:** Conduct workshops to educate staff on the principles of Nagara and their role in sustaining flow.

Step 6: Monitor and Adjust

Continuously monitor the workflow and adjust as necessary to ensure that smooth flow is maintained.

- **Example:** Regularly reviewing performance metrics can highlight areas needing adjustment.

Practical Example: The Toyota Production System

Toyota is renowned for its successful implementation of Nagara principles within its production system. By designing their assembly lines for continuous flow, they achieve rapid production while minimizing waste. Key aspects of their approach include:

1. **Just-in-Time (JIT) Production:**
   Toyota ensures that each component is produced only when needed, reducing excess inventory and storage costs.

2. **Flexible Workstations:**
   Workers are trained to perform multiple tasks,

allowing for adjustments in workload as demand changes.

3. **Visual Controls:**
   Toyota employs visual signals to indicate workflow status, ensuring everyone is aligned with production goals.

Case Study: A Food Manufacturing Company

A mid-sized food manufacturing company struggled with irregular production schedules, leading to excessive inventory and long lead times. To implement Nagara:

1. **Process Mapping:**
   The company created a detailed process map to visualize the flow of raw ingredients through to finished products.

2. **Identifying Waste:**
   They discovered significant waiting times between stages due to equipment downtime.

3. **Redesigning Workflow:**
   By reconfiguring the production layout and investing in preventive maintenance, they achieved smoother transitions.

4. **Visual Management:**
   Kanban systems were introduced to manage raw materials and packaging supplies effectively.

Results:

- **Lead time reduced by 30%.**
- **Inventory levels decreased by 40%.**
- **Overall throughput increased by 25%.**

Nagara in the Age of Technology

Modern technologies can greatly enhance Nagara

implementation:

- **IoT Sensors:** Monitor equipment health in real time, allowing for proactive maintenance to avoid downtime.
- **Automation:** Robotics can perform repetitive tasks more efficiently, contributing to smoother workflows.
- **Data Analytics:** Analyzing production data helps identify patterns and areas for continuous improvement.

Nagara vs Muda and Muri

While **Nagara** focuses on the **flow of work**, it is essential to understand its relationship with the other two forms of waste:

- **Muda:** Refers to wasteful activities that do not add value.
- **Muri:** Involves overburdening people or machines beyond their capacity.
  By achieving a smooth flow with Nagara, companies can reduce both Muda and Muri, creating a more efficient and sustainable production environment.

Conclusion

Nagara is integral to Lean manufacturing, emphasizing the **importance of smooth, continuous flow** in production processes. By implementing the principles of Nagara, organizations can achieve significant improvements in efficiency, waste reduction, and overall responsiveness. A commitment to continuous improvement, combined with the use of modern technologies, enables businesses to sustain a Nagara system, ensuring they remain competitive in an ever-changing market. Through meticulous planning and execution, companies can create a production environment that flows seamlessly, ultimately delivering greater value to customers.

CHAPTER – 24
Poka-Yoke

A Strategy for Mistake-Proofing in Lean Manufacturing

Introduction to Poka-Yoke

Poka-yoke (ポカヨケ) is a Japanese term meaning **"mistake-proofing"** or **"error-proofing."** Developed by Shigeo Shingo, a key figure in the Toyota Production System, Poka-yoke aims to prevent errors before they occur, thereby eliminating defects and enhancing quality. By designing processes and systems that inherently avoid mistakes, organizations can create more reliable and efficient operations.

The essence of Poka-yoke lies in its proactive approach to quality management. Instead of inspecting finished products for defects, Poka-yoke focuses on designing processes that minimize the potential for errors from the outset. This philosophy aligns closely with Lean principles, emphasizing waste reduction and continuous improvement.

The Importance of Poka-Yoke

1. Defect Prevention

Poka-yoke systems are implemented to prevent defects at their source, ensuring that products and processes meet quality standards without the need for extensive inspection. This is especially vital in industries where safety and precision are paramount.

2. Cost Reduction

By preventing errors, Poka-yoke can significantly reduce costs associated with rework, scrap, and warranty claims. The financial impact of defects can be substantial; thus, investing in mistake-proofing techniques often yields a strong return on investment.

3. Improved Efficiency

Mistake-proofing helps streamline operations by minimizing disruptions caused by errors. When processes are designed to prevent mistakes, employees can focus on their tasks without the constant fear of making errors, leading to increased productivity.

4. Enhanced Customer Satisfaction

Delivering high-quality products consistently leads to improved customer satisfaction and loyalty. By implementing Poka-yoke techniques, organizations can enhance their reputation and market competitiveness.

Key Principles of Poka-Yoke

To effectively implement Poka-yoke, several principles should be adhered to:

1. Simplicity

Poka-yoke solutions should be simple and easy to understand. Complex systems can lead to confusion and may defeat the purpose of mistake-proofing.

- **Example:** A simple fixture that only allows components to be inserted in one orientation prevents assembly errors.

2. Error Detection

Incorporating systems that can detect potential errors before they lead to defects is crucial. These systems can trigger alarms or notifications, alerting operators to issues that need attention.

- **Example:** Sensors that detect whether a part is missing before a machine starts can halt operations until the error is rectified.

3. Standardization

Establishing standardized procedures ensures that everyone follows the same steps, reducing variability and the likelihood of errors.

- **Example:** Standard operating procedures (SOPs) that include Poka-yoke measures help create a consistent approach to tasks.

4. Feedback Loops

Incorporating feedback mechanisms allows for continuous improvement. If a mistake does occur, it is essential to analyze the root cause and adjust the Poka-yoke solution accordingly.

- **Example:** A team conducts regular reviews of error reports to identify trends and enhance existing Poka-yoke measures.

Implementing Poka-Yoke: Practical Steps

Step 1: Identify Critical Processes

Analyze processes to determine which areas are prone to errors and require mistake-proofing.

- **Example:** In a manufacturing line, the assembly of complex products may have multiple points where errors could occur.

Step 2: Analyze Error Types

Identify the types of errors that could occur within the critical processes. This may involve consultations with employees who perform the tasks regularly.

- **Example:** A bakery may identify that employees often forget to add a key ingredient during the mixing process.

Step 3: Develop Poka-Yoke Solutions

Create simple devices or systems that will prevent identified errors from occurring.

- **Example:** Installing a weight sensor in the mixer that alerts the operator if the correct ingredient amount is not added.

Step 4: Implement and Train

Introduce the Poka-yoke systems and provide training to employees. Ensure that they understand how the systems work and the importance of their role in maintaining quality.

- **Example:** Conduct workshops to explain how the weight sensors function and their impact on product quality.

Step 5: Monitor and Improve

Continuously monitor the effectiveness of Poka-yoke solutions. Gather feedback from employees and make adjustments as necessary to enhance the systems.

- **Example:** Regularly reviewing production data to see if errors have decreased after implementing Poka-yoke measures.

Practical Examples of Poka-Yoke

1. Assembly Line Fixtures

In an automotive manufacturing plant, a fixture designed for engine assembly only allows parts to be assembled in a specific order. If the operator tries to fit a part incorrectly, the fixture prevents it from being attached.

2. Color-Coded Components

In electronics manufacturing, using color-coded wires and connectors helps prevent incorrect connections. Each wire is color-coded to match its corresponding connector, reducing the chance of errors during assembly.

3. Checklists

In the aviation industry, pilots use pre-flight checklists to ensure that all necessary steps are completed before takeoff. This systematic approach minimizes the risk of overlooking critical tasks.

4. Automated Alerts

In a pharmaceutical plant, an automated alert system notifies operators if certain conditions (e.g., temperature or humidity) are outside specified limits during the production process, allowing for immediate corrective action.

Poka-Yoke in the Age of Technology

Advancements in technology have significantly enhanced the effectiveness of Poka-yoke systems:

- **IoT and Sensors:** Smart sensors can monitor processes in real time, providing instant feedback and alerts.
- **Automation:** Automated systems can perform repetitive tasks with precision, reducing the potential for human error.
- **Data Analytics:** Analyzing production data helps identify patterns of mistakes, allowing for targeted Poka-yoke implementations.

Case Study: A Electronics Manufacturer

An electronics manufacturer faced high rates of defects in their circuit board assembly due to incorrect component placement. To implement Poka-yoke:

1. **Identify Critical Processes:**
   The assembly line was identified as a critical area due to frequent errors.

2. **Analyze Error Types:**
   Employees noted that components were often placed incorrectly due to similar shapes.

3. **Develop Poka-Yoke Solutions:**
   The company designed a custom assembly tray with shapes that only allowed the correct components to be placed in the designated slots.

4. **Implement and Train:**
   Employees were trained on using the new trays and the importance of proper component placement.

5. **Monitor and Improve:**
   After implementation, defect rates dropped by 60%, and regular feedback sessions helped refine the system.

Conclusion

Poka-yoke is an essential tool in Lean manufacturing, focusing on preventing mistakes before they occur. By implementing mistake-proofing techniques, organizations can significantly enhance product quality, reduce costs, and improve operational efficiency. Through the use of simple, effective solutions and a commitment to continuous improvement, Poka-yoke can create a culture of quality that benefits both employees and customers. Embracing Poka-yoke is not just about fixing mistakes; it is about fostering a proactive approach to quality management that leads to sustainable success.

CHAPTER- 24
Shojinka

Optimizing Workforce Flexibility in Lean Manufacturing

Introduction to Shojinka

Shojinka (常駐化) is a Japanese term that translates to **"workforce optimization."** This Lean manufacturing concept focuses on the continuous adjustment of the number of workers in a work center to align with fluctuating demand. The primary objective of Shojinka is to create a flexible and efficient work environment where human resources can be dynamically allocated based on the needs of the production process.

In today's fast-paced manufacturing landscape, where customer demands can change rapidly, Shojinka plays a crucial role in maintaining productivity while minimizing waste and costs. By effectively managing the workforce, organizations can adapt to variations in demand, ensuring that production processes remain efficient and responsive.

The Importance of Shojinka

5. Flexibility in Production

Shojinka allows manufacturing facilities to quickly adapt to changes in customer demand. By adjusting the number of workers, organizations can scale operations up or down as needed, minimizing idle time and maximizing resource utilization.

6. Cost Efficiency

Maintaining an optimal workforce helps organizations control labor costs. By employing the right number of workers at the right times, companies can avoid the costs associated with overstaffing during low-demand periods and the overtime expenses incurred during peak times.

7. Enhanced Productivity

A well-implemented Shojinka approach leads to more efficient work processes. When workers are trained in multiple disciplines, they can be reassigned to different tasks based on demand, reducing bottlenecks and downtime.

8. Employee Development

Training workers in various skills enhances their capabilities and job satisfaction. A versatile workforce is better equipped to handle diverse tasks, fostering a culture of continuous improvement and engagement.

Key Principles of Shojinka

To effectively implement Shojinka in a manufacturing setting, several key principles should be adhered to:

9. Cross-Training Employees

Employees should be trained in multiple disciplines to increase workforce flexibility. This ensures that workers can shift roles as needed without compromising productivity.

- **Example:** In an automotive assembly plant, workers trained in both assembly and quality control can rotate between tasks depending on demand fluctuations.

10. Dynamic Workforce Planning

Manufacturers should continuously assess and adjust their

workforce needs based on real-time demand data. This requires accurate forecasting and a responsive scheduling system.

- **Example:** A food processing facility utilizes historical sales data and trends to anticipate peak demand periods and adjust staffing levels accordingly.

11. Adaptable Work Center Layout

The physical layout of work centers should support variable worker numbers. This includes having modular equipment and flexible workspace arrangements that can accommodate changes in staffing levels.

- **Example:** A clothing manufacturer employs movable assembly stations that can be reconfigured based on the number of workers assigned to a specific task.

12. Utilizing Technology

Implementing technology solutions, such as workforce management software and production scheduling tools, can enhance the effectiveness of Shojinka. These tools facilitate real-time monitoring and adjustments to workforce allocation.

- **Example:** A manufacturing plant implements an automated scheduling system that tracks production levels and alerts managers when additional workers are needed.

Implementing Shojinka: Practical Steps

Step 1: Assess Current Workforce Practices

Analyze existing workforce practices to identify areas for improvement. Understand how many workers are needed for various tasks under different demand scenarios.

- **Example:** A semiconductor manufacturer conducts a study to determine how many operators are needed for each stage of production during low and high demand periods.

Step 2: Develop Cross-Training Programs

Create training programs that enable employees to learn multiple skills. This can include job rotation or skill-building workshops.

- **Example:** A manufacturing facility sets up a mentorship program where experienced workers train others in different functions, enhancing skill diversity.

Step 3: Establish a Flexible Work Center Design

Design work centers that can accommodate varying numbers of workers. Ensure that equipment and tools are easily accessible and adaptable to different tasks.

- **Example:** A packaging company designs its workflow with adjustable conveyor systems that can be lengthened or shortened based on the number of workers available.

Step 4: Implement Real-Time Monitoring Systems

Adopt technology that provides real-time insights into production needs and workforce allocation. This could involve using dashboards that display current workloads and staffing levels.

- **Example:** A furniture manufacturer installs digital dashboards that display production metrics, helping managers quickly assess whether additional workers are needed on the assembly line.

Step 5: Continuously Evaluate and Adjust

Regularly review workforce performance and production outcomes. Solicit feedback from employees on the effectiveness of cross-training and the flexibility of work center layouts.

- **Example:** A pharmaceutical company conducts quarterly assessments of workforce utilization and gathers employee feedback to improve cross-training programs.

Practical Examples of Shojinka

13. Automotive Manufacturing

In an automotive plant, the assembly line employs Shojinka by using flexible workstations that can accommodate varying numbers of employees. During high demand periods, more workers are assigned to the assembly line, while during slower times, workers are reassigned to quality control or training roles.

14. Electronics Production

An electronics manufacturer adopts Shojinka by cross-training employees in both assembly and testing. This allows the company to shift resources based on production needs, significantly reducing lead times for product delivery.

15. Food Processing

A food processing plant uses Shojinka principles to adjust staffing based on seasonal demand fluctuations. During peak seasons, additional workers are hired temporarily, while off-peak times see staff reductions to optimize labor costs.

16. Textile Industry

A textile manufacturer employs Shojinka by utilizing mobile workstations that can be easily reconfigured based on the number of workers available. During busy seasons, the plant can rapidly increase capacity by deploying additional workers to specific tasks.

Shojinka in the Age of Automation

The rise of automation in manufacturing presents new opportunities for Shojinka:

- **Collaborative Robots (Cobots):** Cobots can work alongside human employees, allowing for dynamic adjustments to workforce levels based on real-time demand.
- **Data Analytics:** Advanced analytics can provide insights into workforce utilization patterns, enabling better forecasting and planning.
- **AI Scheduling Tools:** Artificial intelligence can optimize workforce allocation by predicting peak demand times and suggesting optimal staffing levels.

Case Study: A Consumer Electronics Company

A consumer electronics company faced challenges with fluctuating demand for its products. To implement Shojinka:

1. **Assess Current Workforce Practices:**
   The company analyzed production data and identified that workforce levels were often mismatched with demand.
2. **Develop Cross-Training Programs:**
   Employees were trained in multiple roles, including assembly, quality assurance, and packaging.
3. **Establish Flexible Work Center Design:**
   Workstations were redesigned to accommodate varying numbers of employees, allowing for quick reconfiguration.
4. **Implement Real-Time Monitoring Systems:**
   The company adopted a scheduling system that tracked production levels and alerted managers to staffing needs.
5. **Continuously Evaluate and Adjust:**

Regular performance reviews were conducted to refine the Shojinka process and ensure optimal workforce allocation.

Results

- Workforce utilization improved by 25%.
- Lead times for product delivery were reduced by 15%.
- Employee satisfaction increased due to diversified skill sets and reduced stress during peak periods.

Conclusion

Shojinka is a powerful approach to workforce optimization in Lean manufacturing. By focusing on flexibility, cross-training, and real-time monitoring, organizations can create adaptable work environments that respond to changes in demand. As the manufacturing landscape continues to evolve, embracing Shojinka will be crucial for companies seeking to enhance efficiency, reduce costs, and improve overall performance. By fostering a culture of continuous improvement and adaptability, organizations can position themselves for long-term success in a competitive market.

CHAPTER – 25
Takt Time

Synchronizing Production with Customer Demand

Introduction to Takt Time

Takt time (タクトタイム) is a pivotal concept in Lean manufacturing that defines the rhythm or pace of production required to meet customer demand. Derived from the German word "Takt," meaning "beat" or "rhythm," Takt time serves as a benchmark for production efficiency, enabling manufacturers to align their output with customer expectations. By understanding and implementing Takt time, organizations can optimize their production processes, reduce waste, and enhance customer satisfaction.

Understanding Takt Time Calculation

Takt time is calculated by dividing the total available production time by the number of units that need to be produced within that timeframe. The formula is as follows:

$$\text{Takt Time} = \frac{\text{Available Production Time}}{\text{Customer Demand}}$$

Where:

- **Available Production Time** is the total time available for production in a specific period (e.g., hours per shift, days per week).

- **Customer Demand** is the number of units that need to be produced to satisfy customer orders during that same period.

Example Calculation

Consider a manufacturing facility that operates for 8 hours (480 minutes) per day and has a customer demand of 240 units per day.

Using the formula:

$$\text{Takt Time} = \frac{480 \text{ minutes}}{240 \text{ units}} = 2 \text{ minutes per unit}$$

This means the production team must complete one unit every 2 minutes to meet customer demand.

The Importance of Takt Time

Takt time is essential for several reasons:

1. Aligning Production with Demand

Takt time helps synchronize production processes with actual customer demand, ensuring that manufacturers produce the right amount of product at the right time. This alignment reduces the risk of overproduction and underproduction, both of which can lead to waste and lost revenue.

2. Enhancing Efficiency

By establishing a clear rhythm for production, Takt time enables teams to streamline workflows and improve operational efficiency. Workers can organize their tasks around the set Takt time, leading to a more structured and efficient production environment.

3. Reducing Lead Times

When production is paced according to Takt time, the overall lead time for delivering products to customers is minimized. This responsive approach allows companies to adapt quickly to fluctuations in demand, improving customer satisfaction.

4. Facilitating Continuous Improvement

Takt time serves as a benchmark for identifying inefficiencies in the production process. By monitoring Takt time performance, organizations can pinpoint areas for improvement, implement solutions, and continuously enhance productivity.

Implementing Takt Time in Production

To effectively implement Takt time in a manufacturing environment, several steps should be followed:

Step 1: Determine Customer Demand

Understanding customer demand is critical for calculating Takt time. Companies should analyze historical sales data, forecast future demand, and consider seasonal fluctuations to determine realistic production targets.

- **Example:** A beverage manufacturer reviews past sales trends and forecasts an increase in demand during summer months, adjusting Takt time calculations accordingly.

Step 2: Calculate Takt Time

Once customer demand is established, calculate Takt time using the available production time. Consider factors such as breaks, maintenance, and other downtime that may affect total production time.

- **Example:** A toy factory operating 10 hours per day (600 minutes) with a demand of 300 units will have a Takt time of 2 minutes per unit.

Step 3: Design the Production Process

Organize the production process around Takt time. Assign tasks to workstations based on the time required to complete each task, ensuring that no single task exceeds the calculated Takt time.

- **Example:** In a smartphone assembly line, each workstation is allocated tasks that can be completed within the 2-minute Takt time to maintain a steady flow.

Step 4: Monitor and Adjust

Regularly monitor Takt time performance and make adjustments as necessary. If demand increases or production efficiency improves, recalibrate Takt time to reflect the new conditions.

- **Example:** A clothing manufacturer finds that they can produce more units per hour due to improved processes. They adjust their Takt time calculation to accommodate the increased output.

Step 5: Train Employees

Provide training to employees on the importance of Takt time and how it impacts production. Encourage a culture of continuous improvement, where team members actively seek to enhance efficiency.

- **Example:** A manufacturing company holds workshops to educate employees about Takt time and how their individual roles contribute to meeting production goals.

Practical Applications of Takt Time

Example 1: Automotive Assembly Line

In an automotive assembly plant, Takt time is critical for ensuring that vehicles are produced efficiently. By calculating the Takt time based on customer orders, the assembly line can be organized to ensure that each station completes its tasks within the allotted time. For instance, if the Takt time is 60 seconds per vehicle, each workstation is designed to complete its assigned task in 60 seconds, enabling a smooth and continuous flow of production.

Example 2: Food Production

A food processing plant calculates Takt time based on daily customer demand for packaged meals. With a Takt time of 90 seconds per meal, the production line is structured so that each step—from cooking to packaging—aligns with this rhythm. This approach ensures that meals are produced at a consistent pace, meeting customer expectations for freshness and availability.

Example 3: Electronics Manufacturing

An electronics manufacturer experiences fluctuating demand for its products. By calculating Takt time on a weekly basis, the company adjusts its production schedule to align with anticipated sales. For example, during the holiday season, if the Takt time shortens due to increased demand, the company may add extra shifts or cross-train employees to handle the workload efficiently.

Challenges and Considerations

While Takt time offers numerous benefits, several challenges may arise during its implementation:

1. Demand Variability

Fluctuations in customer demand can complicate Takt time calculations. Organizations must have robust forecasting methods to adjust Takt time accurately.

2. Balancing Workloads

Ensuring that workloads are evenly distributed across workstations can be challenging. Tasks must be carefully analyzed to prevent bottlenecks and maintain a steady flow.

3. Employee Resistance

Changes to production processes may meet resistance from employees accustomed to existing workflows. Proper training and communication are essential to foster buy-in and understanding.

4. Integration with Other Lean Tools

Takt time should be integrated with other Lean tools and methodologies, such as Kanban and 5S, to maximize its effectiveness. Organizations should consider how Takt time fits within the broader context of Lean practices.

Conclusion

Takt time is a fundamental concept in Lean manufacturing that helps organizations synchronize production with customer demand. By establishing a clear rhythm for production, companies can enhance efficiency, reduce lead times, and improve overall productivity. Implementing Takt time requires careful analysis, employee training, and ongoing adjustments to respond to changing demands. When effectively utilized, Takt time serves as a powerful tool for achieving operational excellence and delivering value to customers.

CHAPTER – 26
Yokoten

Spreading Knowledge and Best Practices Across the Organization

Introduction to Yokoten

Yokoten (横展) is a Japanese term that translates to "horizontal deployment" or "lateral spread." In the context of Lean management, Yokoten refers to the practice of sharing best practices, knowledge, and improvements across various departments or teams within an organization. This collaborative approach fosters a culture of continuous improvement and learning, enabling companies to leverage the collective expertise and experiences of their workforce to drive operational excellence.

The concept of Yokoten recognizes that knowledge is not confined to a single team or location; rather, it can be harnessed from multiple sources within the organization. By encouraging the flow of information and practices, organizations can achieve significant improvements in quality, efficiency, and customer satisfaction.

The Importance of Yokoten

Yokoten plays a crucial role in modern organizations for several reasons:

1. Enhancing Collaboration

By facilitating the sharing of knowledge and best practices, Yokoten promotes collaboration among teams. This interconnectedness helps break down silos within the organization, fostering a culture of teamwork and mutual support.

2. Accelerating Continuous Improvement

Yokoten accelerates the process of continuous improvement by enabling teams to learn from each other's successes and failures. When one team identifies an effective solution or improvement, it can be shared with others, leading to quicker implementation and wider adoption.

3. Building a Learning Organization

Yokoten contributes to the development of a learning organization where employees feel empowered to share knowledge and insights. This culture of learning encourages experimentation, innovation, and proactive problem-solving.

4. Maximizing Resource Utilization

By sharing best practices, organizations can optimize resource utilization. For example, if one department develops a more efficient process, others can adopt that process rather than reinventing the wheel, saving time and effort.

5. Gaining Competitive Advantage

Organizations that effectively implement Yokoten can gain a competitive advantage by being more agile and responsive to market changes. By leveraging the collective intelligence of the workforce, companies can adapt quickly and make informed decisions.

Implementing Yokoten in the Organization

To effectively implement Yokoten, organizations can follow these steps:

Step 1: Foster a Culture of Sharing

Create an environment where employees feel comfortable sharing their knowledge and experiences. Encourage open communication, recognize contributions, and celebrate successes to reinforce the value of sharing.

- **Example:** A manufacturing company hosts regular team meetings to discuss challenges and successes, providing a platform for employees to share insights and learn from one another.

Step 2: Establish Best Practice Repositories

Create centralized repositories or databases where best practices, lessons learned, and improvement stories can be documented and easily accessed by all employees.

- **Example:** A healthcare organization develops an online platform where staff can upload case studies, improvement initiatives, and effective practices that can be accessed by other departments.

Step 3: Utilize Visual Management Tools

Implement visual management tools such as dashboards, charts, and process maps to highlight successful practices and improvements. These tools can serve as visual reminders of what has been achieved and encourage further adoption.

- **Example:** A logistics company uses visual boards to display key performance indicators (KPIs) and improvement projects, allowing teams to see progress and learn from one another.

Step 4: Conduct Cross-Functional Workshops

Organize workshops that bring together employees from different departments to share ideas and brainstorm solutions to common challenges. This collaborative approach encourages diverse perspectives and innovative thinking.

- **Example:** A software development company holds

hackathons where teams from various departments collaborate on projects, sharing coding practices and problem-solving techniques.

Step 5: Measure and Share Results

Track the impact of shared best practices and improvements through measurable outcomes such as reduced cycle times, increased efficiency, or improved quality. Regularly communicate these results to reinforce the benefits of Yokoten.

- **Example:** A retail chain measures the impact of a new inventory management system implemented in one store and shares the positive results with all locations, encouraging them to adopt the same practices.

Practical Applications of Yokoten

Example 1: Automotive Industry

In the automotive industry, Yokoten is commonly applied to share successful manufacturing practices across different plants. When one facility implements a new assembly technique that improves efficiency, that practice is documented and shared with other plants. This enables each facility to benefit from the insights gained, leading to overall improvements in production processes and quality.

Example 2: Healthcare Sector

A healthcare organization adopts Yokoten by creating a platform where nurses and doctors can share successful patient care strategies. For instance, if a specific approach to patient education results in improved health outcomes, that information can be shared with other departments, allowing them to implement similar strategies and enhance patient care across the organization.

Example 3: Software Development

In a software development firm, teams frequently encounter similar challenges in coding and project management. By utilizing Yokoten, teams share their successful practices in agile development methodologies, version control, and testing procedures. This collaborative learning helps streamline processes and improves the overall quality of software delivered to clients.

Challenges and Considerations

While Yokoten offers numerous benefits, organizations may encounter challenges during implementation:

1. Resistance to Change

Employees may be resistant to sharing their knowledge or adopting new practices. It is essential to address cultural barriers and emphasize the benefits of collaboration.

2. Information Overload

With the influx of shared information, employees may feel overwhelmed. To mitigate this, organizations should prioritize and categorize information for easy access.

3. Lack of Standardization

Without a standardized approach to documenting and sharing best practices, valuable insights may be lost. Organizations should develop clear guidelines for capturing and sharing knowledge.

4. Measuring Impact

Quantifying the impact of shared practices can be challenging. Organizations should establish metrics to assess the effectiveness of Yokoten initiatives.

Conclusion

Yokoten is a powerful tool for organizations seeking to

enhance collaboration, accelerate continuous improvement, and leverage collective knowledge. By spreading best practices across departments, companies can drive operational excellence, maximize resource utilization, and gain a competitive advantage. Implementing Yokoten requires a commitment to fostering a culture of sharing, establishing best practice repositories, and measuring results. When effectively embraced, Yokoten not only improves processes but also cultivates a culture of learning and innovation that propels organizations forward in a dynamic business environment.

CHAPTER – 27
Practical Six Sigma Methodologies

Define Phase in Six Sigma: Establishing the Foundation for Improvement

Introduction to the Define Phase

The **Define Phase** is the first phase of the Six Sigma methodology, which is part of the DMAIC (Define, Measure, Analyze, Improve, Control) framework. This phase is crucial as it lays the groundwork for a successful Six Sigma project by clearly identifying the problem to be solved, setting project goals, and outlining the scope of the improvement effort.

In the Define Phase, teams work to understand the customer's needs, the current processes, and the critical factors that affect the quality of the output. By effectively defining the problem and setting specific objectives, organizations can align their resources and efforts to achieve meaningful improvements.

Objectives of the Define Phase

The primary objectives of the Define Phase include:

1. **Identifying the Problem:** Clearly articulate the

problem or opportunity for improvement.
2. **Understanding Customer Requirements:** Define what the customer values and needs.
3. **Establishing Project Goals:** Set specific, measurable objectives to guide the improvement effort.
4. **Defining Project Scope:** Identify the boundaries of the project and what will be included or excluded.
5. **Building a Project Team:** Assemble a cross-functional team with the necessary skills and knowledge to address the problem.

Key Tools Used in the Define Phase

Several tools and techniques can be employed during the Define Phase to ensure a thorough understanding of the problem and to set the foundation for the subsequent phases. Here are some of the most important tools:

1. Project Charter

The Project Charter is a formal document that outlines the purpose, objectives, and scope of the Six Sigma project. It serves as a roadmap for the team and includes:

- **Problem Statement:** A clear description of the issue to be addressed.
- **Goal Statement:** Specific objectives and success criteria.
- **Scope:** Defines the boundaries of the project.
- **Team Members:** Identification of key stakeholders and project team members.
- **Timeline:** Estimated duration and key milestones.

Example: A manufacturing company experiencing high defect rates might create a Project Charter that states, "Reduce defect rates from 5% to 1% in the production line within six months."

2. Voice of the Customer (VoC)

The Voice of the Customer (VoC) refers to the process of capturing customer expectations, preferences, and feedback. Understanding the VoC is essential for aligning improvement efforts with customer needs.

- **Techniques for Gathering VoC:**
    - Surveys
    - Interviews
    - Focus Groups
    - Customer Complaints Analysis

Example: A software development team conducts surveys to gather feedback on user experience, identifying key areas for improvement in their product.

3. SIPOC Diagram

A SIPOC (Suppliers, Inputs, Process, Outputs, Customers) diagram is a high-level visual representation that helps teams understand the key elements of a process. It provides a snapshot of how the process functions and the relationships between different components.

- **Components of a SIPOC Diagram:**
    - **Suppliers:** Entities that provide inputs to the process.
    - **Inputs:** Resources required for the process.
    - **Process:** The series of steps involved in delivering outputs.
    - **Outputs:** The final products or services delivered to customers.
    - **Customers:** Recipients of the outputs.

Example: For a pizza delivery service, a SIPOC diagram may include suppliers like cheese and tomato vendors, inputs such as dough and toppings, the process of making and delivering the pizza, outputs like the delivered pizza, and customers who receive the pizza.

4. Problem Statement

Crafting a concise problem statement is essential for clearly communicating the issue being addressed. A well-defined problem statement should include:

- A description of the current situation.
- Quantitative data to illustrate the extent of the problem.
- A focus on the impact of the problem on customers or the organization.

Example: "Our customer satisfaction rating has declined by 20% in the last six months due to delayed order fulfillment times averaging 5 days instead of the promised 2 days."

5. Goal Statement

The Goal Statement outlines the desired outcome of the Six Sigma project. It should be Specific, Measurable, Achievable, Relevant, and Time-bound (SMART).

- **Components of a Goal Statement:**
    - Desired improvement (e.g., reduction in defects).
    - Measurement criteria (e.g., percentage decrease).
    - Timeline for achieving the goal.

Example: "Reduce order fulfillment times from an average of 5 days to 2 days within the next three months, achieving a customer satisfaction rating of 90% or higher."

6. Stakeholder Analysis

Stakeholder analysis identifies individuals or groups that have an interest in the project or will be affected by its outcomes. Understanding stakeholder perspectives is critical for managing expectations and ensuring buy-in.

- **Steps for Stakeholder Analysis:**
    - Identify stakeholders.
    - Assess their influence and interest in the project.
    - Develop strategies for communication and engagement.

Example: A healthcare organization identifies stakeholders such as doctors, nurses, patients, and administrators, evaluating their interests and influence on the quality improvement initiative.

7. High-Level Process Map

Creating a high-level process map helps visualize the overall flow of the process being examined. It outlines the major steps and interactions within the process, providing a foundation for deeper analysis in the Measure Phase.

- **Components of a High-Level Process Map:**
    - Key process steps.
    - Inputs and outputs for each step.
    - Decision points and flow direction.

Example: A retail store may create a high-level process map of the customer shopping experience, detailing steps from entering the store to making a purchase.

Conclusion

The Define Phase is a critical step in the Six Sigma methodology that sets the stage for successful improvement efforts. By using tools such as the Project Charter, Voice of the Customer, SIPOC diagram, problem statements, goal statements, stakeholder analysis, and high-level process maps, organizations can clearly articulate the problem, understand customer needs, and establish specific objectives.

A well-executed Define Phase not only aligns team efforts but also fosters a shared understanding of the improvement initiative, ensuring that the project is focused, strategic, and impactful. As teams move into the Measure Phase, the insights gained during the Define Phase will serve as a valuable foundation for deeper analysis and improvement activities.

Measure Phase in Six Sigma: Quantifying the Problem

Introduction to the Measure Phase

The **Measure Phase** is the second step in the Six Sigma DMAIC (Define, Measure, Analyze, Improve, Control) framework. This phase is crucial as it focuses on quantifying the problem defined in the previous phase and establishing a baseline for measuring performance. By collecting and analyzing data, teams can gain insights into the current state of the process, identify variations, and understand the factors contributing to the problem.

Effective measurement is essential to understanding how well a process is performing and provides the information needed to drive improvements in subsequent phases. In this chapter, we will explore the objectives of the Measure Phase and the key tools that can be utilized during this stage.

Objectives of the Measure Phase

The main objectives of the Measure Phase include:

1. **Quantifying the Current Process Performance:** Collect data to establish baseline performance metrics.
2. **Identifying Key Performance Indicators (KPIs):** Define metrics that will be used to evaluate success.
3. **Assessing Process Variability:** Analyze the variability within the process to identify areas of inconsistency.
4. **Validating Measurement Systems:** Ensure that the data collection methods and measurement systems are reliable and valid.

Key Tools Used in the Measure Phase

Several tools and techniques can be employed during the Measure Phase to collect and analyze data effectively. Here are some of the most important tools:

1. Data Collection Plan

A Data Collection Plan outlines the approach for gathering data needed to measure process performance. It defines:

- **What data will be collected:** Specifies the type of data (qualitative or quantitative) and which variables are relevant.
- **How data will be collected:** Describes methods and tools for data collection (surveys, observations, existing records).
- **When data will be collected:** Establishes the timing and frequency of data collection.
- **Who will collect the data:** Assigns responsibilities to team members.

Example: In a manufacturing setting, a data collection plan might specify that defect rates will be tracked daily for one month, with data collected from production logs.

2. Process Capability Analysis

Process Capability Analysis measures how well a process meets specified performance criteria or customer requirements. It helps assess whether a process can consistently produce products or services that meet quality standards.

- **Key Metrics:**
    - **Cp (Process Capability Index):** Measures how well a process can produce output within specified limits.
    - **Cpk (Process Capability Index):** Measures how centered the process is relative to the

target value and its ability to produce within specification limits.

Example: A manufacturer may find that a process has a Cp of 1.33, indicating it is capable of producing products within specifications but could be improved for better consistency.

3. Measurement System Analysis (MSA)

Measurement System Analysis evaluates the accuracy and reliability of measurement systems used to collect data. It identifies potential sources of variation in measurement and ensures that the data collected is valid and usable.

- **Key Components of MSA:**
    - **Gage R&R (Repeatability and Reproducibility):** Assesses how much variation in measurements is due to the measurement system rather than the process itself.
    - **Bias:** Measures the difference between the average of measurements and the true value.
    - **Linearity:** Examines how measurement accuracy changes across the range of measurements.

Example: In a laboratory setting, an MSA might reveal that a particular scale consistently underestimates weight, requiring recalibration or replacement.

4. Descriptive Statistics

Descriptive statistics provide a summary of the data collected during the Measure Phase. They help in understanding the distribution and characteristics of the data.

- **Common Descriptive Statistics:**
    - **Mean:** The average value of a data set.
    - **Median:** The middle value when data is sorted.
    - **Standard Deviation:** Measures the

dispersion of data points from the mean.
- **Range:** The difference between the highest and lowest values.

Example: In a service industry, analyzing customer satisfaction scores using descriptive statistics can help identify trends and areas needing improvement.

5. Control Charts

Control charts are graphical tools used to monitor process performance over time. They help identify variations and trends in data, distinguishing between common cause variation (natural to the process) and special cause variation (due to external factors).

- **Types of Control Charts:**
    - **X-bar and R Chart:** Monitors the average and range of a process over time.
    - **p-Chart:** Used for attribute data, monitoring the proportion of defective items in a sample.
    - **c-Chart:** Used for counting defects in a sample.

Example: A bakery might use an X-bar and R chart to monitor the weight of loaves of bread produced, ensuring they remain within specified limits.

6. Histogram

A histogram is a graphical representation of the frequency distribution of a set of data points. It provides a visual interpretation of data variability and helps identify patterns, outliers, and distributions.

- **Uses of Histograms:**
    - Visualize data distributions and identify the shape of the data.
    - Understand the spread and central tendency of the data.

Example: A healthcare provider may use histograms to display patient wait times, revealing patterns and areas for improvement.

7. Pareto Analysis

Pareto Analysis helps identify the most significant factors contributing to a problem. It is based on the Pareto Principle (80/20 rule), which suggests that a small number of causes typically account for a large proportion of the problem.

- **Steps for Pareto Analysis:**
    - Collect data on defects or issues.
    - Categorize the data into major causes.
    - Create a Pareto chart to visualize the frequency of each cause.

Example: A manufacturing plant might use Pareto Analysis to discover that 80% of defects come from just three common causes, allowing them to prioritize their improvement efforts.

Conclusion

The Measure Phase is a critical step in the Six Sigma methodology, providing the necessary data and insights to understand the current state of a process. By utilizing tools such as Data Collection Plans, Process Capability Analysis, Measurement System Analysis, Descriptive Statistics, Control Charts, Histograms, and Pareto Analysis, organizations can effectively quantify performance, identify variations, and establish a solid foundation for analysis and improvement.

A well-executed Measure Phase not only ensures accurate data collection but also sets the stage for the subsequent Analyze Phase, where deeper insights into the root causes of problems will be explored. By prioritizing measurement and analysis, organizations can drive meaningful improvements and achieve their Six Sigma goals.

Analyze Phase in Six Sigma: Uncovering Root Causes

Introduction to the Analyze Phase

The **Analyze Phase** is the third step in the Six Sigma DMAIC (Define, Measure, Analyze, Improve, Control) methodology. This phase focuses on evaluating the data collected during the Measure Phase to identify the root causes of the problems defined earlier. By thoroughly analyzing the data, teams can gain insights into the factors that contribute to defects, variations, or inefficiencies in a process.

The goal of the Analyze Phase is to use statistical tools and techniques to drill down into the data and uncover relationships and patterns that can lead to informed decisions for process improvement. By establishing a clear understanding of the root causes, organizations can implement targeted solutions in the Improve Phase.

Objectives of the Analyze Phase

The main objectives of the Analyze Phase include:

1. **Identifying Root Causes:** Determine the fundamental reasons behind the defects or inefficiencies.
2. **Analyzing Data:** Use statistical and analytical methods to interpret the data collected during the Measure Phase.
3. **Validating Causes:** Confirm the identified root causes through testing or further analysis.
4. **Prioritizing Issues:** Rank the identified issues based on their impact on the process and overall business goals.

Key Tools Used in the Analyze Phase

Several tools and techniques can be employed during the Analyze Phase to help uncover root causes effectively. Here are some of the most important tools:

1. Fishbone Diagram (Ishikawa Diagram)

The Fishbone Diagram is a visual tool used to systematically identify and organize potential causes of a problem. It resembles the bones of a fish, with the "head" representing the problem and "bones" branching off for different categories of causes.

- **Steps to Create a Fishbone Diagram:**
    - Define the problem and write it in the "head" of the fish.
    - Identify major categories of causes (e.g., People, Process, Equipment, Materials).
    - Brainstorm possible causes within each category and add them as "bones."

Example: In a manufacturing environment, a Fishbone Diagram might reveal that defects in a product are caused by issues related to materials, machinery, and operator training.

2. 5 Whys

The 5 Whys technique involves asking "why" repeatedly (typically five times) to drill down to the root cause of a problem. It is a simple yet effective method for identifying underlying issues without complex analysis.

- **Steps for the 5 Whys Technique:**
    - Start with a problem statement.
    - Ask "why" the problem is occurring.
    - For each answer, continue to ask "why" until reaching the root cause.

Example: If a machine breaks down, the first "why" might be that it was not maintained. The next "why" could reveal a lack of maintenance training, leading to the identification of the root cause as inadequate training programs.

3. Pareto Analysis

Pareto Analysis, based on the Pareto Principle (80/20 rule), helps identify the most significant causes of a problem by categorizing issues and visualizing their impact. It is used to focus improvement efforts on the most critical factors.

- **Creating a Pareto Chart:**
    - Collect data on defects or issues.
    - Categorize the data into major causes.
    - Plot a bar chart to visualize the frequency of each cause, adding a cumulative line.

Example: A restaurant may find that 80% of customer complaints come from just three issues: long wait times, incorrect orders, and poor service. This insight allows management to prioritize improvement initiatives.

4. Histogram

A histogram is a graphical representation of the frequency distribution of a dataset. It helps visualize data variability and identify patterns or trends that may indicate issues in a process.

- **Using Histograms in Analysis:**
    - Create a histogram of key metrics (e.g., cycle time, defect rates).
    - Analyze the shape and spread of the data to identify anomalies or trends.

Example: A call center may analyze call resolution times using a histogram, revealing that most calls are resolved quickly, but a few outliers take significantly longer, indicating areas for improvement.

5. Control Charts

Control charts are used to monitor process performance over

time and help identify trends and variations. They distinguish between common cause variation (inherent to the process) and special cause variation (due to specific factors).

- **Types of Control Charts:**
    - **X-bar and R Chart:** Monitors the average and range of a process.
    - **p-Chart:** Monitors the proportion of defective items in a sample.

Example: A manufacturing plant may use an X-bar and R chart to analyze production output over time, identifying points where the process deviates from expected performance.

6. Process Mapping

Process mapping involves creating a visual representation of a process to understand its flow and identify bottlenecks, redundancies, or inefficiencies.

- **Steps to Create a Process Map:**
    - Define the process to be mapped.
    - Identify and document each step in the process.
    - Analyze the map to identify areas of concern.

Example: A software development team may map out their workflow, revealing unnecessary steps that can be eliminated to streamline the process.

Conclusion

The Analyze Phase is a critical component of the Six Sigma methodology, providing the analytical framework needed to uncover the root causes of problems identified in earlier phases. By utilizing tools such as Fishbone Diagrams, 5 Whys, Pareto Analysis, Histograms, Control Charts, and Process Mapping, organizations can gain deeper insights into process variations and defects.

By successfully identifying and validating root causes, teams can develop targeted solutions during the Improve Phase, ultimately leading to enhanced performance, increased quality, and greater customer satisfaction. The Analyze Phase emphasizes the importance of data-driven decision-making and fosters a culture of continuous improvement within the organization.

Improve Phase in Six Sigma: Tools and Techniques for Effective Solution Implementation

Key Tools Used in the Improve Phase

Several tools and techniques can be employed during the Improve Phase to facilitate solution development and implementation. Here are some of the most important tools:

1. Brainstorming

Brainstorming is a group creativity technique aimed at generating a large number of ideas for solutions to a problem. It encourages open discussion and the free flow of ideas, allowing team members to build on each other's thoughts.

- **Steps for Effective Brainstorming:**
    - Set a clear objective for the brainstorming session.
    - Encourage participants to share ideas without judgment.
    - Record all ideas for later evaluation.
    - After the session, prioritize the ideas based on feasibility and impact.

Example: A hospital team might brainstorm ways to reduce patient wait times, generating ideas such as improved scheduling systems, triage training for staff, and patient flow analysis.

2. Prioritization Matrix

A prioritization matrix helps evaluate and rank potential solutions based on predefined criteria, such as cost, feasibility, impact, and alignment with business goals. This tool assists teams in focusing on the most promising solutions.

- **Creating a Prioritization Matrix:**

- List potential solutions in rows.
- Define evaluation criteria in columns.
- Score each solution against the criteria and calculate a weighted score to prioritize options.

Example: A manufacturing team might use a prioritization matrix to evaluate several automation solutions based on cost, expected ROI, and ease of implementation.

3. Process Simulation

Process simulation involves creating a digital or physical model of a process to visualize how changes will impact performance. This tool helps assess the effectiveness of proposed solutions before implementation.

- **Steps for Process Simulation:**
    - Develop a model of the existing process.
    - Incorporate proposed changes into the model.
    - Run simulations to observe the potential impact of changes on performance metrics.

Example: A logistics company might simulate changes to their shipping process, evaluating the impact of new routing software on delivery times and costs.

4. Pilot Testing

Pilot testing involves implementing a solution on a small scale to assess its effectiveness and gather data before full deployment. This allows teams to make necessary adjustments based on real-world performance.

- **Steps for Conducting a Pilot Test:**
    - Select a limited scope for the pilot (e.g., a specific location or product line).
    - Implement the solution and monitor performance closely.

- Gather feedback from stakeholders and analyze results to identify issues or opportunities for improvement.

Example: A software development team might pilot a new code review process with one project team before rolling it out company-wide.

5. Failure Mode and Effects Analysis (FMEA)

FMEA is a structured approach to identifying potential failure modes of a process and assessing their impact. It helps prioritize risks and develop mitigation strategies.

- **Conducting an FMEA:**
    - Identify potential failure modes for each step of the process.
    - Assess the severity, occurrence, and detectability of each failure.
    - Calculate the Risk Priority Number (RPN) and prioritize risks for mitigation.

Example: An automotive manufacturer may conduct an FMEA to identify risks associated with a new assembly line process, ensuring that potential issues are addressed before full implementation.

6. Standard Operating Procedures (SOPs)

SOPs provide detailed instructions for executing specific tasks and processes. Developing SOPs helps ensure consistency and quality in process execution after improvements are implemented.

- **Creating Effective SOPs:**
    - Document each step of the improved process clearly.
    - Include any necessary diagrams or visual aids.
    - Train employees on the new procedures and provide access to the documentation.

Example: A restaurant may create SOPs for food preparation to ensure that new recipes and cooking techniques are consistently followed by all staff.

7. Plan-Do-Check-Act (PDCA) Cycle

The PDCA Cycle is an iterative approach for continuous improvement that emphasizes planning, implementing, monitoring, and refining solutions. It helps ensure that improvements are sustained over time.

- **Steps in the PDCA Cycle:**
    - **Plan:** Define objectives and develop a plan for improvement.
    - **Do:** Implement the solution on a small scale.
    - **Check:** Monitor performance and analyze results.
    - **Act:** Refine the solution based on feedback and extend implementation if successful.

Example: A call center may use the PDCA cycle to improve its customer service process, implementing changes, gathering feedback, and adjusting based on customer satisfaction metrics.

Conclusion

The Improve Phase is a vital step in the Six Sigma DMAIC process, focusing on developing and implementing effective solutions to enhance process performance. By employing tools such as brainstorming, prioritization matrices, process simulation, pilot testing, FMEA, SOPs, and the PDCA cycle, organizations can systematically identify and implement solutions that drive significant improvements.

Successful implementation of the solutions identified in this phase sets the stage for the Control Phase, where organizations establish mechanisms to sustain and monitor the improvements made. The Improve Phase encourages innovation, collaboration, and a commitment to continuous improvement, essential for achieving long-term success in any organization.

Control Phase in Six Sigma: Ensuring Sustained Improvements

Introduction to the Control Phase

The **Control Phase** is the final step in the Six Sigma DMAIC (Define, Measure, Analyze, Improve, Control) methodology. This phase focuses on establishing mechanisms to sustain the improvements made during the Improve Phase and ensure that the processes remain stable and efficient over time. The primary goal is to monitor the process performance and maintain the gains achieved through the implementation of new solutions.

Effective control measures are critical for preventing regression to old habits and ensuring that improvements become an integral part of the organization's culture. This phase often involves the use of various tools and techniques to monitor processes, analyze data, and engage employees in sustaining the improvements.

Objectives of the Control Phase

The main objectives of the Control Phase include:

1. **Monitoring Process Performance:** Continuously track key performance indicators (KPIs) to ensure processes remain within desired limits.

2. **Standardizing Processes:** Implement standard operating procedures (SOPs) to ensure consistency and quality in process execution.

3. **Training and Engaging Employees:** Involve and train employees in the new processes to foster a culture of continuous improvement.

4. **Implementing Control Plans:** Develop and execute plans that outline how processes will be monitored

and controlled over time.

Key Tools Used in the Control Phase

Several tools and techniques can be employed during the Control Phase to facilitate the sustained success of improvements. Here are some of the most important tools:

1. Control Charts

Control charts are a statistical tool used to monitor process stability and variability over time. They help identify trends, shifts, or outliers in process performance, enabling teams to respond proactively to any deviations from the established control limits.

- **Types of Control Charts:**
    - **X-bar Chart:** Monitors the mean of a process over time.
    - **R Chart:** Tracks the range of variation within a sample.
    - **P Chart:** Monitors the proportion of defective items in a process.

Example: A manufacturing plant may use control charts to monitor the dimensions of a critical component, allowing them to identify any deviations from specifications early.

2. Standard Operating Procedures (SOPs)

SOPs are documented processes that outline the steps necessary to complete a specific task. Developing and implementing SOPs helps standardize processes and ensures that all employees follow the same procedures, reducing variation and maintaining quality.

- **Creating Effective SOPs:**
    - Clearly outline each step of the process.
    - Use visual aids or diagrams to enhance understanding.

- Ensure SOPs are accessible to all employees and regularly updated.

Example: A laboratory might create SOPs for conducting experiments to ensure consistency and compliance with safety standards.

3. Control Plans

Control plans are detailed documents that specify how processes will be monitored, what measures will be taken to maintain quality, and how corrective actions will be implemented when necessary. Control plans help ensure that all critical factors are consistently monitored and managed.

- **Components of a Control Plan:**
    - Description of the process and its key inputs/outputs.
    - Identification of critical control points (CCPs) and performance measures.
    - Procedures for monitoring, responding to deviations, and documenting results.

Example: A food processing company may develop a control plan to monitor temperature, pH levels, and other critical factors during production to ensure food safety.

4. Process Audits

Process audits involve systematically reviewing processes to ensure compliance with established procedures and standards. Regular audits help identify areas for improvement and ensure that the processes are functioning as intended.

- **Steps for Conducting Process Audits:**
    - Develop an audit checklist based on SOPs and control plans.
    - Schedule regular audits and assign auditors.
    - Analyze audit results and implement corrective actions as needed.

Example: A service organization may conduct process audits to ensure that customer service representatives follow established protocols for handling inquiries.

5. Employee Training and Engagement

Training employees in the new processes and engaging them in continuous improvement efforts are crucial for sustaining gains. Providing ongoing education and opportunities for feedback fosters a culture of accountability and commitment to quality.

- **Strategies for Effective Training:**
    - Conduct regular training sessions on new processes and tools.
    - Use interactive methods, such as simulations or workshops, to enhance learning.
    - Encourage employee feedback and suggestions for process improvement.

Example: A healthcare organization may implement ongoing training programs for staff to ensure they are familiar with new patient care protocols and technologies.

6. Root Cause Analysis (RCA)

RCA is a problem-solving technique used to identify the underlying causes of issues that arise after improvements have been implemented. By understanding the root causes of problems, teams can take corrective actions to prevent recurrence.

- **Common RCA Techniques:**
    - **5 Whys:** Asking "why" multiple times to uncover the root cause.
    - **Fishbone Diagram (Ishikawa):** A visual tool that categorizes potential causes of a problem.

Example: If a manufacturing process experiences increased defects, a team may use RCA to identify whether the issue is due to equipment failure, operator error, or material quality.

7. Key Performance Indicators (KPIs)

KPIs are measurable values that indicate how effectively a process is performing against established goals. Monitoring KPIs helps teams assess whether improvements are being sustained and provides insights for future enhancements.

- **Choosing Effective KPIs:**
    - Align KPIs with business objectives and desired outcomes.
    - Ensure KPIs are measurable, relevant, and actionable.
    - Review KPIs regularly to identify trends and areas for improvement.

Example: A retail organization may track KPIs such as customer satisfaction scores, inventory turnover rates, and order fulfillment times to assess the effectiveness of new operational processes.

Conclusion

The Control Phase is critical for ensuring the sustainability of improvements achieved through the Six Sigma DMAIC process. By employing tools such as control charts, standard operating procedures, control plans, process audits, employee training, root cause analysis, and key performance indicators, organizations can effectively monitor and maintain process performance over time.

Successful implementation of the Control Phase fosters a culture of continuous improvement, empowering employees to take ownership of quality and ensuring that processes remain stable and efficient. By committing to ongoing monitoring and refinement, organizations can drive long-term success and achieve their business objectives.

ABOUT THE AUTHOR

Bhargavi Rao

Bhargavi Rao is a seasoned professional with 15 years of experience and a Lean Six Sigma Black Belt. Over the course of her career, she has successfully led and executed numerous Six Sigma projects, driving operational excellence and sustainable improvements. Bhargavi's expertise lies in identifying inefficiencies, implementing data-driven solutions, and fostering a culture of continuous improvement. Her practical insights and deep understanding of Lean principles position her as a leader in transforming business processes across industries.

www.ingramcontent.com/pod-product-compliance
Lightning Source LLC
Chambersburg PA
CBHW031607210526
45464CB00004B/1462